ADVANCE ACCLAIM FOR
THE PRODIGAL

"For all of us who have had our fill of guilt, religious performance pressure, hypocrisy, and shame, *The Prodigal* reads like a needed vacation for your soul. Emotional Impact Warning: you'll need a box of tissues nearby as you read."

—BRIAN D. MCLAREN, AUTHOR/
SPEAKER/ACTIVIST, BRIANMCLAREN.NET

"Brennan Manning's last work continues the powerful message of grace and forgiveness that has transformed so many lives. *The Prodigal* will transform you too."

—MARK BATTERSON, *NEW YORK TIMES*
BEST-SELLING AUTHOR OF *THE CIRCLE MAKER*

"Finding out what kind of person you are and finding out what kind of God you believe in are uncomfortably interlinked. This vivid and often moving novel explores some of those links, not offering glib happy endings but a sense of truthfulness painfully achieved and love and grace painfully absorbed. For anyone who hopes one day to be a grown-up Christian."

—DR. ROWAN WILLIAMS, RETIRED
ARCHBISHOP OF CANTERBURY

"Fr. Brannon Manning did not live quite long enough to see the publication of *The Prodigal*, his last novel. But he did live long enough to work with Greg Garrett in creating it. Colorful. Well-written. Engrossing. Totally engaging. *The Prodigal* is all these things and several more that I can think of. But it is also more than any of them. Fr. Manning will no longer write such stories for us, of course, but what he and Garrett have created in this one is the consummate final tale. What they have created is the Ragamuffin at his best, full of hope, full of love, and finally, full of belief in the goodness of God."

—PHYLLIS TICKLE, FOUNDING EDITOR,
RELIGION DEPARTMENT, *PUBLISHERS WEEKLY*

"This story contains all the elements of true beauty . . . pain, loss, sin, and regret, yet overshadowing every bitter tear there is love, forgiveness, and grace. You will find yourself in these pages, in things you admire and things you detest, but more than that, you will be reminded of a Father who stands with arms wide open for every prodigal who would turn their heart toward home."

—SHEILA WALSH, AUTHOR
OF *THE STORM INSIDE*

THE PRODIGAL

A RAGAMUFFIN STORY

BRENNAN MANNING AND GREG GARRETT

ZONDERVAN®

ZONDERVAN.com/
AUTHORTRACKER
follow your favorite authors

ZONDERVAN

The Prodigal

Copyright © 2013 by Brennan Manning and Greg Garrett

This title is also available as a Zondervan ebook. Visit www.zondervan.com/
ebooks.

Requests for information should be addressed to:

Zondervan, *Grand Rapids, Michigan 49530*

Library of Congress Cataloging-in-Publication Data

Manning, Brennan.
  The prodigal : a ragamuffin story / Brennan Manning and Greg Garrett.
    pages cm
  ISBN 978-0-310-33900-7 (trade paper : alk. paper) 1. Clergy--Fiction. I.
Garrett, Greg. II. Title.
  PS3563.A5365P76 2013
  813'.54--dc23
                              2013027003

Scripture verses taken from the King James Version of the Bible as well as the
New Jerusalem Bible, Henry Wansbrough, ed. New York; London: Doubleday;
Darton, Longman & Todd, 1985. And from the Holy Bible, New International
Version®, NIV®. Copyright © 1973, 1978, 1984, 2011 by Biblica, Inc.™ Used
by permission. All rights reserved worldwide.

Authors are represented by the literary agency of Alive Communications,
Inc., 7680 Goddard Street, Suite 200, Colorado Springs, CO 80920, www
.alivecommunications.com

Any Internet addresses (websites, blogs, etc.) and telephone numbers in
this book are offered as a resource. They are not intended in any way to be
or imply an endorsement by Zondervan, nor does Zondervan vouch for the
content of these sites and numbers for the life of this book.

Printed in the United States of America

13 14 15 16 17 18 19 20 /RRD/ 20 19 18 17 16 15 14 13 12 11 10 9 8 7 6 5 4 3 2

"I'm a cad but I'm not a fraud.
I set out to serve the Lord."

Mumford & Sons, "Whispers in the Dark"

NOTE FROM THE AUTHOR

by Greg Garrett

I wish Brennan Manning had crossed my path a long, long time ago.

And I wish he were still alive to cross my path now.

I was raised by loving parents in a legalistic and not particularly grace-blessed corner of the Church. Although there were many good people, a lot of great music, and a ton of great food in our tradition, what I absorbed from worship more than anything else was my own worthlessness. If God loved me—and the songs said he did—the preaching and teaching Sunday after Sunday didn't indicate it. In fact, if you paid attention to the preacher—and I did—God seemed to be angry with us, really angry, and nothing I did would ever measure up to his notice.

As a sensitive and already guilty soul, I took on that worthlessness down to my very marrow. How could God—or anybody—love me, flawed and broken as I was?

I fled that church, fled the tradition, fled Christianity itself, and might have stayed fled forever if I hadn't been rescued by another church decades down the road at the lowest point of my life.

Brennan Manning could have saved me from some of that. In the face of a contemporary American Christianity that argues that human beings have to earn their way to God, Brennan offered the necessary correctives that we are pursued irresistibly by the One who created us, that fail as we might (and do, daily), we are offered forgiveness, that no one can ever sin so badly as to remove him- or herself from the love of God. He also offered the example of his own story, of his life as a Roman Catholic priest who left the priesthood to marry, of his struggles with alcohol, and of his firsthand knowledge of suffering, sin, and redemption.

I didn't discover Brennan's work until after I'd finally returned to the faith, but when I found his message of love, grace, and forgiveness, when I discovered that this inspiring writer and storyteller was an imperfect and damaged soul just like me, just like all of us, I felt that I was discovering a friend and kindred soul.

I fell in love with Brennan Manning, with his honesty, with his gentle spirit.

And again, I wished that I had encountered him long before, that I had somehow heard his message that God loved me— messed up as I was and am—beyond reckoning.

As he neared the end of his life, Brennan wanted to write a novel that would dramatically illustrate the things he had spent his life teaching and doing: grace, love, forgiveness, faith, service.

It was no surprise that he would want to utilize the story format for his last work despite a lifetime of preaching, writing, and blessing others. In *The Ragamuffin Gospel*, Brennan used examples from great novels like *The Moviegoer* and *The Brothers Karamazov*, and I remembered he explicitly argued that stories, poems, and music might be the most powerful ways we understand and experience love, grace, and forgiveness:

> If God is not in the whirlwind, He may be in a Woody Allen film or a Bruce Springsteen concert. Most people understand imagery and symbol better than doctrines and dogma. One theologian suggested that Springsteen's *Tunnel of Love* album, in which he symbolically sings of sin, death, despair, and redemption, is more important for Catholics than the Pope's last visit when he spoke of morality only in doctrinal propositions. Troubadours have always been more important and influential than theologians and bishops.[1]

So it made sense to me that in addition to telling his own story, Brennan would want to turn to fiction to help people see his life's teachings come to life. As I knew from seeing the video trailer for his memoir, *All Is Grace*, which came out in 2011, Brennan was in declining health, mentally alert but in a rapidly failing body. Coauthor John Blase had helped Brennan complete *All Is Grace*, and he would need at least as much help this time— maybe more, since although Brennan had told stories about his life for decades, he had never written a novel.

I was honored to be chosen to write alongside Brennan. In my three previous novels, grace, love, and forgiveness are major themes. My main characters are often deeply flawed, but thanks

---

1. Brennan Manning, *The Ragamuffin Gospel* (Colorado Springs, CO: Multnomah, 2005), 96.

to the power of miraculous love, they find their way back to where they ought to be. I was also excited about the idea of dramatizing the work of a great Christian teacher, because I have some experience wrestling with the artistic challenge of how to strike the balance between being a writer of fiction and a person of deep faith.

It's one thing to say you want to write a novel about grace or forgiveness or faith, which is what Brennan wanted to do. It's another thing to tell a powerful story in which those concepts are allowed to get up and walk around in the form of characters' lives. Stories are about people, not about ideas; if you start with themes or ideas, the book can become nothing more than slogans, the characters just protesters carrying picket signs. To create a successful novel incorporating Brennan's teachings on grace, compassion, and forgiveness, we had to populate a story with real people facing real problems, with the real possibility of their failure, with real desires and fears.

Brennan wanted his last book to be a powerful story that people could read, enjoy, and learn from. We wanted it to be a worthy bookend to Brennan's faithful life and engaging words. And we quickly found the dramatic framework that would be true to all those objectives.

A few weeks after I'd been asked to work with Brennan on the project, we had agreed on a retelling of the parable of the Prodigal Son. It was Brennan's favorite story. As a recovering alcoholic, a failed husband, a priest who left the Church, it was a story that resonated with him: he had plenty of wandering on his ledger.

Like many of us, Brennan knew what it felt like to stray, to slip into mire of our own making, to wish we could go home. Like many of us, he knew what it felt like to think you are unworthy, that you have worn out your welcome, that there is no home left at home. But Jesus' story of the son who insulted his father by demanding his inheritance while his father was still living, who shamed his father by blowing through that inheritance with wine and women until nothing was left, is a story of the purest grace and of a love that will never write us off.

For Brennan, the story of the Prodigal was *the* story explaining Christian faith, and it was certainly the most meaningful in regard to his own life. The idea of a loving and forgiving Father was essential to his personal faith and to his teaching. He talked often about God as "Abba," using that loving name for "father" that Jesus uses when he talks to God. The Prodigal's story acknowledges that we have all wasted our substance on riotous living (as the King James Version has it in Luke 15:13). We have all wandered away from God at some point, some of us farther than others. We have all thought we could never return. But one of Brennan's favorite Bible verses describes the reunion of the Prodigal Son with his father: "So he got up and went to his father. But while he was still a long way off, his father saw him and was filled with compassion for him; he ran to his son, threw his arms around him and kissed him" (Luke 15:20 NIV). Brennan often used to draw attention to the fact that this is the only time the Bible says, "God ran." If we will just turn in the direction of God, we will find that God is already coming to meet us, has already forgiven us, has never stopped loving us.

In *The Ragamuffin Gospel*, just before he discussed the story of the Prodigal at length, Brennan put it this way: "The gospel of grace announces: Forgiveness precedes repentance. The sinner is accepted before he pleads for mercy. It is already granted. He need only receive it. Total amnesty. Gratuitous pardon."[2] When we imagined an earthly father, like the father in the story of *The Prodigal*, coming to rescue the son who has insulted and shamed him, it was a startling insight into a story—and an article of faith—I think I had taken for granted. As our protagonist says in the book, if an earthly father can love and forgive so well, can we imagine our heavenly Father is capable of less?

So: it had to be the story of the Prodigal Son. But, that settled, there are all sorts of prodigals out there. We could have written about any kind of person—whether original gangsta, suicide bomber, dishonest banker, or simply rebellious daughter—since we are all, as Brennan said, ragamuffins. That is the human condition. But Brennan wrote in *The Ragamuffin Gospel* that once we truly believe in God's amazing grace, the love and forgiveness embodied in the story of the Prodigal, it allows us all to be honest about our failings. Because it opened lots of dramatic doors for us, we decided our main character should be a megachurch pastor who had fallen from grace. That would give us a logical reason to engage faith, to speak about God, and to put church front and center, and it also gave us a chance to talk about one of Brennan's biggest problems with American religion.

Despite his great popularity and devoted following, Brennan was ever suspicious of religious celebrities. Early in *The Ragamuffin Gospel*, he actually called out "our adulation of televangelists, charismatic superstars, and local church heroes," and this adulation could easily become a story line.[3] Our Jack Chisholm would

---

2. Ibid., 188.
3. Ibid., 25.

be the sort of celebrity pastor delivering a mainstream gospel of fear and striving, a message ignoring the marvelous grace of God—but who, through his own sin and suffering, would discover how very central that grace is in understanding God, faith, and Christian practice. As you'll see as you read the book, Jack has to learn not only how badly he was mistaken about God and God's grace, but about the sufficiency of his own ministry, in which he was a public figure but never a pastor, in which he helped people on the other side of the world, but never those with whom he had to be in daily relationship.

Both Brennan and I had faced rock bottom. We knew what it felt like to lose everything, to have fallen into bad habits that threatened to destroy us, and Jack Chisholm would benefit from our experience—and be a better character because of it. Even if his failings made him seem a little unsympathetic at the opening of the story, we believed people would come to recognize themselves in him. We had also both been the beneficiaries of amazing grace, been forgiven not because we deserved it but purely out of love, and Jack comes to recognize the power of grace and forgiveness—and to become an authentic agent of it himself.

Jack, it turns out, was also informed by current events. Champion cyclist Lance Armstrong was suffering through his own scandal as we planned and began this book. As you probably remember, although he had for many years been accused of cheating by using performance-enhancing drugs and other illegal practices, Lance had denied it—and tried to ruin everyone who told the truth. Then in January of 2013, he did his famous interviews with Oprah Winfrey, in which he acknowledged that he had, in fact, been guilty of everything he was accused of all those years.

I watched those interviews with my girlfriend, Jeanie, and when they both were over, we turned to each other and shook our heads.

"He doesn't seem the least bit sorry," I said.

"He's sorry he got caught," she said.

Lance's nonapology inspired our characterization of Jack Chisholm early in the novel. Like so many other celebrities, Jack follows the playbook—deny, deny, deny, then say you're sorry that anyone was offended. But so rarely do public figures accept responsibility for their actions, truly repent of them, and offer a genuine apology to the people they hurt. In the Christian tradition, offense is supposed to be accompanied by remorse and what we call "amendment of life." That's what the original Greek word translated in the Bible as "repent" actually means—not just regret, but turning your life around, becoming a different and better person. The Lance Armstrong story suggested a wonderful way of thinking about where our character Jack might start off—and what he had to overcome—in the course of our story.

But even after we had settled on our core concepts, plot, characters, and settings, I was still thinking about an additional idea: I wanted Brennan himself to be a character in the novel. What better way to make sure that Brennan's teachings emerged from the book than to have a character embody them? Richard Francis Xavier Manning, whom the world knew as "Brennan," is the obvious inspiration for Francis Xavier Malone, the character in our novel known as "Father Frank." Father Frank is the moral center of the novel. He speaks in Brennan's cadence and sometimes in his very words, and he teaches the other characters of the book about grace, love, and compassion. I hope that Father Frank comes across as an honest and loving tribute to Brennan himself—and now that Brennan has gone to be with his Abba, that he feels like a reminder of the humor, the gentleness, the wisdom, and the faith that made Brennan a guiding light to so many.

I wish Brennan Manning had crossed my path a long, long time ago.

And I wish he were still alive to cross my path now.

But I hope that *The Prodigal* is a worthy monument to him, and a worthy companion to *The Ragamuffin Gospel* and the amazing body of books, sermons, and teaching he left behind.

Thanks for reading our story.

1.

Jack Chisholm woke slowly from a dream where he had been walking the beach with his father, hand in hand. In the dream, he was again a boy of six or seven, and his family was in Florida on summer vacation.

His father had always loved the beach, and when Jack was a boy, they had driven down every summer to vacation on the warm, white sands at Destin. Jack; his older sister Mary; her twin, Martha—dead now thirty years; his mother, Marie—dead for the past ten; and his father, Tom—still alive, though dead to Jack.

The dream felt so real. He could feel his father's strong hands holding him upright as the waves crashed against them. Jack felt a powerful sense of loss. He had not talked to his father in a decade, not since his mother's funeral. When he thought about his father in waking life, it was always with more anger than grief. The man had made his childhood a misery. No way was Jack going to let his adult life be held to the same impossible measuring stick.

At the graveside, they had quarreled. At the funeral, Tom had shamed him, and so Jack had walked away, leaving his family and Mayfield, Texas, forever.

The slow, steady crashing of waves had been the soundtrack to his dream, but it continued even now after he felt himself rise up through layers of sleep, even now that the sunlight forced him to open his eyes.

He had put it off as long as he could, the knowledge of where he was, the awareness of why he was there, but now there was no denying it.

It was Christmas morning. Jack was alone, lying on a chaise lounge on the balcony of a hotel room overlooking the dark-blue Caribbean. The sound of the ocean masked the hotel workers who were rapping on the bolted door and calling out in Spanish or broken English, their entreaties growing more emphatic. Meanwhile he could drink tequila and slumber fitfully and try to forget the hard facts that he had no more money and no place to go.

In a couple of hours, thousands of members of Grace Cathedral in Seattle, the church he had built, would be filing into one of three campuses for Christmas services, cups of steaming coffee in one hand, Bibles in the other. Some of them would be dressed in their Christmas best; some would be in ragged jeans and flannels. Some of them thought alcohol was a sin; some brewed their own craft porters. Some of them were scandalized when he preached his sermon series on the joys of sex with your spouse; others were so grateful they couldn't stop thanking him. The people of Grace were Anglo, Asian, Hispanic, African American, rich, and poor. However much they differed, though, they all had one thing in common: their pastor, Jack Chisholm.

Yet today when it came time for the Christmas sermon, the members of Grace would look up at the pulpit—or at the giant video screens—and they would see Danny Pierce, their junior pastor, stepping in to preach. They would be wondering where Jack Chisholm was, why he had left them, how he could have failed them so completely.

They would be wondering what was going to happen next.

Jack himself had no idea what was going to happen next, although he suspected the worst, at least for himself. He had managed to keep his head above water since the news broke six weeks ago. But he feared the end was approaching fast. The only way Jack could stop himself from jumping off the balcony and into the crashing sea was to start drinking when he woke up. Then he could try to forget.

Could try.

He reached under the lounge and found what might be the last of the tequila he had bought before the church canceled his American Express. He unscrewed the cap and brought the bottle to his mouth.

This was his first drink of the day. The clear liquid was smooth and powerful as it slipped down his throat. *Tequila is a sledgehammer wrapped in velvet,* he thought, and smiled in satisfaction before taking another swig.

"Merry Christmas," he whispered.

He slipped a hand into his pajamas pocket and pulled out his cell phone, miraculously still connected. Maybe the church didn't know they were still paying for it; maybe they were being generous. It didn't matter. The phone was his one connection to the larger world and it worked.

"Call home," he said. It dialed the number, but as had been the case for five weeks, he was greeted by an electronic voice and a beep, not by his wife, Tracy.

It rattled him, but after a few moments, he took a deep breath and left another message. "Tracy," he said. "If this is still your phone. If you're even listening to these messages. It's Christmas morning. Christmas morning." His voice broke, and he blinked back tears before regaining control. "I'm just wondering what Alison is getting from Santa," he said, in a tone much breezier than he felt. Alison was their eight-year-old daughter, the best thing he had ever made, although he was sure he had never said that out loud. That thought—the thought of her—made his voice catch again. "No. I'm wondering if you're ever going to talk to me again. I know things haven't been right for a long time. I know that. But, Tracy, I think if you would just talk to me—"

We could work it out?

I could explain?

There was nothing he could say. He hung up, then sat surveying the phone as though it held some secret.

Things hadn't been right for a long time. He wasn't one to let people get close, wasn't good at relationship. Work was the one thing he did well, the one thing with an obvious and immediate payback. His whole life he had been losing things, and maybe that had made him afraid to love too much. But that didn't mean he didn't love, that he didn't miss his family.

It didn't mean that at this moment he didn't feel utterly and completely lost.

On Christmas morning last year, Jack stood onstage at the main campus of Grace Cathedral with Tracy and Alison on either side, beautiful in matching red velvet dresses, smiling and singing carols.

At this time last year, he had been with his family.

After the eight-person worship band finished leading an alt-rock version of "O Come, O Come, Immanuel," he gathered Tracy's and Alison's hands the way he did every Sunday, squeezed them, let them go, and slowly and purposefully walked the twelve steps to his pulpit.

Then he stood still, his head bowed. Jack loved the moment before he began to preach, loved the moment before he spoke hard words to the world and they loved him for it. He rested his hands on the fine polished oak of his wide pulpit, looked down at the sermon notes on his iPad, then looked out at the four thousand people gathered here in this beautifully renovated former department store. Just as many were worshiping in the other two campuses across town, watching him on video screens. Many times more were watching him live on TV or on the church's webcast.

A year previous, the *Guardian* had called Jack "the people's pastor," and although they might be a newspaper for radical leftist Brits, they weren't far wrong. Few American pastors had more listening when they talked; few had more people paying attention to what they wrote. Jack's words seemed to resonate perfectly with the American values of hard work, achievement, self-improvement, guilt.

It was a perfect marriage of man and message.

Behind him, the giant worship screens were emblazoned with the words "Let Us Pray." He closed his eyes now and held his silence until he felt their silence, until he felt those untold thousands here and everywhere else hanging on his every word.

Then he spoke, and his warm, resonant voice reached out into those open spaces and caressed those open minds. "Father

God. You created us good, but we fell, the victims of our own desires. You loved us, but we turned our backs on you. You sent prophets to teach us right from wrong, but we chose wrong, every single time. You gave us your holy Word so we could know your will, but we ignored it, and we ignore it still. And on this day, over two thousand years ago, you sent your Son, Jesus Christ, to show us the life you wanted us to live—and we killed him for it.

"At every step, we fail you and we fall again. We fall farther and farther, until the distance between us is unbelievable, unbearable. We are so far from you, so wrecked by our own sin and desire, so lost that we can barely even see you anymore. And why would you want to see us? We fail you, again and again and again."

He paused for effect, to let people know what was coming, to build their anticipation, and then he said it, pausing slightly between each word so the people could join their voices to his as the phrase rolled out: "We have got to do better."

He felt the skin on his arms prickle and knew a similar shiver was running through this congregation and all those listening as he prayed. These were his most famous words, the catchphrase that appeared on billboards across Seattle, the title of his first best-selling book, of a children's Sunday School curriculum, of a twelve-week Twelve Step course.

He nodded, eyes closed, and whispered, "If we are ever going to deserve your love, God, we have got to do better."

He had them now, he could feel it. His heart was pounding and he suppressed the crazy grin that always threatened to spill across his face when he felt the waves of attention crashing over him. He gripped the pulpit more tightly. Anyone watching would see his knuckles whiten as he introduced the theme of this sermon, of every sermon, even on this Christmas morning. "Today, on another anniversary of your reaching out to us and our failing you, we commit ourselves to bridge the gap between us. We commit ourselves to live worthy lives, to be spotless and blameless, to—for once—get your attention for the right reason.

"'Be perfect, therefore, as your heavenly Father is perfect.' That's what the Bible tells us. But because we are so far from doing that, God has turned his back on us."

He stopped, smiled, though his eyes showed only sadness, looked out at the congregation. Some heads bowed, many looked his direction.

"And so we have got to do better."

After he finished, he held that last silence, then raised his hand like a conductor. He formed a fist and shook it a few times, then dropped it solidly onto the wood of the pulpit. He looked up and out at the crowd and said, "Amen."

The houselights came up, the screens behind him changed, and he flipped to the next page on his iPad.

"Turn with me in your Bibles to the second chapter of the gospel of Matthew," he said, and the rustle that followed as they complied began like aspens fluttering in a strong mountain breeze, then became waves crashing on the shore.

In the front row, five steps below the dais, Danny Pierce flipped him a thumbs-up. *You tell 'em, boss.*

Three seats over, his dark-eyed personal assistant, Sally Ramirez, looked up from her Bible to give him a warm smile, and Jack gave her a tiny nod and looked back down at his notes before he could get distracted, before his thoughts went in a distinctly unholy direction.

Oh my, she was a sexy girl.

Now it was Christmas morning a year later, and everything had changed.

Jack shifted on the chaise lounge. Even though she had been his downfall, he couldn't be angry at Sally. She should write a book, pose for *Playboy*, capitalize on the fifteen minutes of fame she hadn't wanted but seemed to be getting nonetheless.

He couldn't find it in him to be upset at Danny, either. A small-town boy like Jack whom he'd turned into another big-city star, Danny was the tool of the church elders, that's all. The most visible face of the church after himself and Tracy, neither of whom would ever be back. The elders needed Danny, needed some kind of continuity if they were going to keep the church together.

They needed Danny to step into his pulpit, maybe even into Jack's shoes as senior pastor.

"Good luck with that, brother," Jack muttered. Danny would need luck to balance on that high wire.

Still, Jack felt bad. He had failed them. Failed them all. Tracy. Alison. Danny. Maybe even Sally.

At that thought, he pulled out his phone again.

"Call Sally," he said.

"Calling Sally Ramirez mobile," his phone affirmed, and then he heard the ring, once, twice, three times. Her message.

"It's Sally. You know what to do."

He'd thought—

Who knows. To finish that thought would require his taking on a whole lot more responsibility for this mess than he was prepared to do.

Still, he felt bad. Or would feel bad, if he didn't drink some more of this good Mexican tequila, and that right soon.

Jack screwed open the bottle, took another swig, then closed it and lay the bottle gently down on the slate floor next to him. The sun was rising over the Caribbean, beating down on him. Soon he'd need to cover up or get sunburned worse than he already had. Even the mild winter Mexican sun was too much for him now after fifteen years in Seattle.

Why was he here?

Why had he come back to the scene of the crime?

Maybe he thought he could fix things by coming back. Maybe he thought nobody would think to look for him here. Maybe he thought Sally would join him. It didn't matter now.

He'd never even been to Mexico until September. That had been because of Sally too. She was there every step of the way.

It hadn't been his idea.

"Nothing was my idea," he murmured.

He took another drink. Things were becoming pleasantly fuzzy. It was better if he didn't remember.

The phone began playing his ring tone—the opening organ chords of Don Henley's "Dirty Laundry." Ridiculously apropos after the media had raked him over the coals these past few weeks. He'd have to change that if he kept this phone, if he decided to keep on answering a phone. But at least Sally was finally calling him back after going missing for weeks.

He raised the phone to his mouth. "Why haven't you called before now?" Jack said, trying to keep the anger out of his voice. They were in this together—or ought to be.

"I always call on Christmas morning," a male voice said softly.

His father.

He pulled the phone away from his ear, looked at it in disbelief.

"Jack," his father was saying, "I'm right—"

Jack pressed the disconnect button, tossed the phone across the balcony, his heart pounding. That had been too close. He checked the recent calls—yes, that was his father's cell. He'd accidentally answered this number three Christmases back, after the old man had backed into the digital age.

But his father had spoken at least this much truth—he had called every Christmas morning for these last ten years.

Jack had always hung up on him without a word. Maybe his father, and Mary, and her dolt of a permanent boyfriend, Dennis, watched *Home Alone* together on Christmas Eve, maybe hope sprang eternal that all Tom had to do was call his son and everything that stood between them would be erased in an instant.

Why was he calling on this Christmas morning, after the whole country knew about his disgrace? To gloat probably. Jack had never lived up to his expectations. Nobody ever could. No matter what Jack accomplished, no matter how much good he preached, how many people he helped, he could still hear the voice of his father, criticizing, calling him to account.

He could hear him even now. Some parents said, "Do your best."

Tom Chisholm had always said, "You can do better."

Well, Dad, Jack thought, *I didn't come to Mexico to screw up. I didn't come here that first time to embarrass you. I came for good reasons. I thought I was doing the right thing, until I wasn't.*

That counted for something, didn't it? He had done more

good things than bad, hadn't he? Grace raised lots of money for causes around the world. He preached good works every Sunday as part of his twelve steps of spiritual recovery, giving of yourself, giving back to God. Let the critics complain about the size of his church buildings, about the TV shows and ad buys, about his salary, which was well deserved; there was no Grace Cathedral until Jack built it.

He had done some good in the world.

Every August at the end of the fiscal year, the church went online and voted on ten charities they wanted to support in addition to the foundations Jack had created and the church supported, End Sexual Slavery and Cleanwater. And every year he took camera crews around the world to show the people of Grace—and to show their critics—what their money did, how it rescued people from brothels in Thailand, how it brought clean water to villages in Africa.

This year, Sally had asked him to consider some action on the drug violence in Mexico. It was a subject on which she had too much knowledge. Her father had been an innocent bystander killed in a gang shootout; her grandparents still lived in a border city.

Jack had asked her to tell the church about how murder and intimidation were transforming the country she loved into a nightmare for many Mexicans. *While the root problems might be too complex to tackle,* she'd said, *the wives and children who've lost husbands and fathers desperately need help.* The stat that got him on board was hearing that in the last four years, over eight thousand children had been orphaned in Ciudad Juárez alone.

Grace Cathedral was also moved by her words. The congregation voted to help fund the widows and orphans of the drug wars, and to study the problem more closely to see if they could do more.

So, in October, Jack and a group from the church had taken a weeklong junket to Mexico with a film crew. They had visited a drug-war refugee camp and an orphanage in Juárez that Grace was now sponsoring. Jack had attended a conference with regional governors, cabinet members, and Mexican clergy to talk about what Americans could do to help. They had closed their week in Mexico by filming a sequence in a village in the Yucatán where a new well drilled by Cleanwater had replaced a contaminated water source. It was a great photo op—lots of smiling children perched on and around Jack, great footage of sparkling clear water.

They were slated to fly out that afternoon from Cancún, but the airline canceled their flight and a lot of others—mechanical problems with the fleet.

"They've pulled fifty 757s off the line for emergency repairs," Sally told Jack after returning from the airline counter in the Cancún airport, "including ours. Apparently seats are coming loose in flight."

"Really?" Jack sipped the Starbucks latte he'd just bought. "I can't see how that's a good thing."

"It's a pretty major deal," she said. "Flooded the whole system with canceled flights. They say they can't get us home through our Dallas connection until Sunday, not even in first class, and there's nothing but standby on the other airlines until then."

"Two days? They can't route us through someplace else? Isn't this their fault?"

"Totally. Well, it's possible they'll be able to get us home tonight or tomorrow through Miami or Newark." Her face did not look hopeful. "What do you want to do?"

Jack thought about the possibility of being stuck in an airport overnight, about the three connections and eighteen-hour travel time, about flying to the East Coast to get to the West Coast, and he shook his head. When you travel a lot, travel gets harder, not easier.

"Forget that," he said. All of a sudden, he wanted something stronger than coffee. He took a deep breath. Then he pulled out his phone, called home, and told Tracy what was happening.

She had already heard about the failing seats. "I wondered if that was you."

"Danny's preaching Sunday," Jack said, "and I'm not scheduled for anything until Tuesday, so I'm going to wait for a direct flight. Sally will make it work."

"She always does," Tracy had said.

He hadn't thought to ask what she meant by that.

"So," he said after she'd hailed a cab back into Cancún, "what's the safest place for us in Cancún?"

"We're not staying in Cancún." Sally gave him that smile that made him uncomfortable. "I booked us rooms on Isla Mujeres, a ferry ride off the coast. Cancún is pretty safe for American tourists, but there has been some violence. Isla is a lot quieter, safer, and the beaches are beautiful. We'll go on R and R until I wrangle us a plane home."

"I don't know how to R and R," he said. "I didn't pack a bathing suit. And I'm white as—I don't know." He considered his Seattle complexion. "Something really, really white."

"Then you can sit under a palm tree and order little drinks

with umbrellas in them," she said. "You deserve something nice, Jack." She fixed him with the usual sad half smile she gave him when she was trying to convince him to take care of himself. "You of all people deserve to have some fun."

"Okay," he said, holding up his hands. "I give. I'll have a margarita. Maybe a couple of hours on the beach. We're in Mexico, let's do Mexico." He even pulled up a tiny smile from somewhere. "I mean, how much trouble can we possibly get into while we're on standby?"

"Not much," she said, and she went off to arrange their passage.

Not much.

Only all the trouble in the world.

2.

They took the ferry across the clear blue waters to Isla Mujeres, where Sally rented them a golf cart, the primary means of transport on the island. They checked into their rooms at a resort on the north end of the island, not the most expensive, she told him, but the nicest location. Great views of the rocky seaward side, white sand beaches on the leeward side, and lots of privacy. Each of their rooms had a private balcony looking out over the ocean.

That night they went into town for dinner, and Jack found himself sitting next to Sally at the bar of an open-air restaurant on Hidalgo Street.

"We're going to have that margarita," she said. "And then some ceviche."

She put her hand on his shoulder.

He looked at it.

He looked at her.

And that, he reflected later, was where it happened.

That was where he could have stopped it, if he'd really wanted to.

After Jack had that one margarita, Sally talked him into a

shot of the clear mezcal from Merida that the persuasive young bartender told them was smooth as glass. The first shot was compliments of the house.

"It's the purest product of the agave plant," she told him. "It's good for you. In Mexico we have a saying: *Para todo mal, mezcal, y para todo bien, también*." She laughed at his raised eyebrow. "'For everything bad, mezcal, and for everything good as well.'"

"I guess it would be rude not to," he said, feeling a little drunk just off that one margarita, just off her smile, and he took the tiny shot glass from her, drank, and felt his face flushing. It was good.

He accepted a second. And then a third.

Before the evening was out, they found themselves throwing back shots with a wedding party from Italy. Much of the evening was a blur—or just plain missing—but he remembered them all chewing tequila-flavored scorpions and washing them down with shots of mezcal to the cheers of a gathering throng in the street. He remembered overhearing Javier, their bartender, happily muttering, "Gringos," as he counted his tips.

Someone had driven them back to their hotel in the golf cart, and Sally held him upright and kept him on the cart when they hit potholes or speed bumps on the cobbled streets.

Someone helped him up to his room on the second floor.

And he had awakened late the next morning to bright daylight and the sound of surf crashing. He sat up, his head pounding, in a bed a little too rumpled to have been occupied by only one person.

He pulled on his pajamas, padded slowly over to close the window—the sound of the waves was setting his head on fire.

Then someone knocked on the door. Sally opened it, a card key in her hand. "You okay, boss?"

He rubbed his forehead and blinked at her. "What—what happened?"

"Ah, *querido*," she said, and she touched his head gently with her index finger, the gesture of a lover, not an employee. "You had a little more than one margarita."

She sighed, dropped her hand to her side, turned a little away from him.

"So did I."

For a moment he thought he might throw up. He hadn't wanted this. Had he? "Please, God," he gasped, even though he wasn't sure exactly what he was asking.

He started to ask Sally the questions that had to be asked. What had they done? And what were they going to do now? How would they make things right?

But Sally said suddenly, "The airline just called. I pulled some strings, got us in first class on the next flight out. We need to be packed up for the ferry in an hour."

"Okay," he said. He looked at her. She looked back. "I'll meet you in the lobby."

She nodded, crossed the room, closed the door. His head was still pounding and he still felt sick to his stomach, but he walked back to the window and opened it. The salt smell and the noise of the crashing waves washed over him. And not for the last time, he wondered what it would feel like to walk out into that water and never come back, to sink into that place where thought and memory no longer existed.

They didn't talk about what happened during the ferry back

over to Cancún, nor in the cab to the airport, nor on the flights back to Seattle.

And so, that Sunday, as he reported on his trip to the people of Grace, since they hadn't said it, then nothing had happened. And if nothing had happened, then there was no reason anyone else should know about it.

Or so he thought, until the following day when Martin Fox walked into Jack's office and shut the door behind him. Martin was a Seattle investment banker and one of Grace Cathedral's elders, the lay leaders of the congregation.

Jack himself had laid hands on Martin to ordain him as a church leader. He thought that they were as close as either of them could permit themselves to be with another human being. And yet, here stood Martin looking at him fiercely, as though they hadn't just enjoyed their best fiscal year ever, as though they didn't continue to add members and ministries, as though they weren't one of the best-known churches in the whole God-forgetting Northwest.

All of a sudden, Jack had a flashback to the pressure of Sally's hand on his shoulder, to the sight of that rumpled bed, and he felt his stomach contract with something that felt very much like fear.

Martin seated himself across from Jack without asking leave to do so, and spoke without being invited. "Why didn't you come to me when there was still time to do some damage control?"

Jack felt his gut contract again, but he kept his face blank except for the arch of one eyebrow. "What are you talking about?"

"I should have known that nobody could live up to what you preached," Martin said. "You've made us a laughingstock, Jack. A cliché."

"Martin," Jack said evenly, "what are you talking about?"

"What am I talking about?" Martin reached into the pocket of his thousand-dollar suit, pulled out his phone, and held it up for Jack to see. "This was posted on Twitter. Someone else posted footage to YouTube. One of the staff saw these and sent them to me."

"Martin—" Jack began, taking the phone.

Then he saw the picture.

It was from the bar in Isla Mujeres. Jack's face looked sweaty, flushed, as he dangled a scorpion by the tail and prepared to eat it. Behind him, Sally cheered him on, her hand on his back. He was surrounded by a dozen other rowdy revelers.

Jack looked across at Martin, who shook his head. "Is that you, Jack?"

"Who took that?" Jack asked, breathing slowly and evenly as he handed the phone back.

"An American tourist passing by thought you looked familiar. Her friend's video is worse. You're kissing Sally. And not like her pastor, believe me." Martin looked disgusted.

"That's not me," Jack said, and he tried to believe it himself. "Nothing like that happened."

"I've spoken with the other elders," Martin said, as though Jack hadn't spoken. "We've made a decision. We want to be forgiving, Jack. Redemptive. To show people that you can sin and still earn forgiveness, just like you've taught us. If you go in front of the church Sunday, acknowledge what you've done, ask them for forgiveness, we might have a chance to save you." He shrugged. "It'd mean a leave of absence. Maybe a long one. We'll plead—I don't know—sex addiction. Alcohol. Something."

"I'm not a sex addict. And I don't have a drinking problem,"

Jack said, stiffening at the very thought of standing in front of his congregation and talking about this. A hard note entered his voice. "I'm not going to confess to something I haven't done."

Martin looked at him. The sadness in his eyes spoke of more than just the situation; he seemed to be disappointed in Jack personally.

Just like Jack's father.

Jack crossed his arms then, looked back across the glassy expanse of his desk. "Forget it. I'm not doing that."

"I'm offering you a chance to save your job, Jack," Martin said. "To do the right thing. Please, Jack, be—"

"You can't take this church away from me," Jack said. "I built it from nothing."

"And you can destroy it just as quickly," Martin said. "We've already had a couple hundred emails from members wondering what we're going to do."

Jack stood up slowly, as if to announce the end of the meeting. "You can't take this church from me," he said again.

Martin stood up and measured him with a glance before buttoning his jacket and nodding. "I'm sorry, Jack. Truly I am." He shook his head, didn't offer a hand.

He turned and let himself out.

Jack sat quietly for a moment, his heart pounding. He reached for the phone and started to call home, then thought better of it. He punched in Sally's extension, listened as it sent him to voicemail.

By midafternoon, the footage had gone viral. His Facebook ministry page was filled with rants and I-told-you-so's, and "#cheatingjack" was trending on Twitter. The church's website had either been overwhelmed by visitors or hacked—either way it was down, dead as Hitler. Three of the country's biggest raw news feeds had posted the video from Isla, and Jack's desk phone and cell were both ringing nonstop. He spoke to the *Seattle Times*, CNN, Fox News, and a local TV station in the space of twenty minutes.

"We have no comment at this time," he said over and over again, until he instructed his secretary, Carly, not to send through any more blasted calls.

"Yes, sir," she said crisply, as though he were a total stranger.

Carly had never called him "sir" in the five years she had worked for him.

He dialed Sally's number again. They had to get their story straight; plausible deniability was still possible.

The truth, in this case, would do anything but set them free.

She still didn't pick up.

Jack walked down the hall to her office. It was dark, the door locked, no evidence that she'd even come in to work that day.

"Please, God," he prayed. Again, he wasn't sure what he was asking, but he needed help, needed something. Things were going south.

He had to think.

He forced himself to breathe evenly, exhale the stress.

Three doors down was Danny's office. He knocked, then opened the door and walked in.

Danny's eyes were red, and for a moment he simply looked up at Jack and didn't speak. When he did, he sounded exhausted. "Jack, what did you do?"

Jack sniffed dismissively, a sort of chuckle. He crossed over to the desk.

Danny looked up at him. "What part of this is funny, man?" He straightened in his seat. "The part where people make fun of Grace Cathedral because our pastor had himself a Girls-Gone-Wild moment on the Island of Women? The part where people call the people's pastor 'the people's hypocrite'? Yeah." He nodded. "That's big today." His voice dropped to a whisper. "Or maybe it's the part where I was God's prize idiot for believing in you."

Jack couldn't listen. He had to stay calm. To stay in control.

"This is nothing," he said. "A mistake. I've confessed worse from the pulpit."

"It's not a 'mistake,'" Danny said, using air quotes. He shook his head, leaned back for a moment in his chair, then leaned forward, elbows on his desk. "A mistake is when you, I don't know, accidentally give somebody the wrong directions because you don't know where you're going. This is worse. Yeah, I've heard you confess from the pulpit. 'I have sinned,' you tell us. 'I'm not perfect.'"

Danny paused, bit his lip as though it pained him to go on. "You tell us we have to earn God's love, that we have to do better. But now it looks like you don't follow your own rules." His voice quavered as he said, "Only an idiot would follow a leader who doesn't lead."

The words felt like shots to his body from a prizefighter. Jack stood up, reeling, his face flushed as red as in the Isla Mujeres picture. "You punk," he said. "You snot-nosed teenager. How dare you talk to me like that."

"I trusted you!" Danny shouted, pushing back his chair and stepping around the corner of his desk to glare at him. "I loved you like you were my father, Jack. I idolized you. Like you were my own father."

Danny's fists were clenched, raised waist high, as though all he needed was the slightest provocation to throw a punch. Jack thought about provoking him—and then he was flooded by memories of Danny, ever helpful, ever thoughtful, ever supportive.

The best Number Two he could have asked for.

"You shouldn't have done that," Jack said at last, and all of a sudden the anger vanished and he felt tired. "Trusted me like that. A father will only ever let you down."

He dropped into a chair, his shoulders slumped. Danny sat back down behind his desk.

They sat in silence.

Jack remembered hiring Danny as an intern fresh out of college, teaching him to preach and teach, ordaining him as a minister to Grace Cathedral.

Good memories, never again to be remembered without grief.

What had he done?

Please, God.

At last, Jack broke the silence. "What's going to happen, Danny?"

Danny looked down at his desk. "The elders are meeting now. Martin told me you refused to submit yourself to the church for discipline. To ask for forgiveness."

Jack took a deep breath, let it out. It was too late. Nothing would change. "That's right," he said.

"Then I'd guess right now they're looking over the charter and figuring out what happens if the church fires you."

"This is my church," Jack said, his voice surer than he felt. "They can't fire me."

"It's God's church, Jack," Danny said. He got up, stepped around the desk again, and dropped a hand to Jack's shoulder. He squeezed once, this boy who had trusted him, and this was worse than any blow.

Jack could not bear it; he must break. He would do anything they asked just to stop things from ending like this.

Then Danny walked out, leaving Jack alone. At last, when it was clear Danny wasn't coming back, he walked back to his office. On the way, no one met his eye. Sally's office was still empty, the lights off. His secretary didn't look up as he passed.

It was as if he were already gone.

And that was that. Before the day was out, Grace Cathedral had fired its founding pastor, contacted his wife with the news, offered her a substantial financial package predicated on her staying out of the public spotlight that was becoming very hot indeed and would only get brighter.

They offered Sally a large but undisclosed settlement to likewise disappear quietly and not make things any worse with disclosures or, God forbid, sexual harassment suits.

They offered Jack exactly nothing.

When Jack came home to the pastorage, the house was dark, his family gone. He made some phone calls to people who he knew would still answer, but they got him nowhere. No one knew where Tracy and Alison had gone—at least, no one would tell him—and no one offered him anything but bad news.

His agent, Sheila, said his publisher was invoking the moral turpitude clause standard in most Christian publishing con-tracts and would not be paying him any more royalties. "They sounded almost gleeful," she said.

"They owe us a lot of money," Jack said. "Of course they're gleeful."

Tracy wouldn't answer his calls, nor would anyone in her family.

Sally apparently didn't want to rescue him after all. She had yet to call him back.

While only hours earlier he had thousands, maybe tens of thousands of admirers, Jack had never had many close friends.

And every time Jack tried to pray, it felt as if he were holding one end of a conversation.

He was on his own.

Which was how he came to be in Isla Mujeres on Christmas morning, homeless, penniless, alone, drinking one last bottle of tequila before the hotel maintenance man pulled his door off the hinges and tossed him out into the empty future.

No one was going to save him from this.

"Merry Christmas," Jack said again, and at those words, something in him broke. He knew it was self-pity, sorrow not for what he had done, but for what was being done to him. But it felt like real heartbreak all the same. Tears flooded his eyes, and he clutched the bottle as though it were his only friend. He sobbed, great, racking sobs that shook his whole body.

And then someone knocked on the door.

Jack bit his lip to silence himself.

He listened.

The knock came again, soft. The past few days the knocking had been staccato, accompanied by angry calls of "Señor Chisholm?"

This was different.

He got unsteadily to his feet, crossed the hotel room, and

prepared to throw himself into the arms of whatever God thought he deserved.

"Okay, then," he said, opening the door. "I'll go quietly—"

He stopped in his tracks, swaying slightly.

Standing on the other side of the door was his father, Tom Chisholm, older and thinner and, yes, sadder than he had been when Jack had walked away from him a decade earlier.

They stood looking at each other. Jack noted with an air of detachment that his father was holding a cell phone in one hand. The other hand was still raised to knock again on his door.

At last, he found his voice, used the word he had not uttered for years. "Dad?"

His father nodded.

"How—" No words could register his disbelief. He could only ask the obvious. "What are you doing here?"

His father dropped his arm, put his phone in his pocket.

There were tears in his eyes.

Jack had never seen his father cry, not at the funerals of his sister or his mother. He was too strong for that, too distant. He was a rock. An island.

And yet a tear was tracing its way down his cheek.

Jack blinked. Was it the tequila? Was this just another chapter of his dream?

But he could feel the weight of the bottle in his hand, the weight of the despair in his heart.

This was real, and it was happening now.

"What are you doing here?"

Tom Chisholm looked away for a moment. He raised one forefinger to wipe the tear from his cheek. "I guess—"

He cleared his throat, paused for a moment.

Then he simply extended his hands to Jack and said, "I've come to take you home."

Home.

Jack looked down at the bottle in his hand, almost empty. He spared a glance at the room behind him, unkempt as if animals had been nesting here. He closed his eyes tightly for a moment to see if that would stop the world from spinning so fast.

At last, he opened his eyes.

His father stood there, arms open, still waiting—as perhaps he had been waiting all this time, all these years.

I've come to take you home.

He decided.

"Okay, then," Jack said.

He put an unsteady foot forward, then another.

Then he stepped across the threshold and into the arms that had once rescued him from the angry waves.

3.

When he woke early the next morning, it was to the familiar childhood smells of coffee and bacon frying. Jack thought for a moment he might be dreaming again. He sat up and looked around. Yes, he was lying in his old room in the queen-sized bed his mother had bought for when he and Tracy came to visit, lying under the flowered Laura Ashley comforter she had picked out. Jack had swept the color-coordinated blue-and-silver satin pillows onto the floor when he fell into bed the night before. They littered the ground now like satin toadstools.

He saw his bookcase, filled with the C. S. Lewis and Tolkien books he'd consumed as a kid, plus what looked like overflow from some of the other bookcases in the house. Was that an old tax guide?

Some of his high-school football trophies and a game ball, dusty now, still adorned the top of his dresser. He could read "Mayfield Wildcats MVP 1990" on the largest trophy and couldn't help smiling. Those had been good times.

Mayfield football—not to mention Mayfield itself—had gone downhill since then.

Next to his dresser was the rocking chair his grandfather had given him when he turned thirteen. "A man's got to have a rocking chair," Grampa Joe had said. He'd been unable to hide his disappointment. Surely Grampa Joe made it mostly because he loved making things with his hands. But Jack spent countless hours in that chair reading, and years later, working on a sermon for his mother's funeral while Tracy snoozed in this very bed. It had been a perfect gift after all. He had learned carpentry in the hopes of making something for his son someday.

That is just one of the many dreams that didn't come true.

Over the chair was the corkboard, plastered with pictures of quarterbacks Joe Montana and Peter Gardere. "Peter the Great," the University of Texas QB who had beaten the University of Oklahoma four times. He looked over the pictures of high-school friends, of him with his high-school girlfriend, Darla Scroggins, now Darla Taylor, long married to his former fullback, the hateful Jamie Taylor. His dad had taken this hunting picture with Jack's best friend, Bill Hall. Jack had shot a twelve-point whitetail buck and with Bill's help was holding the rack steady for the picture.

He hadn't seen Bill Hall, or Darla Scroggins, or James Taylor, may he rest in pieces, in a decade. The room was like a museum of his life, cut off years ago. There were no pictures of Grace Cathedral, no evidence of his life as "the people's pastor," only one small picture on the bedside table of him and Tracy, taken one Sunday after church on what was their last visit before his mother's funeral.

The room reminded him of an episode of *The Twilight Zone.* Or maybe that Kurt Vonnegut novel he'd read in college where aliens kept human beings in zoos for observation.

He could hear his father listening to the morning news on KLBJ-AM as he got ready to go open up the hardware store and lumberyard that had been in their family for three generations.

Jack threw off the covers, got to his feet, and went to the front window to look out at the world.

It was the day after Christmas in Mayfield, Texas. Snow lay drifted inches deep in the front yard. Jack guessed that in back of the house, Live Oak Creek was frozen over, something that had happened only a few times in his memory.

He stood at the window listening to his father move around downstairs and wondered what he must be thinking about. Although it had been a positive beginning, they had made the long trip home mostly in silence. By the time Jack sobered up enough to absorb the explanation of how Tom found him, he was also sober enough to wonder if he'd made a good choice returning.

It was his only choice. That was true enough.

But what was he going to do next?

Tom told him that he had been asking the church for weeks about Jack's whereabouts. At last, Danny Pierce called him. He had tracked Jack back to Isla Mujeres by the trail of credit card charges.

"Of course," Jack had said, nodding. "They will know you by your trail of credit charged."

In the end, nothing was magical about Tom arriving on his doorstep, although the thought of his father, who was neither young nor wealthy, traveling to another country to bring him home was humbling.

So humbling that they had danced around the hard truth

throughout the trip and he hadn't known what to say late last night when they arrived home. The closest they'd come to acknowledging it was when his father saw him up to his old room.

"It's not much, I know," Tom said. "But maybe the familiar is good just now."

"It's fine," Jack said. He set his suitcase down on the bed and unzipped it. It was, he realized now, filled mostly with shorts and T-shirts. "Too bad I wasn't on the lam in an arctic climate."

"Some of your old jackets are still in the closet downstairs," his father said. "And I'll bet you have some sweaters up in your closet."

"I'm sure they are both warm and stylish," Jack said.

Appropriate clothing was the least of his problems, and both of them knew that.

They stood for a while saying nothing.

"Well," Jack said, turning to see his father with his hand on the doorknob. "It was really good of you to come and get me. Thank you."

His father raised a hand, waved off the thanks. They looked at each other.

Whatever needed to be said was not forthcoming. Not at that moment, anyway.

"Good night, son," Tom said, turning to go. "Tomorrow maybe things will look better."

"I doubt it."

That caused Tom to pause for a moment at the bedroom door. "You know, Jack," his father said, "whatever you've done, it can be forgiven."

"No," Jack said. "I don't think so."

"Well," his father said with that old gruffness in his voice again, "you're the pastor. But I hope to God you're wrong." And he closed the door and left Jack with his own thoughts.

Jack tossed for hours before finally falling asleep.

This morning would be just as awkward, he was sure. What could they possibly talk about? His childhood? The sermon he'd preached at his mother's funeral? Before yesterday, he hadn't spoken to his father in years, and they shared so few good memories to fall back on.

Sometime today or tomorrow, he imagined he would have to see his sister Mary. They'd exchanged nothing but innocuous Christmas cards since he left home. He also imagined that sooner or later he would start encountering people who knew his past and recent history. He couldn't remain in this place forever.

When he agreed to come home with his father, he stepped across that threshold of deciding whether or not to live, but living wasn't going to be easy. He needed money, first of all, and he needed to get his family and church back. He needed to show the world he was still good, that this mistake wasn't the measure of who he was, and the sooner he got started, the better.

"Jack," his father called from the bottom of the stairs. "Breakfast."

"I'm up," he called back—feeling fifteen again. "I'll be right there."

He threw on his lone pair of jeans and a ripped University of Texas sweatshirt he found in the closet, padded downstairs, and found his father seated at the kitchen table. Beside him waited a plate of scrambled eggs, bacon, and toast.

"Hot breakfast," Jack said, and against his will he smiled. His mom had always insisted they eat a hot breakfast when it was cold outside.

"Yeah," his father said. He looked down at his plate, then across at Jack. "Will you say grace?"

Jack hesitated, then shook his head. "Why don't you," he said.

Tom nodded slightly. "For this food we are about to consume and for all your good gifts, we are truly thankful, oh Lord. Amen."

The clinking and clanking of utensils against plates was the loudest noise for the next few minutes. Jack looked up now and then to see his father chewing slowly, thoughtfully.

Bacon was crunched, coffee slurped.

"How are things at the store?" Jack managed when it became clear he would have to be the one to start.

"Oh," Tom said, swallowing, "we get by. Things are tough for everyone."

"Is Mary still working for you?"

Tom shook his head. "Not for years."

"Really?" Jack shoveled some eggs onto his fork. "I thought—" He shook his head. Well. "What does she do, then?"

"She went to work for herself," Tom said. "She's got her own accounting office now. Busy during tax time."

"Wow," Jack said. "I guess I thought she'd die at the cash register."

Tom actually chuckled a bit at that. "She and her MBA got too expensive to keep," he said. "I'm sure she'll tell you about it."

Jack's half smile vanished. "I doubt that," he said. "Is she still with Dennis?"

Tom nodded as he buttered a slice of toast. "That's the cash register she'll die at," he said softly.

Jack seized this topic gratefully. "They've been engaged since I left for college. Are they ever getting married?"

His father glanced up, then back down at his toast. "Ask me something I know the answer to."

Jack hesitated. "Did you tell her you were bringing me home? What did she say?"

"About what you'd expect." Tom shrugged. He looked across the table at Jack. "You know her. She's a hard one. Told me I ought to leave you where you lay." He shook his head. "Her exact words. Just didn't see how I could do that."

"Yeah," Jack said. He sighed. "I guess I would have advised you the same." He had a thought—salvation!—about something else they could discuss. "How are things at Saint Paul's sort-of-Lutheran Church? How's Pastor John, the modern-day Martin Luther?"

Pastor John Heinrich had led his church out of the national denomination some fifteen years ago over some theological issue or other. As a result, the sign out front said "Lutheran" in big letters, and below it, in much smaller letters, "Independent."

Jack had been away at school. When he returned, it was a *fait accompli*.

His father smiled for a moment, then looked out past Jack and then down at the table again before he spoke. "Not so good, I guess. Pastor John died three years back, and we can't afford a full-time pastor anymore. We've had guest preachers, but it's not the same." He shrugged. "And most of us are old and getting older. I guess it's time to admit defeat."

"It sounds like times are hard all over." Jack knew from his reading, and from years of talking to other pastors, that small-town churches were drying up.

"That they are," his father said. "All the churches are down. Except First Baptist. They're circling the wagons against the liberals." Tom shrugged his shoulders slowly. "In scary times, people like to have their fears confirmed, right?"

"I don't know," Jack said. "Maybe."

Was that what his father thought he'd been doing?

Was it what he was doing?

He cast his mind about for a way to put that back in the box. "Can't—can't you get some seminary kid who needs some on-the-job training?"

His father looked at him. "What does a young person today know about my life? The life of Sister Clanton? She's ninety-four, buried two husbands and seven kids." He sighed again. "No. We tried that. We had some Lutherans from the program in Austin. Two boys and a girl. She was the best, actually. At least she could feel for you."

"Wow," Jack said. "I'm—sorry." Truth be told, he had always hated that little church. Pastor John had beaten him down throughout his childhood with talk about his unworthiness until finally he'd accepted it as a theological truth. But he also knew that little church had been a rock in the lives of his parents, and he remembered the joy on his mother's face when she had sung the old hymns. "There is wonder-working power in the precious blood of the Lamb."

The clock chimed eight times, and both of them looked up with something like relief at the interruption.

"Your sister is coming for dinner tonight," Tom said, dabbing at his mouth with a napkin and rising from his chair. "I expect I'll stop and get some chicken on the way home."

"Okay," Jack said. "Is Dennis coming too?"

Tom shrugged. "Do you want him to?"

"Yeah. I don't know. Whatever you think." Dennis Mays had been two years ahead of Jack in school. They had played football together, but as with many of the people in his life, he was coming to realize, they had been friendly but never friends.

His father was putting his dishes in the sink. He wiped his hands on a dish towel, then spoke without turning. "I figure you'll need a few days to sort this out. Figure out what's next. Take whatever time you need. But I wanted you to know—you're welcome here, Jack."

Jack thought he should say something, make an appropriate noise, but he couldn't think of the right guttural response, so he sat in silence.

"I know I'm not much good at saying things," his father went on. "I just wanted you to know. You can stay as long as you need. As long as you want."

"Thank you," Jack said. "Really."

Tom nodded, turned from the sink, and went to the hall closet. Jack could hear the rustle of clothing as his dad pulled on his winter coat, gloves, and Grampa Joe's old gray felt Stetson fedora.

"You know," Tom said, coming back into the kitchen, "my father bought this hat in 1950 at the haberdashery downtown. It was the newest style. The Whippet, they called it."

"Really?" Jack put his dishes in the sink. "The Whippet?"

"When I'm gone"—Jack could hear the clinking of keys as his father pulled them out of the bowl on the hall table—"I want you to have this hat."

"It's a nice hat," Jack said, thinking he would not wear that hat if his life depended on it. "But you're going to be around for a long time."

"I'll see you this evening," Tom said. He was bundled up tight. "Should be a quiet day, day after Christmas."

"Batteries," Jack said, remembering. "You'll sell a lot of batteries."

"Maybe so." Tom nodded, raised a hand in good-bye, and was gone.

Jack sat down at the fine oak table his Grampa Joe had crafted before Jack was born. He sipped his coffee and looked down at his dim reflection. He rubbed his finger over the glossy dark finish. Beautiful.

As a boy, he sat here, his mother to his immediate right, his sisters across from him. Mary and Martha had been a year older, as identical as pieces of bread in a sandwich. When they switched places at the table to fool him, he never even noticed.

That old sadness washed over him in an instant and he was plunged into a pool of grief. In the week after Martha's death, his father had taken the leaf out of the table and hauled the extra chair out to the shop. The four of them had sat without speaking at an abbreviated feast, his mother drawn and red-eyed, while his father drew away from them, his words even fewer and more hard-edged, and Jack sank into himself, the one thing that could never be taken away from him.

The stupid comments some people made, that it was some-how a blessing that the girls were twins, that you'll always be able to see her sweet face in the one who's left.

A blessing?

Or a curse?

Jack put his head in his hands. The past was hard to visit. He suddenly felt exhausted.

He let out a deep sigh and took a final sip of his coffee. Maxwell House. If those people in Seattle could possibly think less of him, this would do it. He trudged up the eleven stairs to his room, rolled back into bed, and pulled the covers over his head.

He wanted to go back to sleep, wanted to dream of his mother laughing, to remember a time when laughter had lived in this place.

She was the only one who could ever make his father laugh. He had been a different man once, long, long ago. Jack remembered the time his mother had imitated Grampa Joe's Thanksgiving prayer at the reception after his funeral. She'd reminded them of that epic annual prayer when the old man built clause by clause, neighborhood by neighborhood—"and, Father, we thank you for rain, and for the birds of the air and the lilies of the field, for they neither sow nor reap nor gather into barns"—until seven-year-old Jack's stomach growled in protest.

He remembered how Tom had, at first, been offended but then had hidden his smile behind a hand. And then how he had been laughing as hard as the rest of them, laughing until tears filled his eyes, laughing until he had to sit down.

Those had been better days.

Better days.

4.

When Jack woke, it was dark outside. He shook himself awake as though he had slept through the morning alarm and had to get to work.

Someone was ringing the doorbell.

Jack got out of bed and looked out the window.

A huge Dodge pickup sat in the driveway. Dennis, no doubt. Always Dodge trucks, one after another. The man was a study in steadiness.

It must be time for dinner.

"Hey, Dad," his sister was saying from the hallway downstairs, and then he heard a rumble of greeting from Dennis.

He couldn't let them know he had slept the day away. He threw water on his face, pulled on a pair of jeans and a black T-shirt, and came down the stairs two at a time. When he got there, the three of them were conversing in low tones in what had once been the living room, that formal and uncomfortable room at the front of the house that was never lived in.

Dennis was spread out across the dusty royal-blue velvet sofa that was perhaps as old as he was. Mary and her dad sat on the perpendicular matching love seat.

Dennis Mays looked up as Jack walked in and a genuine smile spread across his face. "Twelve," he said, and he hoisted his considerable bulk off the couch to greet him.

Jack had worn the number twelve as Mayfield's starting quarterback for three years, one of which Dennis had been his starting left guard. Dennis had been a considerable presence even as a young man. Now he was roughly the size of an oil tanker. Jack wondered clinically how a human being could carry a stomach that size around without collapsing. It was a feat of engineering, for certain.

"Seventy-Eight," Jack said, stepping forward, a smile creeping across his face. Their handshake was unsettling. Jack wasn't sure his hand would recover without surgery.

"Sis," he said as Mary offered her hand from her seated position.

"Jack," she said. She nodded, let go, and he stepped back. Not the warmest of greetings, but just about what he'd expected.

He settled into the ugly La-Z-Boy recliner.

"It's good to see you, Twelve," Dennis was saying. "Good to see you."

"Your sister brought a casserole," Tom said. "I told her she didn't need to—"

"You'd eat that fried food from Chicken Express every night if I didn't cook for you," she complained. She turned to Jack. "He knows better, he's not supposed to—"

Tom cleared his throat. Mary stopped midsentence. Jack noted this and filed it away for later.

"It's my ham casserole," she began again. She looked across at Jack. "You always used to like that."

He was strangely touched that she remembered. Mary had taken over the family cooking after Martha died. Their mom had been severely depressed for years and rarely cooked. She would often spend the day in bed and then eat supper in the pajamas she'd worn all day.

"Thanks," he said. "You'll have to give me that recipe someday."

"It's in the Fannie Farmer cookbook in the kitchen," she said crisply. "You would know if you were ever in there."

"Well," Dennis said, raising a hand to stop her, "he's here now, isn't he? Twelve, why don't you break out that cookbook and make us something for dinner tomorrow? You always were a good little homemaker." He laughed, a big, rolling belly laugh that filled the room.

It was famous in Mayfield lore: Jack and his friend Bill had taken Home Ec as seniors, had been the only boys in the Future Homemakers of America picture in the yearbook. Although the strategy had been to avoid taking Calculus—and it had worked—Dennis still found the Home Ec thing hilarious these twenty years later. But nobody had ever impugned Jack's manhood. Being the starting quarterback, "QB 1," inoculated you against that for all time.

"How was your day?" Tom asked, his voice quiet after that ringing laughter. "Productive?"

"Good," Jack said. "Yeah. Good. I've got some leads." He nodded, too many times.

The silence stretched. Jack guessed his father had spilled that the house was dark when he returned home.

"How long you here, Twelve?" Dennis asked. "I can get some of the guys together. Maybe we can go hunting this weekend—"

Mary inclined her head in that way she was known for. She, too, was interested in Jack's response.

"I don't know. Just 'til I figure a few things out. Get my second wind. Not long."

Mary's gaze was cool, remote. "Until the reporters find you?"

Dennis raised a finger again as if to stop her, and she turned angrily to him and spat, "I am so tired of being shushed," before delivering her next words to Jack. "Do you know how many calls I got from TV stations and newspapers in places I've never even heard of? How many news trucks have been set up in front of Dad's store? How many headlines in the tabloids at the grocery store checkout?" She humphed. "'The People's Pastor in Mexican Love Nest'?"

"Mary—" Tom turned to Jack. "They were only here for a few days. I told them I didn't know where you were, that I didn't imagine you'd ever come here. They left." He shrugged.

"They'll be back," Mary said. "And they will make our lives a living hell."

Jack looked around the room, at his sister, father, and Dennis.

"If I'm an embarrassment to you," he said steadily, trying to keep the edge out of his voice, "I can go. I can just walk out the door."

"Oh yes, Jack," Mary said. "That's what you always do. Just walk out the door. You haven't wanted to be a part of this family for ten years."

"There hasn't been a family here for ten years," he said.

"So go, Jack," she said, her face flushed. "Go back to your

perfect family and your big life." She immediately regretted her words. He could see her lip crumple as she realized her comment had staggered him.

But it stayed said, all the same.

Jack got to his feet. He couldn't stay, and he couldn't go. Maybe all he could do was forget about things for a few hours. "I'm sorry," he told his father. "I'll leave in the morning. Could— can I borrow a twenty?"

His father looked as though he'd been smacked in the head with a two-by-four. "I–I–Jack, I don't think I have a twenty."

Jack actually laughed. He shook his head. Of course he didn't. "Don't worry about it. Really."

Tom took out his wallet, counted out a ten and three ones, handed them to Jack with a quavering hand.

"I hope you enjoy the casserole," Jack told the room. He turned and walked through the hallway and out the front door, into the cold night. After the door shut, he stood on the front porch shivering for a moment. He didn't have a coat, but he didn't care about that.

Of all the ways to die, this wasn't the worst of them.

He set out across the front lawn toward town.

Behind him he heard the front door open, and Mary called out his name. She ran to catch him.

"Jack," she repeated, taking him by his elbow.

"Go back inside, Mary," he said. "You'll freeze out here."

"Jack," she said, and he could see that she was crying. "If you leave, you will break his heart. Again. Do you know why he came to get you after all this? Do you even know?"

"No," Jack said. He yanked his elbow free. "And I don't care.

He was a lousy father. That was a nice thing he did, bringing me home from Mexico. I don't know why he did it. But one nice thing doesn't make up for—"

"He's dying," she said, and she took his elbow again. "He's already on borrowed time. I don't think he could go without—without—"

She stopped. She sobbed so hard that for a moment she couldn't speak. Against his will, Jack felt himself swallowing, felt his stomach contract.

"I'm sorry," he said. "But what can I do? I don't have a dollar to call my own. I can't even—"

"You could not break his heart!" she wailed. "Just this once, you could stop before you break his heart."

Jack looked at her.

He shook his head, pulled his arm gently from her grasp.

"Maybe we should have had this conversation a long time ago," Jack said. "It's too late now."

"Jack," she pleaded.

"It's too late," Jack repeated. He stumbled away from her, his feet crunching through the snow.

She didn't follow him this time, and he didn't look back.

He walked the eight blocks into what people still called downtown, past the bank, Chisholm's Hardware, and the Buy-n-Buy convenience store. The town got smaller every year, more threadbare, closer to death. What kept people here?

At last, he stepped into the warmth of Buddy's, the perpetually run-down bar that at least didn't pretend to be anything other than what it was: the only place in town where you could drink your troubles away.

Including him, three people sat at the bar. He recognized the bartender, a girl who had been two grades below him in school. She'd been married and divorced twice since then, and as Jesus might have said, the man she was living with now was not her husband. A white-headed man was at the bar with his back to him.

Jack paid him no attention as he bellied up, said, "Hi, Shayla. Pitcher of Bud Light. One glass." It was the best he could afford on his borrowed thirteen-dollar stake.

She goggled at him. "Hey," she said. "Umm. Okay. Coming right up."

"Why, if it isn't Jack Chisholm," said the wry and surprisingly kind voice to his right. He turned to see the speaker scoot his drink down the bar and slide into the next chair. The voice belonged to a priest—or at least the man was dressed like a priest, all in black and wearing a clerical collar. "It's Francis Xavier Malone."

Jack recognized him at once, although he took the outstretched hand and shook it nonetheless.

"Father Frank," he said. "What are you doing here? I thought—"

He caught himself. Frank Malone had been the priest in Mayfield from before Jack was born. And Jack had grown up knowing two sure things: in Mayfield, football was king, and Father Frank had to be kept away from alcohol.

Oh well. He had put his foot in it already. So he nodded over at the amber liquid on the rocks in Frank's glass. "I thought you couldn't get a mixed drink in this county."

Frank smiled grimly. "A sad thing it is when your private shame becomes public knowledge." He raised his glass and swirled the liquid around, the ice clinking. He took a sip, smacked his lips. "Only ginger ale, Jack. Although you recall aright. One still cannot order a mixed drink anywhere in this county, although I don't think I could get one here even if it were legal."

"That's God's truth, Father," Shayla said, bringing Jack's pitcher, which had inches of foam atop the watery beer, and his one glass. "I'm not allowed to serve him anything but ginger ale," she told Jack. "It'd be my job."

"That's the way it is in Mayfield," Frank said, "as I'm sure you remember. Everyone knows your business. But on the good days, no one lets you struggle alone." He rolled the ice cubes around in his glass again. "So what brings you here?"

"Family visit," Jack said nonchalantly. "I'm just here for a few days." He started to pour a beer.

"So," Father Frank said, steepling his fingers in front of his face, "I observe that you are here in Buddy's, where I have never known you to be, on the day after Christmas. On the feast day of Saint Stephen."

He cocked his head to one side. "I also observe that you set out from your house without jacket or hat on the coldest night of the year. And," he said, nodding his head toward the light beer Jack was pouring into his mug, "I observe that you are drinking for two. And not too particular in the drinking, if you'll forgive my saying so."

"Trying to keep my girlish figure," Jack said. He drank, grimaced at the bitter, watery taste. "Ugh."

"I know." Father Frank sighed. "And yet even that, I pine for."

Jack looked at Father Frank's open, smiling face and he

prepared to stand up and sit elsewhere. "No offense, Father. I just wanted to drink alone. Not bother anyone. Not be bothered."

Frank nodded, took a drink of his ginger ale. "Sure. I get it. You wanted to pretend."

Jack almost spat out the beer he was swallowing. "Excuse me?"

He tried to glare at Frank, but the old priest was having none of it. That grin had slid back across his face. "'Excuse me' because it's bad manners to acknowledge the elephant in the room? Or because you think that perhaps your recent experience is unique in human history?"

Jack could only look at him and blink.

"We did have reporters lined up from there to there," Shayla said, indicating from one end of the bar to the other. "It's not like what you did is a secret."

"I didn't do anything," Jack muttered, pouring himself another beer. One more glass and he would be in a good place; if only he could get there before anyone said anything else he couldn't ignore.

"What you did or didn't do is of no consequence," Frank said softly. "Not to God."

"Excuse me?" Jack repeated.

"The world is full of the bedraggled, the beat up, and the burnt out," Frank said. "The ragamuffins. You did get that one thing right in your preaching. Yes, I've followed your career," he said to Jack's wide-eyed stare. "We don't send forth many famous men of God from Mayfield. We are a mess. All of us. Your case is just a little more visible in a day and age when everybody seems to know everybody's business."

Jack poured himself that third magical beer, chugged a long drink, which gave him the courage to go on. "Father Frank, you've been stuck in this town for—what—forty years? What do you know, really?"

"What do I know about people who don't have it all together?" Frank fixed him with his gaze. "Only that I am one. But there is grace, Jack. Amazing grace. When we acknowledge that we are all just beggars at the door of God's mercy, God can make something beautiful out of us."

Jack dropped his gaze and finished his beer. "That's lovely, Father," he said. "But I didn't come to Buddy's to talk shop. Why don't you save that for your best-selling book *Beggars at the Door of God's Mercy*. I expect it'll get you on all the talk shows."

Father Frank shook his head. "A small-town priest is all I have ever been, and it has been the joy of my life. But if I were to write a book—if I were to leave behind something of my life's work—it would be to tell people that broken and worthless as we are, we are nonetheless loved beyond all reckoning."

Something wet itched at the corners of his eyes. He rubbed them, then turned away. This pitcher had one more glass in it before he had to do something—to sober up and trudge back to his father's house or to walk off into the endless night.

"I read your books," Father Frank was saying as Jack poured this last beer. From down the bar, Shayla chimed in, "I started the first one, Jack, but I couldn't get all the way through it." She made an *I'm sorry* face. "It made me feel bad about myself."

"That was sort of the point," Jack muttered. "We don't feel bad enough about ourselves."

"Oh, I think you feel bad enough. More than bad enough,"

Frank said. "And you taught everyone else to feel the same." He patted the top of the bar. "When you were inviting people to open their Bibles, did you ever invite them to turn to that lovely spot in Romans? 'For I am certain of this: neither death nor life, nor angels, nor principalities, nothing already in existence and nothing still to come, nor any power, nor the heights nor the depths, nor any created thing whatever, will be able to come between us and the love of God, known to us in Christ Jesus our Lord.'"

That last glass of beer had worked wonders; he could say what he was actually thinking. Jack turned to Father Frank and smiled for several seconds. "I was the people's pastor. You're a broken-down, alcoholic priest in a broken-down town. And you think you're going to teach me something about God?"

Frank inclined his head, and Jack thought maybe he'd gone too far.

He'd never been punched by a priest before.

Then Frank raised his head and looked Jack square in the eyes. He saw pain, but there was something else. "You've spoken God's truth there, lad. But perhaps you might try and answer the question that yours begs: How is it that, late one night on the first day of Christmas, the people's pastor finds himself in a bar in this nothing town, talking about God with this broken-down alcoholic who calls himself a priest?"

"I'm sorry," Jack said, raising a hand. He sighed. "That was cruel."

Frank shrugged. "You asked me a real question," he said. "I'm asking you one in return."

Jack raised his pitcher. Nothing but the dregs was left.

"Can I get you anything else, Jack?" Shayla asked.

"No," Jack said. "Thanks, Shayla." He laid his last two dollars on the bar as a tip and took a deep breath.

Back out in the cold? Back to a house full of memories?

He wondered where Tracy was tonight, if Alison was asleep or lying awake. He imagined her sleeping, probably at her grandparents' in California. Maybe they were nervously listening for the door, wondering if he was going to track them down. Why hadn't he even considered it?

More likely the church had helped them start a new life somewhere far away from TV cameras. And tonight, the grandparents were visiting, helping Tracy and Alison ease into their first Christmas without him.

Not even that fourth glass of beer could soften the blow. He would never find them, never get his church back, never be anything but a punch line for the rest of his life.

"I'm finished," he said. He sat back in his chair, feeling it in his bones. Everyone had abandoned him. God had abandoned him. He was done for.

"What's that?" Frank asked.

"Nothing," he said. He laughed, a sardonic "huh," and slid unsteadily to his feet. "Thanks for the company. I guess I'll go"— he exhaled slowly—"home."

"Let me drive you," Frank said, stretching out a hand to steady him. "You've had a lot to drink in a little time, and Shayla has had enough of my company for this one night."

"Go on," she said, looking up from polishing a glass. "Who needs you?" But she smiled at Frank, and despite his own extremity, Jack could see love in her eyes.

"Okay, then," Jack said. "I'd be grateful."

They walked out to the sidewalk. The wind was whipping down the street, and Jack hugged himself for warmth.

Father Frank still drove that ancient Chrysler LeBaron, maroon, with a white vinyl top.

"I know," Frank said, opening Jack's door. "1986. Beat up as its driver."

"You've had this car as long as I've known you. Known about you," he corrected himself as they got inside. Frank turned the heat on high as soon as the engine warmed up.

"It still gets me where I'm going. That's enough. And I don't think I could ever replace all my cassette tapes. Not on a priest's salary."

"Well, there you go," Jack said. He was beginning to warm up, and he felt pleasantly buzzed. Father Frank pulled something from the backseat—a cassette. He pushed it in and an Irish reel filled the car.

"Really?" Jack asked. "You are a walking stereotype, Father Frank."

"What can I say?" Frank shrugged. "We love what we love."

"I expected Van Morrison," Jack said.

"Ouch," Frank said, backing into the empty street and pulling forward onto the snow-blown main street. "And here I was just listening to 'Moondance.'"

It was a short drive, and they let the silence sit. It was not uncomfortable.

"It's the corner up ahead," Jack blurted out, perhaps unnecessarily, because Frank pulled easily into the drive behind his father's car. Dennis and Mary had left.

"Your father and I have had the odd conversation of late,"

Frank said, after he shifted into park. He looked meaningfully across at Jack. "You've come home at a good time."

Again, Jack could not help but laugh, a bark of amusement totally out of proportion to the mirth he felt. "Is that how it seems to you?"

"Yes," Frank said. "Indeed it does."

Jack reached for the door handle, but Father Frank reached his hand out. "This broken-down old priest would enjoy a word or two with you again sometime."

Jack turned to go. Then he nodded. "It's a small town," Jack said.

"That it is. Give my best to your father. Good night, Jack."

He waved as he backed onto the street, then drove off into the night. Jack stood watching him go, shivering, wondering if he would wake up his father. Wondering if he really wanted to go inside at all.

He walked up to the lighted porch, raised his fist to knock, but hesitated.

It opened then, of its own accord. Or so it seemed.

His father stood in his plaid flannel robe, thin white legs exposed beneath it.

"Come inside," he said. "I made coffee."

"Hey," Jack said, closing the door behind him. "I—"

"I made coffee," Tom repeated. He led Jack by the arm to the table. They sat and sipped and thought about what they might say to each other.

"I'm sorry about your sister," Tom said at last. "She shouldn't have said those things."

Jack shrugged. "She's got a right. She's been here. I wasn't. I'm—I'm sorry I ruined the evening."

His father waved it away. "You can't ruin ham casserole. I left you some if you want to warm it up."

"I think I do," Jack said, making his way to the fridge. He hadn't eaten since breakfast, and not much then. "Father Frank said I should tell you hello."

"Did he?" Tom asked. "Father Frank?"

Jack was spooning some casserole onto a plate and paused. "I guess because he's been keeping an eye out for you." Jack looked back at his father. "Since you've been sick and all."

Tom nodded, his head down. "He has."

"I'm sorry," Jack said, returning to the table. "I'm sorry you couldn't tell me. It's no wonder Mary's mad at me. I'd be furious."

"Well," Tom said. He shrugged. "You're here now."

"It doesn't make up for—" Jack stopped himself; it sounded horribly familiar.

They listened to the microwave hum, the fan breathe out the scents of melted cheese and diced ham.

"Why don't you come to work with me tomorrow?" his father asked after neither had said anything for a minute or two. "I could use your help with year-end inventory. Back room mostly. You wouldn't have to talk to customers. And you could do with something to occupy your mind."

The microwave dinged, and Jack pulled out his steaming food. "I'm not saying no," he said. "But how is counting hammers going to get back what I've lost?"

"I don't know," his father said. "But it seems to me that we do what we can with what we have where we are." He spread his hands, indicated the table, the town, the planet. "And this is where we are."

"Sounds like something Father Frank would say," Jack said, seating himself.

"It probably is," Tom said. He inclined his head. "Don't forget to say grace."

Jack looked at his father, waiting.

He looked at his sister's ham casserole, steaming on the plate.

He looked around the table, empty of so much for so long.

He looked at himself, a dark shadow in his grandfather's dining room table.

He looked back at his father, head bowed.

And then he, too, inclined his head.

"Grace," he said.

Then Jack picked up his fork, and slowly and with gathering strength, he began to eat.

5.

Some things never change. In Jack's lifetime alone, the world had moved from rotary dial to cell phones, from three networks to YouTube and Netflix, but in Chisholm's Hardware, Eisenhower was still president—or maybe Roosevelt.

Teddy Roosevelt.

Jack walked in and turned in a circle, taking in its rough-plank floors and tall shelves filled with hacksaw blades, plumbing supplies, and four-penny nails.

He was amazed that customers could slide a credit card at the cash register now. Otherwise, it didn't seem that anything had changed since his childhood, including the dirty tile at the front desk.

"You know, they've developed a wonderful new flooring," Jack said. "I think it's called linoleum." He shook his head. "And that stool. You should use it for kindling."

"Your mother used to sit on this stool," Tom said after they had unlocked the door, hung up their coats, and stepped behind the front counter.

"I remember," Jack said. "You used to work the back room,

and she'd sit out here and make people laugh. That was before—" Jack stopped.

"Yes," his father said, sighing as he eased himself slowly up onto the stool. "That was before."

"So, what can I do?" Jack said, looking around. He had worked at the store through high school, and in the summers when he was home from college. He had worked the register, loaded lumber, signed in shipments, made deliveries, counted loose nails. He'd done every task in the store except bookkeeping, which was Mary's province. Running this store was second nature to him.

Like preaching a sermon, he thought, shaking his head.

Like shaking hands after the service. Like smiling until your face hurts.

"I tried to let things sell down here at the end of the year so there'd be less to count."

"Like always." Jack nodded.

Tom pulled a black binder from next to the cash register. "I was hoping maybe you could do a rough count of the lumber. Manny and I can't shift the piles the way we used to."

Manny was older than Tom—had worked for Tom's father, in fact. No one, maybe not even Manny himself, knew how old he truly was. Jack guessed that about all he was good for anymore was sweeping the floor and companionship. Not that those were unimportant.

"Loose and bundled lumber both, okay?"

"Of course." Jack felt a tiny smile flicker at the corners of his mouth. He'd be outside where he didn't have to talk to anybody, and two days after Christmas, surely nobody would be in the lumberyard. It was as close to hiding out as he could get in plain sight.

As if on cue, the bell at the front door jingled, and an elderly woman in a red-and-green Christmas-themed pantsuit and tennis shoes stepped inside. Her agility belied her age. Nora Calhoun was in her eighties, but she was apparently still able to take her morning walk.

"Jack Chisholm," she was saying now. He looked left and right, as though perhaps she was speaking to someone else. But her eyes—and her grin—were directed straight as an arrow. "That's right, son. I am talking to you."

Against his better judgment, he returned her smile. "Mrs. Calhoun," he said. "Can I show you some hammers on this lovely morning?"

"Don't give me any of your lip," she said, but she had a twinkle in her eye. Nora Calhoun had been his Sunday School teacher when he was in fifth grade, the first grown-up outside his family to tell him how sorry she was about Martha's death. She was also the custodian of a secret recipe for fried-chicken seasoning that was the pride and envy of a town full of women who still cut up fryers and put them in a pan of hot oil. "I came as soon as I heard you were back. I hope you'll stay a good long time."

"Good Lord, no," Jack blurted, his eyes going wide. "I mean, I'm just here for a while. Just helping out."

Nora Calhoun shook her head. "It's good timing," she said. "Your father needing the extra help. And your recent troubles."

It's a sad thing when your private shame becomes public knowledge, he remembered. He had better grow a tougher skin—or regrow the one small-town living had once taught him.

"What can I do for you, Mrs. Calhoun?" he said. "Exactly?"

"Oh, you're not getting off that easy, Jack," she said. "I don't need anything this store can offer."

"You need a new roof," Tom said, and Jack turned to him, grateful for the opportunity to edge away.

"As though I could afford a new roof, Tom," she said. "The materials alone would set me back a pretty penny."

"We could sell it to you in installments," Jack said, heading toward the coatrack. "A nail at a time."

"Oh," she said in mock indignation. "I don't suppose I'm quite that hard up."

"We'll work with you," Tom said. "Nora, you do need a new roof."

"I do," she admitted. "Lyndi climbed up and put that tarp over the leaky spot. And it still leaks." She turned to Jack. "Lyndi is my great-granddaughter. She comes to see me every week or so from Austin." She smiled wryly. "I believe her mother makes her."

"I've got to go out to the yard," Jack told her, pulling on his coat. "It's good to see you, Mrs. Calhoun."

"Oh, I'll see you again," she said. "That's a promise. Now, I'm off to practice for Sunday." Nora Calhoun had been the organist at Saint Paul's since before Jack was born. She smiled and turned to go, and he stepped out the back door and into the lumberyard, clipboard in hand.

It was chilly. He pulled on his gloves, tugged on the wool cap he'd found in the top of his closet, knitted by his mom years ago in the maroon and white of the Mayfield Wildcats. As he slipped it over his head, it felt a little like a hug across the great divide. *Thanks, Mom.*

The lumberyard was a small space—unlike in the big box

stores where the lumber stretched into the distance like a studio back lot. The racks and shelving were built into the walls of the building behind them, which Grampa Joe had bought, gutted, and opened to the sky back in his day.

Jack wondered, illogically, if maybe it had been the haberdashery.

Not much wood was out here. When contractors bid a big project, they usually went into Kerrville to Home Depot, or all the way into San Antonio or Austin. Jack wondered what his dad thought was going to keep him occupied for long in this store, in this town.

In this life.

He pulled out his phone, checked again: no messages. That morning, as every morning, he had already called Tracy, called her parents, called Sally. No answer, no reply, nothing from any of them.

Would he ever hear from them again?

He didn't have many personal contacts in his phone book. Not for somebody who had been CEO of a multimillion-dollar nonprofit, pastor of a megachurch, best-selling author, and media figure.

He didn't have that many people he wanted to talk to, or who wanted to talk to him.

Maybe he never had.

On an impulse, he called Danny Pierce's number. It was a Thursday, two days after Christmas. He didn't figure Danny would be at work, but who knew? Maybe he'd pick up.

He didn't. Jack took the phone down from his ear, looked at it, frowned.

Then he shook his head and left a message. "Danny. Jack. Wanted to see how things went on Christmas Day. I hope it was okay. Better than okay." He paused, bit his lip. "And to tell you my dad found me. Thank you, I guess. I was in a pretty bad place. Still am. But at least—"

That was all he had. He didn't know what the silver lining was. He couldn't finish that sentence. Not yet. Maybe not ever.

"I've got to count some lumber," he said instead. "I hope you're okay, Danny. I know I left you in a terrible spot." He stopped, shook his head, sighed. "Listen. Take care of yourself, man. That place will eat you alive."

He hung up. It wasn't an apology. He knew that. He had witnessed enough non-apologies in his years of ministry. But the sentiment was true. All of it was true.

He did hope Danny was okay.

He did realize he had left him in a horrible spot.

And that place—like any church—would eat him alive if he wasn't careful.

He looked down at the pile of lumber in front of him, raised his pencil and clipboard, and amused himself by estimating the total board feet. After Mary taught him how, he used to waste time out here in the summers of his high-school and college years doing calculations, something alien to his English-major mind. That thought brought a smile to his lips. He remembered sweltering summers with Darla, before she left him. And with Bill, down at the creek at day's end with a cold beer and the radio turned up loud in his Chevy truck.

It was the first time he had remembered being happy in Mayfield. Maybe that's why he didn't hear the footsteps behind him before he heard the voice—blustery, gruff, and not particularly friendly, "Well, looky looky. I heard you were back. I just couldn't hope to believe it."

Jack felt his stomach do a slow roll as he was yanked from the creek and his college years to the dusty playground behind the middle school. He knew that voice immediately, and it was connected to a long, looping left hook caroming off the side of his head. To a ring of boys in a schoolyard shouting encouragements to one or both of them. To the thud of blows landing on each side.

That was not the only time he and Jamie Taylor had come to blows. They had never been friends, not as far back as he could remember.

Which, for the two of them, would be kindergarten at Mayfield Elementary School.

Jack let out his breath slowly, breathed in, and turned around slowly.

"Sweet Baby James," he said. "Or should I say 'Mr. Mayor'?"

"Either is fine," James Taylor said, his arms crossed, a smile flickering across his face. He stood there with Randy Fields, a follower from kindergarten days onward. Randy was now Mayfield's police chief, if a force of four people, two of them part-time, could be considered worthy of a chief. Still, he did have a uniform.

"Nice hat," Jack told Randy.

James cocked his head to one side, sizing Jack up. He stared at him so long it went from being simply rude to being a challenge. Randy, too, just stood there, his hands in the pockets of his leather jacket, smiling. He wasn't the sharpest tool in the shed, but he could read a room. Randy surely shared his mayor's joy at Jack's cataclysmic fall.

Jack felt the heat spread up his neck, and he was grateful his head was covered by maroon and white so nobody could see how he was flushing.

"Can I help you with something?" Jack said at last. "Does the bustling city of Mayfield require some lumber?"

"No," James said, smirking. "I was just cementing this moment in my memory. I don't ever want to forget this. Right, Randy?"

"Never," Randy said, nodding.

"How's Darla?" Jack said, a conversational stab. Maybe James had got the girl—but not before Jack had spent years in the neighborhood.

"She's very happy," James said. "We all are. The girls are off at college. Cameron was QB 1 this year, and we're looking through college offers. Maybe Texas."

"That's great," Jack said. He examined his feelings and discovered that he actually meant it. However much he might dislike James, Darla was a good girl. He had forgiven her a long time ago for breaking his heart. And anybody who played quarterback for the Mayfield Wildcats got a free pass, no matter who his father was. "It sounds like things are going well for y'all."

He nodded and prepared to turn back to his inventory. But James wasn't done yet. "So, is this really happening? Please, God, let it be true. Are you really stuck in Mayfield for good?"

Jack considered what would upset them the most. "I'm just here for a while. You'll be glad to see me go, I'm sure."

"No, man," James said. He took a step forward. "I'd love for you to be here forever." He took another step closer, and now he was uncomfortably close, had penetrated Jack's personal comfort zone. "I'd love to walk in here every day for the rest of my life and see you counting two-by-fours." He smiled, flicked Jack's clipboard with the back of his hand. "Nothing would make me happier."

Jack's face flushed again as he juggled and caught the clipboard. Not for the first time, he imagined launching a long, looping left at that smug smile.

That smile dimmed a few watts as James saw Jack's expression. He had seen that face before. He took a step backward.

Jack held the clipboard tight, his knuckles clenched. He would not give in, would not give James that satisfaction, would not invite Randy to do riot control.

"Enjoy it while you can," Jack said. "I'm not done yet." At that moment, he meant it, meant it from his heart. He would not give James the satisfaction of lying where he fell. "I'm not anywhere near finished." And as he spoke, he felt his spine draw straighter, his shoulders pull back.

He was not finished.

Please, God, let it be true.

He took a deep breath. "Now, if there's nothing else?"

James shook his head and took another step back. "This should last me all day. All week."

"Sweet Baby James," Jack said. "You are a piece of work." He gave Randy a raised fist of solidarity. "Back the blue. Right, Randy?"

"Right," Randy said.

Then he blinked, unsure whether he was being complimented or insulted.

Randy would have to parse that in his off time. Jack was through with them both. He turned and began counting boards again.

The footsteps started away, paused, resumed. Jack heard the door to the store open, then close.

He let out his breath. How long had he been holding it?

"I didn't punch him," he muttered to himself, claiming what little scrap of victory he could. "I didn't punch him."

This time.

Jack spent the rest of the morning shifting and counting lumber, making entries on his clipboard, and transferring them to the notebook at the front counter. At lunchtime, his sister walked over from her office two blocks over. She carried a paper bag with three Styrofoam bowls of chili from The Lunch Counter. She offered one to him without looking at him.

He hadn't considered what he might do for lunch, but his stomach was growling. So he pulled up another stool, sat down opposite them at the front counter, and took the plastic lid off his bowl. Inside were chunks of ground beef, kidney beans, big slices of translucent onion, in a sauce that was equal parts Campbell's tomato soup and chili powder. Betty had run The Lunch Counter for Jack's whole life, and this was her mom's chili con carne recipe from the Depression.

He was surprised how happy he was to eat it again.

"Thanks, sis," he said as they all dug in. "I was hungry."

"I thought you could use something to get your strength back," she said. "I heard Jamie Taylor came by to gawk at you this morning."

"Who told you that?" Jack asked, slurping his chili.

"Who didn't?" she said. "There are no secrets in Mayfield."

"Yeah," he said. "I keep forgetting about that."

"Everybody asked me if you punched him. I heard no blood was spilled." She arched an eyebrow. It made her look just like their mom for a moment.

"Mary, I'm a pastor," Jack said. "Or I was." He gestured at her with his white plastic spoon. "Anyway. The point is, I'm not supposed to punch people."

"You're not supposed to do a lot of things," Mary said. Her father looked up sharply at her. "Sorry," she said.

"You're still a pastor, Jack," Tom said. "It's just that, today, you're a pastor counting lumber."

Jack got a chuckle out of that. "Right," he said. "Tomorrow, who knows?"

"I know, right? You could be counting nails," Mary said. "I've got the greatest confidence in you." And she gave him what actually looked a little like a tiny smile.

The bell at the front door jingled once during their lunch as Charlie Gobel limped in, leaning heavily on his cane, and looking for a float for his toilet. Jack got up and pulled one down off the shelf for him. Tom rang Mr. Gobel up, asked some questions about Molly, his wife, and gave him change for a twenty.

"I didn't punch him," Jack said as the bell jingled behind Mr. Gobel. "Although God knows I wanted to." He shook his head. It made no sense. They were grown men.

"What did he say?" Tom said.

"Well, first he just stood there for a long time." Jack tilted his bowl to get the last of the chili. "Said he was enjoying it so much he wanted to fix the moment in his memory forever."

"Son of a . . ." Mary spat, her face flushed.

"Mary," Tom said, eyes wide.

"He is. Always has been."

Jack suddenly remembered a time in elementary school when Jamie Taylor had gotten him down on the playground, was sitting on his chest and flailing away at his head with his fists. Maybe they were just second-graders, but it seriously hurt.

That was the moment when Mary had barreled into Jamie and knocked him sprawling into the dust. At that time, she and Martha were both far taller than any boy in the second grade, and Martha had joined Mary in offering to do some serious violence to Jamie if he got back on his feet. Jack had never lived it down, of course. Jamie had continued to ask if Jack's sisters were coming to rescue him long after there was only one sister, which Jamie knew full well.

"He is," Mary insisted.

"It's just not very Christian," Tom said, looking across at Jack for reinforcement. Tom did not, apparently, disagree with the assessment, just the expression of it.

"It's not very Christian," Jack said, but he laughed.

Mary snorted. Then she started laughing too.

Tom looked back and forth between them and smiled.

Blood is thicker than water.

"Your numbers are off on the eight-by-tens," she said to Jack after lunch. "We've never had that many at one time."

He checked his clipboard. "Oh. I stuck in an extra zero." He recalculated, showed it to her again.

She nodded and began to gather up their trash. Mind like a calculator.

"Dennis tells me that you're both coming for dinner tonight," she said.

"You don't have to—" Jack began, and that's as far as he got before Mary fixed him with a steely stare.

"I know full well what I don't have to do," she said. "Dennis is smoking ribs for you. And you don't have to hang out at Buddy's every single night of the year, do you?"

He looked blankly at her. "How—"

"Remember, no secrets in Mayfield," she repeated. "Anyway, Father Frank will have plenty of drunks to talk to. He always does."

They looked at each other.

"Okay," Jack said. "If he's smoking ribs."

"He is," Mary said. "See you at six."

Tom slowly got up from the counter. "Thanks," he said. "You're a good girl, Mary." He kissed her on her forehead.

"Yes, I am," she said briskly. "Jack."

"Sis." He nodded.

His phone began to buzz in the pocket of his coat. He dug it out, checked the caller.

It was Danny.

"I need to take this," he said, and he stepped through the store to the back door before answering. His heart was pounding.

It was the first time anyone from his old world had spoken to him since the day he was tossed unceremoniously out of Grace Cathedral.

"Danny," he said. He noticed his hand was trembling. "Hey. Danny."

"I'm not supposed to be talking to you," Danny said. "I'm not supposed to be in contact with you in any way at any time. They say you're going to sue us, try to get your old job back."

Jack felt his shoulders slump. "Really?" he managed to get out. "Danny, I would never do that."

"All the same," Danny said. "I'm not supposed to be talking to you."

"And yet you are," Jack said. He stepped out into the sunlit section of the lumberyard and leaned against the south-facing wall where he wouldn't be quite so chilly.

"Jack, where are you now? Are you, you know, in your right mind? You said you were counting lumber. I thought—oh, man, I don't know what I thought. Some elaborate scaffold to hang yourself." He laughed nervously. "That's why I called."

"I'm in Mayfield," Jack said. "My dad brought me home. I'm working in the hardware store. Right now, I'm standing in the lumberyard."

Danny was silent. Jack checked to see if he had bars. Yes, three of them. It was Danny he didn't have.

"Danny?" he asked. The silence stretched a bit longer.

"Wow," Danny said at last. "Hardware?"

"Yeah," Jack said. "Listen, Danny. Have you heard from Tracy? Are she and Alison okay?"

"Listen—" Danny began.

"No," Jack said. "I deserve to know at least that much. I'm pretty sure it's against the law to keep Alison away from me. And I miss them. Both." He did, he realized. His stomach was clenched with grief. "If it was you—Danny, if it was you, wouldn't you be climbing the walls, worried out of your mind?"

"Yeah," Danny admitted. "But, Jack—"

"Come on, Danny," Jack said, pulling the phone away from his face and looking at it as though it had offended him. "I just want to know—"

"I haven't heard from them, Jack," Danny said. "Why would they talk to me? And I don't know where they are. I think that was part of the deal. They'd go away, they'd be quiet, and we'd take care of them. Protect them. The church pays the lawyers. That's all I know."

"Protecting them from who? Me?" He knew the truth immediately. "No. Protecting them from the media." He let out a disgusted *whoosh* of air. "Like Tracy would ever talk." His stomach slowly rolled again. "Like I didn't shame her so bad she'd ever want to talk about it."

"Your dad asked me where they were," Danny said. "He's called me more than once. A lot more. I told him I didn't know anything." Danny paused. "I don't think he believes me."

"I believe you," Jack said. "And I think you'd tell me something if you could." He sighed. It was a dead end on finding his family, but at least not the end of his and Danny's friendship. "Are you okay? What's it like up there?"

"It's like riding a bucking bronco, Jack," Danny said, and against his will, Jack smiled.

"Like holding a live power line," Jack said.

"Like drinking from a fire hose," Danny offered, and it sounded like he, too, was chuckling a little. All of those had been the comparisons Jack had made when Danny asked what it was like to be the Number One in a big church.

"I haven't been online to look," Jack said. "I've been afraid to find out what's happening, I guess. Are you bringing in an interim?"

"Jack," Danny said, and even without seeing him he knew he was shaking his head. "Who would they bring in? Billy Graham? The pope? No, they're calling me acting lead pastor, we've brought in some administrative help, and we're trying to figure out what to do next."

"Wow," Jack said. He paused for a moment with a thought he could not let go of but was afraid to verbalize. "I don't guess anybody's said anything about me coming back."

"Some things have been said," Danny admitted. "But nobody knew where you were. If you were ready to . . ." His voice trailed off.

"Yeah," Jack said. "I don't know myself where I am. Or what I'm ready to do." He pushed himself off the wall, started pacing across the lumberyard. "I miss it. I miss everyone. But I miss my family most of all."

"I wish I could help you, man," Danny said. Both men were silent, and then Danny said, as though he'd made up his mind about something, "If I hear anything, I'll let you know. Scout's honor."

Both of them had been Eagle Scouts; it was not an idle promise. It was a solemn oath.

"Danny, if you need anything—any help, whatever—you call me." He stopped pacing. "I'm not so busy with my lumber that I can't talk." He smiled sadly. "Really. I'll help you out any way I can."

"Are you preaching?" Danny asked. "You should be preaching." He stopped, caught himself. "I mean, if you're right with God."

Jack shook his head. "Really. You think I should be preaching?" Jack said. "No. Don't answer that. No way. I'm done with that." It was chilly out here without his coat. "Anyway. Thanks for calling. Thanks."

It was quiet on the other line, and for a second, Jack wondered if they were still connected. Then, spoken softly, the words, "You're not going to sue the church?"

That hurt his heart. "No," he said. He shook his head. What made Martin Fox or anyone else think he would destroy the thing he'd built?

Maybe that he'd done what he did without thinking what it might do to all the things he'd built?

He shook his head again. If he wasn't sure who he was these days, should he be surprised that nobody else knew?

"No, Danny," Jack said in a low voice. "I'm not. Scout's honor."

He hung up and walked back inside. His sister had left, but Tom was settled on his stool behind the cash register, reading what looked like an ancient *Reader's Digest*. He used to buy them at garage sales, maybe he still did. At the register were also recent issues of *People* and *Us*. Jack's mom used to read them, and he suspected that his father kept subscribing to them—and maybe even read them in slow times—to keep that connection.

Tom looked up as the door opened, then commenced to reading again as Jack walked across the store to reclaim his clipboard. Behind him in one of the aisles he could hear Manny sweeping; he was always around, though rarely seen these days.

"Did you know Napoleon was poisoned?" Tom said without looking up.

"Is that the most current hypothesis?"

Tom smiled, closed the magazine, checked the date. "It was as of the early 1980s," he said.

"A lot has changed since the eighties," Jack said. He stood for a moment, looking for the right words. "Listen," he said. "I was on the phone with Danny. Danny Pierce. From Seattle?"

"Oh?" his father said without looking up.

Where to start? With the most immediate. "He said you'd been trying to find Tracy."

"About time he called you back."

"Have you been asking him about Tracy? About where they are?"

Tom simply nodded once, looked up, looked back down. "Of course I have," he said.

Of course.

For an instant, Jack felt Tracy's and Alison's hands in his as he prepared to preach. It was the best part of his week, he realized now. Not because he was getting ready to speak, but because he was connected to them, drawing strength from them, claiming them.

And they were claiming him.

He felt tears burning at the corners of his eyes. He covered his face with his hand and turned away so his father couldn't see. Jack had been taught at an early age not to cry—or at least not to let anyone see you doing it. In his family, men didn't cry. Or in Mayfield, for that matter.

"Hey," Tom said. He heard his father slowly getting off his stool and stepping from behind the counter. "Jackie," he said, crossing over to him. "What's wrong?"

Jack had not been called "Jackie" in thirty years. It's what his mom used to call him when he'd fallen out of a tree or been stung by bees or gotten the bad end of a tussle with Jamie Taylor.

"Tracy hasn't talked to me since—since I left," Jack said, his back still to his father, tears continuing to threaten. "I can't believe she could hate me so much. And she's going to teach Alison to hate me."

"Hey," his father said, putting a hand on his shoulder and turning him slightly. "We don't know what she's thinking."

"We know they're gone," Jack said. "We know she won't call me back." He dropped his hand, felt a tear run freely down his cheek. "And the worst thing is, I deserve it." His shoulders slumped. "For what I did. I deserve it all."

"Nobody deserves to be abandoned by the ones they love," his father said quietly, and Jack felt a sting of conscience, knew Tom could have brought forward long years of reproach, and yet didn't.

"It's the worst," Jack admitted. "It's tearing me apart."

"We'll find them," Tom said. "Don't you worry about that. It's a small world, what with the Internets and all." He patted Jack's shoulder gently. "We'll find them."

Jack laughed, wiped his face. "Sure we will," he said. "The Internets are our friend."

He patted his father's hand, which was still resting on Jack's shoulder. He never expected that hand to feel comforting. He wondered what else he'd been wrong about.

He stepped back. "It's okay. It is what it is."

They exchanged a long look and both nodded. Then Jack picked his clipboard off the counter, shrugged on his coat, and went out to count the rest of the lumber.

6.

He was taking a break and sipping on a can of Dr Pepper. Heat radiated off the sun-baked wall he was seated against and his eyes were closed, when he heard footsteps again.

"Didn't get a good enough look the first time?" he called out, trying and failing to hide the hostility in his voice.

"I don't believe I got a first look," a calm female voice said.

He opened his eyes, stumbled awkwardly to his feet, spilling some Dr Pepper on his shoe in the process. "I'm sorry," he said. "I thought you were—someone."

"I like to think I am someone," she said, not unkindly. "Are you feeling like a zoo animal, Jack Chisholm?"

He laughed despite himself. "Yeah, you could say that. I'm sorry. Do I know you?"

She laughed. "Jack," she said. "It's Kathy. Kathy Branstetter."

"No," he said. He looked more closely at her. Thirtyish, tiny, attractive, wavy blonde hair, a legal pad in one hand. She was dressed too well for Mayfield, in a skirt, knee-high boots, and a nice jacket. He remembered a dumpy gray little girl. Not this. "No. You're not."

"I'm pretty sure I am," she said mildly.

"Sorry. It's just —I heard you were working for the *Washington Post*. I've read your political stuff. And I haven't seen you—"

"I was away for a long time," she said. "Then my dad got sick. He needed someone to help run the *Courier*."

"I'm sorry," he said. "I hadn't heard. I always liked your dad. Is he—better?"

"He died last year," she said.

"Oh," Jack said. "Man."

"You were away for a long time too," she said. "No worries."

He took a sip of what remained of his Dr Pepper. "Your dad used to cover all our games," he said. "He made me feel like I was a media star. He'd ask such good questions about the defenses, about what I was seeing. He really knew his job."

"He should have been a sports reporter for a big-city paper. We used to watch football together. At the end, that was all we could do. He was too weak to even tell me what was happening."

Jack looked down at the brown drops on his tennis shoe, then wiped his toe on the back of his jeans. He looked up at her. "So, that was last year. Why are you still here?"

She looked around, her eyes taking in six kinds of lumber. She took a deep breath, let it out. "Well," she said, "there was a lot to wrap up. The estate and all. And nobody to step in and take over the paper. And I—" She worried her bottom lip with her teeth.

He understood, or thought he did, and he let her off the hook. Sometimes you don't know what else to do.

"And you're still here," he finished for her.

She nodded. "I think I could go back," she said. "I want to. I miss it. Breaking the big story. Balancing on the high wire."

"Oh yeah," he said.

"But I feel like, right now, this is where I'm meant to be."

He smiled. He had heard this kind of language a lot as a pastor. *Meant to.* "Did, umm, God give you that message?"

She sniffed. "Does God ever tell me anything?" she said, then her shoulders released a bit. "Sorry. God and I aren't currently on speaking terms."

"It happens," he said. "We seem to be on a break ourselves."

"Really?" she said. "The people's pastor? I guess—I guess I just wanted to believe that maybe you were still holding on to something despite, you know. Despite everything."

"Kathy Branstetter," he said, draining the can, "I don't know you well enough to talk to you about God. In fact, I probably shouldn't be talking to you at all. The media and I are also not on speaking terms these days."

"I did come to talk to you as a journalist," she admitted. "I need something for the 'Around the River' column," she said. "Something small." She held up her thumb and forefinger, pinched together.

He looked at her with some curiosity. No journalist had ever politely asked him for a quote for a column, let alone a column about the comings and goings of townspeople.

"I can't ignore the fact that you're here, Jack," she said. "Not and feel like I didn't leave every ounce of my journalistic integrity back in DC." She opened her notepad, took out a pen, stood ready to write. "So, I hear you've come back to visit your dad."

"Is that what you hear?" he said. Apparently his dad was not the only one in his family who could arch an eyebrow.

"You know full well what I hear," she said, a touch of heat

in her voice. "Some of it is even true. But if you tell me that you've come back for a visit," she said, pointing her pen at him, "then I publish that you've come back for a visit. And for now, we can leave it at that." She wrote something down. "For now. And if *TIME* or the *Seattle Times* or whoever calls me, again, I can tell them what I have verified myself, which is that and nothing more." She smiled. "Doesn't mean they won't be back down here harassing honest Texans about you."

"I'm sorry," he said. "I didn't want my troubles to complicate anyone else's life. But they have. They do." He saw that she was still waiting.

He took a deep breath.

"I've come back to visit my father," he said with no particular emphasis.

"Right." She nodded at him. They had signed a contract.

She capped her pen, closed the legal pad, stuck out her hand, and shook his. "It's good to see you, Jack. I've followed your work too. Didn't like it. But I followed it." She checked her watch, made a face. "And now I've got to go cover a junior-high basketball game." Her eyes had a hint of regret in them. "'Lo, how the mighty have fallen.'"

"'The beauty of Israel is slain upon thy high places,'" he said. It was from David's lament for Saul and Jonathan in 2 Samuel. "It's where that phrase comes from. 'How are the mighty fallen,'" he explained in response to her raised eyebrows. "You know," he said, as much to himself as to her, "I have never preached from that. It's one of the most honest expressions of grief in the Bible."

They stood without speaking for a moment, both of them

looking at the ground between them. At last, she checked her watch and groaned. Basketball would not wait.

"I hope you find what you're looking for," she said. "Tip-off is in four minutes."

"Thanks," he said. "You too. Break a leg. Or something."

"Or something," she said, and hurried off.

He went inside to put his drink can in the trash. They were adding up. How come Mayfield didn't recycle aluminum cans? How hard would that be? Everybody recycled aluminum now, right?

After a decade in Seattle, he was green down to his bones. Maybe he could lobby the city council, encourage James to take some bids from a recycler. They weren't that far from Kerrville, or from San Antonio, for that matter. Somebody might make a paying concern out of it.

He suddenly realized that he was thinking about a future in Mayfield.

"No way," he said aloud as he opened the back door and walked into the store. "Absolutely not."

"Absolutely what?" his father asked.

"Nothing," he said.

"How was *Meet the Press*?" Tom had done a poor job of hiding the *People* magazine he'd been reading. Katie Whoever, who had married Tom Cruise, was peering out at Jack from under a ledger. She was getting on with her life, Jack read.

"I didn't remember her at all," Jack said. He came around the counter, sat down on one of the other stools, and set his drink can in front of him to dispose of later. "Kathy Branstetter, I mean. Not your Katie person."

"You probably haven't seen her since she was in junior high," Tom said. "Maybe some Sunday in church. You wouldn't have taken a second look at her. Nobody did. Plain little girl." He smiled. "But so smart. Weren't we all proud of her? That school in the East—Radcliffe?"

"Smith," Jack said absently. "Maybe. All those radical lesbian colleges sound alike to me." He smiled. His congregation had been full of radical lesbians.

He was also smiling because he had just said the word "lesbian" in front of his father, something he never expected to do.

"Anyway," his father said. "She want an interview?"

Jack pursed his lips. "That's the funny thing. She didn't, really." He shook his head. "It's like she wanted to give me some breathing room. She said she'd heard I'd come for a visit. That's all. Asked me to confirm it."

"You're sitting right here," his father said. "That seems like confirmation enough."

"I think she wanted me to know—" Jack shook his head again. Something. "It's odd. Small-town people get all up in your business. And then, when you least expect it, they leave you alone."

"Mayfield 101." His father laughed. "Welcome home." He checked his watch, looked out onto the pavement to see if anyone was coming. It was five o'clock—closing time. He slid off the stool, put the Closed sign in the front door, turned the lock.

"Manny," he called out into the store. "Quitting time."

He rang up a No Sale on the cash register, counted out some bills, and gave them over to Manny, who appeared from nowhere. Manny was as thin as his father now and even more crooked, ancient, and ageless.

Manny's mother had known Pancho Villa. The man knew stories that could make you laugh and break your heart.

Manny shuffled out the back door. Jack knew he would let himself out of the back of the lumberyard, then walk the seven blocks to his trailer on the east side of town. Jack began to button up his coat and turned to see why his father hadn't moved from the register.

"Jack," Tom said, "do you ever think about your mother's funeral?"

And immediately he was back there, the shame, the anger. It was instantaneous. When did he not think about the funeral? Jack could remember every detail—the floral spray on top of the gunmetal-gray coffin, the packed church, his father, thin and wan in his only dark suit.

He remembered stepping up to preach, launching into how we were not good enough, how we needed to remember that our lives could end while we were far from God, how we all needed to do better.

Above all, he remembered his father slowly pushing his way to his feet in the middle of his sermon, standing like a silent accuser. Jack had lost all momentum and stopped preaching. His father had said, in a voice that echoed in the silent sanctuary, "Jack. Please. Sit down."

And he remembered how his face boiled with shame. He had stood there for a long moment in the pulpit, felt the tension spread outward like ripples in a pond. There, on this most public and personal of stages, his father was once again telling him he was not good enough.

It was his whole childhood delivered up in a moment.

Jack had stepped back from the pulpit.

He dropped his hands to his sides.

He nodded once to himself, as he made a decision that would have consequences from that moment forward.

He walked down the steps of the dais, laid a hand on his mother's casket as he passed, and then he had passed out of that church, out of his family's life, out of Mayfield forever.

No more shame from his father. No more regrets. No more wishing he could be better, do better.

Or so he thought.

Now it was happening again.

"Really?" he said, his face flushing. "I've got nowhere to go, I am at your mercy— literally at your mercy, Tom—and this is what you want to talk about?"

"We've never talked about it," his father said, settling himself back onto the stool. "And while I don't want to hurt you, this story now has a clock ticking in the background." He paused, fixed Jack with his eyes. "I know your sister has already told you that I am not only ailing, but laboring under a death sentence." He smiled. "That sounded very melodramatic. Like bad TV dialogue. I apologize."

"I—" Jack began, and couldn't figure out what came next. "How did you know?"

"Because I know Mary," Tom said. "And I know your sister has had at least three opportunities to beat you over the head with this news since you returned." He shrugged, raised his hands, palms up. "And being Mary, she has clubbed you with it at least once. I love her. As I love you. But she is still very angry."

Jack nodded. She was, deservedly. "I'm sorry. Really. I don't know what to say. But why—"

"The reason I bring up that hard thing from the past is this," Tom said. "I don't have much time. I am trying to be gentle with you, Jack. I know what a hard spot you are in, and life has finally taught me to be kind to people who are in a bad way. I am not trying to shame you. Please believe me."

He nodded, bit his lip, then nodded again before repeating, "But I don't have much time. I want to meet my only grandchild before I die. I want you to understand that I have never stopped loving you." He shook his head. "And I want to understand—" He sighed deeply, as though the thought still pained him. Perhaps it did. "I want to understand why you chose at your mother's funeral to tell us grieving souls what horrible sinners we were."

"I was concerned about your grieving souls," Jack said heatedly, before realizing it was a stock answer he'd given a thousand times in the past. He wasn't even sure now why he had done it, except that was how he had always done things.

"What about our hearts?" his father asked. "What about some understanding of your mother's very difficult life? What about an honest expression of grief?"

"I—"

"Surely, Jack," his father said, "being a man of God is about more than shaming people for their imperfection. Especially at such a time."

Again, he had nothing. He had preached a thousand funerals, given that same we-have-got-to-do-better sermon, been thanked by people for being concerned for the souls of those in attendance.

Never once, he suddenly realized, had a loved one thanked him for bringing them comfort, for soothing their pain. It prompted something that he couldn't help but say aloud, the verse from 2 Samuel again: "'The beauty of Israel is slain upon thy high places: how are the mighty fallen!'"

Jack shook his head, more filled with shame than before.

What had he done?

Those words from 2 Samuel had floated out into the store and remained there.

His father inclined his head, took a deep breath, looked up at him. "Jack, I don't know if I have a week, a month, three months. I have to be honest with you now. We have to be honest with each other. And we haven't been honest with each other. We haven't had to."

Jack started to say something and his father raised a hand—it was neither the time to protest or explain. "However much it is, it's not enough time for me to pretend. You've accomplished great things by every measure we hold dear. But where are those great things now? You've stood in front of tens of thousands of people. Where are those people now? You've proclaimed that we are sinful to anyone who would listen. Who was willing to stand by your side and love you when you proved the truth of that?"

Jack felt his stomach clench. He had asked that same question a hundred times since that first trip to Mexico. But he couldn't acknowledge it. It was easier to pick a different fight, not to talk about his own failures, but instead imagine someone else's.

"You are always judging me," Jack said, crossing his arms.

He sighed. Even to himself, he sounded fifteen years old again.

Tom looked Jack in the eyes. "I have been guilty of that, yes. I'm sorry. But I was always loving you. I hope that counts for something, son. Here at the end."

They looked at each other now and said nothing. A pickup truck with dual exhausts rumbled down the street. Jack wondered if it was Dennis, on his way home to check on the ribs.

Perhaps his father wondered the same thing. He nodded, let out his breath, let the matter drop.

"Come on," he said. "Let's get cleaned up before dinner. You've been working outside all day."

"Maybe tomorrow I can sweep some floors," Jack said.

"And put Manny out of work?" his father said, and he smiled a little. "Heaven forbid." He slid off his stool and went to shrug on his coat, his own father's hat.

Jack was filled with an unaccountable love and sadness as he watched the old man dress for the cold.

"Dad," he said.

He meant to say something else. Something more.

Something like, "I love you."

Something like, "I'm sorry."

But he couldn't make that happen. Not yet.

"Yes, Jack?" Tom said as he wrapped his scarf around his neck a second time.

Jack hesitated. He couldn't bring himself to name the elephant in the room. At last he spoke. "What am I going to do?"

His father considered. That was the question, wasn't it?

Tom pulled on his gloves, slapped his hands together, looked over at him. "What do any of us do, Jack? The best we can." He stepped forward, took his son by both arms, looked up into his face. "I know that this feels like a dark time. You have known your share of them. We both have. But I also know this: Your best days are still ahead."

Jack didn't, couldn't, believe him. But he nodded, once, twice, three times, and a tiny smile made its way across his face.

It felt like a benediction. Like a blessing.

"Okay," he said. "Maybe so."

His father smiled. For him, the matter was settled, and other things loomed. "Let's go eat some ribs."

Because you had to keep things in the proper perspective. Maybe the world was falling down around you.

But it still admitted of this much: baby back ribs, smoked over low heat and served with a side of homemade barbecue sauce, spicy and tart, a foretaste of heaven.

7.

A small-town hardware store is open Monday through Saturday. Jack had remembered this in some part of his mind, and yet, he felt a momentary and ridiculous disappointment that first Saturday morning when he heard his father making breakfast downstairs and realized that this was a day like any other. He had been a working pastor for fifteen years, had gotten into the rhythm of Friday and Saturday off, even if it rarely worked out that they were totally free of church duties.

People had a way of dying or being in car wrecks or having their husbands leave them even on the pastor's day off. And no matter how many staff he had doing pastoral care, he couldn't remove himself entirely from that duty. It occurred to him now that he was glad of that. His best memories were of those agonizing times when his life actually intersected with another's.

He threw on some clothes, the same jeans he had been wearing all week, another T-shirt, and bounded downstairs.

"Morning," Jack said to Tom as he came into the kitchen. "You know, I should really be fixing you breakfast."

"It brings me pleasure to cook," his father said. "And I love to eat. Couldn't do it during the chemo. So if I want to eat eggs every morning for the rest of my life," he said, sliding beautifully fried eggs onto the plates, "by God, I'm going to do it. A man should be able to eat what he wants!"

"I'd make eggs for you," Jack said. Although his eggs wouldn't be nearly so well cooked as these, the whites delicate fried lace, the yolks still runny.

"You can make the toast," his father said. "You always had a gift for that."

Jack popped four slices of bread into the toaster. "Done."

"Do you mind working this morning?" Tom paused from retrieving orange juice and butter from the refrigerator. "I could really use your help making some deliveries from the lumberyard."

"I don't mind at all," he said. "Really, Dad. What else would I do?"

"Well," his father said, "I was going to pay you today. And advance you a bit for clothes. If I have to look at that same pair of tight jeans for another week, I can't be held responsible for what happens to them."

Jack looked down at his skinny jeans. They were black, hip, fit him pretty well, and didn't fit Mayfield one tiny bit. In fact, truth be told, his soul patch, his ironic T-shirts, his whole look was wrong for this place.

"Anyway," his father said, "I thought maybe you'd like to take the truck and do some driving today. Buy something in Mayfield if you can manage it. But take the afternoon and drive. I remember how you used to love that."

Jack nodded. A day driving through the Texas Hill Country,

the twists and turns of the wooded hills, suddenly sounded like a little bit of heaven.

"I would like that," he said. "I would like that a lot."

The day seemed a little more promising now. He had already made his morning calls to Tracy, to Tracy's parents, added in calls to her brother and sister. Nobody answered.

It's like a spiritual discipline, he thought. You make the effort, and maybe no one answers.

But nobody will ever answer if you don't call.

He had realized that morning, though, as he paused on the verge of dialing, that he should stop calling Sally. She had apparently decided that whatever her future held, he was not a part of it—and that felt right to him too. It made much more sense now than when he was drinking on the balcony over the sea in Mexico. Misery had wanted company, and—he supposed—maybe misery had not been so particular about whom that company was.

Because now, stone-cold sober, he could face the reality that what he—they—had done was wrong.

It wouldn't make it any more right, no matter what they did now.

And really, all he wanted was another chance with his family. Nothing else.

So he had skipped that call, breathed a silent prayer for Sally, and gone downstairs to breakfast.

"Dad," he asked, once they'd sat and his father had said grace, "Have you seen Bill?"

Jack had not encountered his best friend from high school since he'd returned, and he wondered why. Everyone else seemed to be finding a reason to stop into the store and see him with their own eyes. Tom had actually come home from the men's basketball game the night before and told Jack that everyone asked about him, wondered why he wasn't there. That made Jack smile. He could not imagine being the focus of so many eyes again, not this soon.

"Maybe when they play Llano," he said, pronouncing their rival's name with the proper Texan *l* instead of a Spanish *y*. "Those are always good games."

"Well," Tom said, "I saw Bill at the game last night. We talked for a good long bit, actually. But not about you." He shook his head. "Not for a long while now. I think he feels like you left him behind." He stopped. "I know he does. And he's taken it kind of hard."

"I did leave him behind," Jack agreed. "I regret it. Maybe I can make it up to him."

"Maybe," his father said, spreading butter onto his toast. "But don't be hurt if you can't. Sometimes—" He set the knife down, thought better of saying more.

"Bill Hall is a good man," is what he said instead. "He's raised five kids alone, girls, all by himself. He's worked hard on that ranch, done his best for our little church. Chairman of deacons this year."

Jack had a vision of Martin Fox, his thousand-dollar suits, his searing judgment. Surely Bill was nothing like that.

Surely.

"Maybe our paths will cross," Jack said. "They have to at some point, right? I'd like to at least tell him I'm sorry." What happened after that couldn't be forced. He either was or was not going to be forgiven. He couldn't, he realized with something that felt a little bit like wonder, earn forgiveness. But saying he was sorry—that was, he now saw, an important and much-neglected piece of the puzzle.

"I'm surprised he hasn't been in the store," Tom admitted. "And a little afraid I know why. Last week, before I went to bring you home, I saw him five days out of six." He pondered that as he chewed. "He better not be driving over to Kerrville."

"He better not," Jack said. "That's a long way. And there's no reason."

"Maybe you could have a tiny word with him," Tom said. "Just to let him know that." He shrugged. "Maybe he thinks he wouldn't be welcome or something."

"Maybe," Jack said. He drank the rest of his orange juice, then the rest of his coffee. When he rose to gather the dishes, he said, "I can at least clear off the table. Those eggs are way beyond my talents."

"And wash," his father said. "You were ever an excellent dish washer."

"They are good eggs," Jack mused. "Fried eggs. Funny. In Seattle I used to have free-range organic frittatas for breakfast. I don't guess there's much call for that sort of thing here."

"Jack," his father said, rising slowly, "I believe truer words were never spoken."

They rode in together, without a word, but the silence was not unpleasant. The cold snap had broken, the snow had melted, and they were enjoying the second day in a row of springlike weather.

"Texas in December," Jack said. "Gotta love it." The temperature was in the fifties, but slated to climb into the seventies that afternoon.

His father grunted. "Got to love that we're not in Amarillo or Lubbock," he corrected. "Those parts of Texas get plenty of hard weather."

"Still," Jack said, "I'll be able to roll the windows down this afternoon." He sighed. "How great is that?"

His father actually seemed to pause and consider the question. At the stoplight, unaccountably red with no other vehicles in sight in any direction, he nodded.

"It is great indeed," he said. "Great indeed."

Jack thought that his father must be developing a true appreciation for the little things. And why not? He was losing all the little things as well as all the big things. Who could say what you ultimately miss more?

Jack started work that morning by beginning to load the store's pickup with the Saturday morning deliveries. Today it looked like a mixed bag of lumber, two dozen fifty-pound bags of fast-setting concrete—pretty much their whole stock—and a roof's worth of brown three-tab shingles. Too much for one trip, for sure. It'd more likely be three or four.

He saw that Mrs. Calhoun was getting the shingles and nails. Someone must be putting on that new roof for her. Three hammers. *Thank God for nail guns,* he thought. He wouldn't want to be doing roofs no matter the time of year. It was backbreaking work.

First, he hauled a delivery out the river road to the Marquettes, a family he knew but not well. They had moved to Mayfield after he graduated high school. Tom said they were members of the church—and like most members, no longer attended much. They had a sign in front of their house, next to a small American flag, that read: God loves you. Always has. Always will.

Mr. Marquette came out to meet him when he pulled into the driveway. He was a big, hearty type in his fifties. "John Marquette," he said, offering a hand. "I don't think we've met."

"Jack." They shook.

"Building a doghouse," John explained, as Jack began to pull boards from the bed.

John Marquette was not one to stand around and watch. Together they pulled and stacked the lumber, and he stood watching as Jack checked it against the manifest, then handed John the clipboard for a signature.

"I need to pay you now?" Mr. Marquette asked as he scribbled.

"It'll go on your account," Jack said. He shook John's hand. "Let us know if we can help you with anything else."

John Marquette smiled. "Welcome home, Jack," he said.

"Thanks." In the truck on the way back to the store, Jack wondered if there was anybody in the county who didn't know that he was back.

It was midmorning by the time Jack drove the second load, sacks of dry concrete, out to the Koenig Ranch, twelve miles west of town. The last two miles were on gravel roads, which were overhung by oak and pecan trees. White dust billowed up behind him as he drove, and goats nibbled at the rocky soil on both sides of the road.

Warren Koenig, the youngest brother, was on the front porch of the big house sipping coffee. He scrambled out of his rocking chair and to the circle drive as Jack pulled in. Jack had played football and basketball with Warren's older brother Van, but Warren was four years behind them in school. He'd mostly been a noisome tagalong kid, cheering from the bleachers, watching practices. Jack wondered how the years might have changed him.

"Hey, Warren," Jack called as he got out of the truck.

"Jack," Warren said, stepping over to shake his hand with both of his. He was still on the small side, the youngest and the shortest of the brothers. "Good to see you. When'd you get in?"

"Early in the week," Jack said. "How're things?"

"We're building a new fence this week," Warren said. *"Lieber Gott!"* Warren was third-generation German-American, but some German apparently had stuck. Jack heard plenty of German in his years in Mayfield. The Germans had settled the Hill Country in the nineteenth century, planted vineyards, made beer, brought their great legacy of smoked meats that eventually became Texas barbecue.

Jack was willing to consider forgiving the Germans a lot because of beer and Texas barbecue.

"Mein Gott!" Jack agreed, shaking his head. Putting in a fence was another backbreaking chore he'd rather not perform again in this life. "You've got a post-hole augur, right?"

"Oh yeah," Warren said. "Man, you remember digging post-holes by hand?"

"Oh yeah," Jack said. He could almost feel the bruises and blisters again on his hands after a hard day of digging postholes without gloves. Because when did tough young men ever wear gloves to do manual labor? "Where should I put this stuff?"

"Over by the shop," Warren said.

Jack pulled the truck around, backed it up to the door of a large tin shed. The shop was about the size of four oversized garages and a good thirty feet tall. Inside were a one-ton truck, a monstrous John Deere tractor, a combine, and a lot of tools and supplies. He spied a small stack of cement bags against one wall. "Over there?"

"Yeah, that'd be great," Warren said. He grabbed a bag under each arm, and the two of them began stacking the concrete.

"Hey, Jack." Warren grunted on their fourth trip as he tossed a bag on top of a pile that was probably a little too high now for safety.

"Yeah," Jack said, beginning another pile.

"Are you back for good?"

"I don't know," Jack said, returning to the truck. He was now carrying the bags on his shoulders. Although he'd been working out until recently, this was a new order of pain.

"Van said you weren't. He said"—his voice became apologetic—"he said you didn't fit in anymore."

"Did he?" Jack looked down at himself, covered in gray dust. "Was it because of my skinny jeans?"

Warren hooted as though Jack had made the prize joke of all time. "*Nein*. No, man." He waved his hands dismissively. "Although ain't nobody around here wears skinny jeans that's not fifteen." He suddenly became serious. "But you know what he meant. You've been a big shot. In the news. On TV."

"Yeah." Jack grunted, shouldering his bag onto the stack. "Once. I think maybe those days are done."

"*Nein*," Warren said. "Don't think that way, Jack. What about second chances?" He paused. "Maybe that's it. Maybe Van thinks you're just here taking a breather."

At that moment, Jack actually was taking a breather, holding on to the tailgate and panting for air. "Warren," he said, when he could. "Why would I stay here?"

"Why does anybody?" Warren asked. Then he answered himself. "For the beer. For the brisket. For the sunsets!"

"For the football," Jack added. "The pecans. The pecan pie."

"For the swimming hole at the creek," Warren said. "When it's a hundred degrees and you feel like the world is going to melt."

Jack picked up two more bags. "I'm a little out of shape," he said.

"You haven't done this kind of work for a long time," Warren said. "You were using your brain, man. Working with your brain."

"Huh," Jack said. It was something less than agreement. He had spared himself backbreaking work, that was true.

Was it honest work?

Could he be proud of what he'd been so proud of?

They stacked the last bags with a thud. Both of them were panting now. Jack hoped Nora Calhoun's workers, whoever they were, would be at the house when he arrived so he wouldn't have to off-load by himself.

"You want a Shiner?" Warren asked.

Jack was covered with sweat. He wiped the dust off the back of his left hand, wiped at his eyes with it, checked his Rolex.

"Oh, *ja*," he said.

They sat in the sun, rocking on the front porch, sipping at cold Shiner Bocks at eleven in the morning.

"Admit it," Warren said. "This is not so bad."

"No," Jack said. "It's great." He thought for a moment about his father and their ride in to work, and he felt a sudden warmth that had nothing to do with the sunlight. "Great indeed," he said.

"Van's in Austin." Warren rocked as he spoke. "The ledge is in session." Jack needed a moment to place the word "ledge." Van had been elected a state senator, and every two years, he had to spend a substantial amount of time in Austin where the legislature met to hammer out bills.

"I thought he'd be home today," Jack said. "Surely the ledge doesn't meet on weekends."

Warren seemed to flush a little. He shifted uncomfortably.

"I'm sorry," Jack said. "I say something wrong?"

"We think—we think Van has gone and got himself a pretty young thing in Austin," Warren said, and now it was the full-blown blush only a pale German complexion can offer.

"What about Candace—" Jack began, scandalized, and he stopped.

He had no right to talk. None at all.

They rocked for a bit in silence, Warren still beet-red with anger or sadness or embarrassment.

They took a drink, then another.

"It is a sad thing," Jack offered at last, "when your private shame becomes a public scandal."

Warren nodded.

Maybe this is a universal truth. Maybe everyone has something they're ashamed of. Some family scandal, some personal failing.

Of course it is, he thought. *We're all broken. We're all fallen.*

"We have got to do better," he murmured automatically. It sounded odd.

"What?" Warren asked. He set his beer next to the rocker with a clink.

"Nothing," Jack said. He drained his Shiner, thanked Warren, and got to his feet.

"Jack, you're still a man of God, right?" Warren asked as they walked to the truck.

Jack paused to think about that. He shook his head. "Warren," he said, "at this moment, I'm not really even sure what species I am."

"No," Warren said. "I watched you preach. A thousand people must have been there."

"Ten thousand," Jack corrected. "Sorry. Not that it matters."

"Well," Warren said. "Would you pray for Van?"

"What would you want me to pray?" Jack said, not committing himself.

"To do better?" Warren asked. He stopped, considered what he might say. "He's really hurting his family." He looked up at Jack. "He's hurting all of us."

"I can pray about that," Jack said. He nodded to himself. "I will pray about that." He climbed into the truck, looked at Warren. "Can you do the hard thing? Can you go on loving him, even while he's hurting you? That's really important."

Warren blinked once or twice. Then, slowly, he nodded. "You can't just stop," he said. "Can you?"

"I don't see how you can," Jack said. "Not if other people go on loving us even when we disappoint them." He started the truck. "Not if God goes on loving us."

They each raised a hand, a Texas wave, good for all occasions.

"I'll see you," he said.

"*Auf wiedersehen,*" Warren said. "I'll tell Van you asked after him."

"You do that," Jack said. He drove back into town and loaded the truck with Mrs. Calhoun's shingles. They weighed in at about eighty pounds per bundle, and Jack actually had to stop, drink a Dr Pepper, and catch his breath again midway. He was totally out of shape for this kind of work. It had seemed so easy when he was twenty. He was too old for this.

He wondered how on earth his father had been managing these past few years.

"Dad," he called, sticking his head into the store.

"I'm with a customer," his father called back, not unkindly.

Jack loaded up the last bundles of shingles and the rolls of felt and then went back into the store ten minutes later. "I'm going out with this last delivery," he said as his father rang up dozens of D batteries for Shirley Martin, the high-school music teacher.

"For my electronic keyboard," she explained. "It eats them like jelly beans."

"You know, we should carry some rechargeables," Jack said without thinking. Must be that Seattle green creeping in. "I mean, Dad, maybe we could—"

"It's a good idea," Tom said, handing her back her change. "And surely a little gentler on the planet." He nodded at Jack. "You can make some shelf room for them on Monday."

Mrs. Martin left, the bell jingling as she exited.

"I'm going now, okay?" Jack said. "Could I have some—"

"Oh," Tom said, stopping himself just in time from closing the till. "Right." He pulled out some twenties, counted them, handed them to Jack.

"Have a great afternoon," he said.

"I'll pick up some chicken on the way home," Jack said. "Okay?" He smiled. "A man should be able to eat what he wants to eat."

"Oh, and football is on tonight," Tom said.

"Football," Jack said. "Is Seattle playing?"

"That's next Sunday," Tom said. "After we get home from church."

Not a chance. That needed to be settled right away.

"Dad," he said. "I'm not going to church. Not tomorrow. Not next week."

"No?" Tom looked a little disappointed. "I'd be happy to show you off."

"I'm sure you'd like that," he said. "But I'm not sure everyone else would."

Tom laughed. "You've not done anything worse than half the people there. Father Frank says you can't trust any church that won't accept that it's made up of sinful men and women." He closed the cash drawer. "Honestly, Jack, it's just like every other place on the planet. Some people would be scandalized if you walked in. Some would welcome you with open arms."

"I'm not ready for that," Jack said. "Too many memories."

"Memories can be good or bad. It depends on what you do with them."

"Well," Jack said, trying hard not to smile, "I have a memory that the last time I was in that church someone ordered me to stop preaching. It's a little hard on the ego."

Tom also struggled to hold a straight face. "Could be that begging you to stop was better than letting you go on preaching."

Jack couldn't hold it; a snicker crept out. "Could be," he admitted.

"Have a great afternoon," Tom said. "And it's the Alamo Bowl tonight. Texas is playing."

"You know," Jack said, "that sounds good." And he meant it. Texas football, fried chicken, some time with his dad. Not bad at all.

He turned to go, and then remembered what he'd come in to ask.

"Dad," he said, "how have you been managing to keep this store going all on your lonesome?"

Tom didn't say anything for a long moment. Jack watched his father shaking his head in puzzlement. He shrugged. "Honestly, son? I don't know. Somehow things get done. Trucks get loaded."

"Things get done?" asked Jack. The English major in him had noted the passive voice, and he pursed his lips. "By whom are these things done, Dad? Elves?"

"Manny and me have held down the fort for thirty years," his father said. He smiled. "I have not seen hide nor hair of any elves."

"But—" Jack's own muscles were aching from one morning of loading and delivering, and he was years younger. And cancer-free, for that matter. "How, exactly, have you held down the fort?"

"I'm glad you're here," was all his father said. "And you've earned your time to play. Go on. Drive safe."

"Okay," Jack said. "Here I go."

8.

Jack's last stop was Nora Calhoun's, and that would launch him on his way out of town. As he walked out to the truck, he considered if he could make any of his purchases locally. The Buy-n-Buy only sold Texas novelty T-shirts, the Sears was mostly an order store now. He needed new clothes this moment.

He'd have to drive to Kerrville. But that was okay. It was a beautiful drive.

On the way over to Mrs. Calhoun's, he stopped at The Lunch Counter for a sloppy joe and crinkle-cut fries that he could eat on the way. He dropped by the Buy-n-Buy and bought a Dr Pepper and some cassette tapes for the truck. The selection was limited, but he found a *Best of Guns n' Roses* and an *Al Green's Greatest Hits*, as well as a number of bands best left forgotten. Not even Father Frank would want these in his backseat.

Jack parked in the driveway, didn't see anybody around, got out, walked up to the door, rang the bell.

Nora Calhoun opened the door slowly, and instead of smiling and telling him she was glad to see him, she stepped forward and sank into his arms.

She was crying, her gnarled fists balled and hard against his chest.

"Mrs. Calhoun," he said, bewildered. He looked down at the top of her gray head. "Nora. What's wrong? What's happened?"

He looked into the house. Was someone hurt? Was something on fire?

"Oh, Jack," she said finally. "Jack Chisholm, I am the stupidest old woman."

"I would not let you say that if I was your worst enemy," Jack said, taking hold of her shoulders. "And I am not your worst enemy."

That must have been what she needed. She sniffed, stepped back, drew herself up with some dignity, and invited Jack inside. They went back to the kitchen, and she seated him at the dining room table, which sat under a spreading water stain on the ceiling.

"I'm sorry, Jack," she said while she poured him a cup of coffee. Maxwell House. It was his fate from now on. She lowered her eyes and shook her head. "I can't accept delivery of those shingles."

"I can take them back," Jack said. "But, Mrs. Calhoun, you need a new roof." It was the first thing he noticed when he pulled up to her house. The shingles were dingy and frayed. He looked up at the water stain—he must be sitting underneath the leak that Lyndi patched.

"I know that," she said. "And after talking with your father the other day, I thought I'd found a good deal on labor. These boys were driving through town, saw my place, told me they'd come this morning to put on a new roof if I'd order the shingles." She passed him the cup, warmed her own, and then sat down at the dining room table. Antique, Jack noticed now, cherry, beautiful grain. All it needed was a new coat of finish.

"I should have known it was too good to be true," she was saying.

"They wanted to be paid up front," Jack said, his heart sinking.

"How did you know?" she said. She shook her head. "That way they wouldn't have to bother me when the job was done. But they didn't show up this morning to start taking off the old shingles. And the phone number they gave me doesn't work."

"Cash or check?"

"They wanted cash," she said. She raised a hand to her mouth. "I should have known. Oh, I am a stupid old woman."

"Stop it," Jack said. "It's a common scam. I had some older members of my church get taken the exact same way. The exact same. And they weren't stupid any more than you are."

"I am so sorry to drag you out here," she said. "Those shingles look heavy."

"You know it," Jack said. "And I still have to unload them."

"But I don't have any more money."

"You need a new roof," Jack repeated.

"There's no more money," she repeated.

They sat for a moment, sipping their coffee and sighing. At last, Jack swallowed the last of his Maxwell House and slid his chair back. Although he didn't know yet how he was going to make it work, he had decided something. "This is going to sound counterintuitive, Mrs. Calhoun, but I am going to unload your shingles because I believe that somehow, some way, that roof of yours is going to get fixed."

She looked at him skeptically. "By elves?"

"Sure," he said. "By elves. Are you going to church tomorrow?"

"Am I alive?" she asked.

"You're a praying woman," he said. "Here's what I want you to do. I want you to go to church and pray that somehow this will work itself out."

Her pursed lips showed how much she believed him. "Is that your advice as a pastor, or as someone who doesn't want to take my shingles back to the hardware store?"

"Both," he said.

"I don't much believe in miracles anymore," she said softly. He knew her life had been fraught with tragedy.

"Miracles come in all shapes and sizes," he said, reaching out to pat her hand. He got to his feet. "You just go to church. You pray. I think something good might happen."

Outside, he unloaded the shingles by the front porch, grunting louder with each bundle. She watched him quietly, her expression something between doubtful and heartbroken. When he was done, he walked over and hugged her.

"Call Randy," he told her. "Tell the police what happened. Let's at least not let these guys scam anyone else."

She nodded. It would be a blow to her pride—but better that blow than someone else be taken in.

"And listen—I want you to start believing something good is going to happen."

She couldn't. He could see that just by looking at her crumpled face, her defeated posture. Any kind of miracle was too much to hope for. She'd been kicked too hard to believe.

He knew that feeling well, and didn't want anybody else to suffer it if he could help it.

"I'll see you soon," he said.

Sooner than she knew.

"Bless you," she said, although he hadn't done much yet worth blessing. "You know, you're a good boy, Jack."

"I'm glad somebody thinks so," he said.

He waved to her, climbed into the hardware store's truck, and was on his way out of town.

He drove the curves and shade of the river road as far as the highway. Then he turned south and let the wind rush through the cab as he lowered both windows, turned up the music, and got his speed up near seventy.

It was the fastest he had driven in a long time—and the farthest. Forty-five minutes later, he arrived in Kerrville blasting "Paradise City" and making a general nuisance of himself at each traffic light. Down past the Guadalupe River—pronounced in Texan "Gwad-a-loop"—he stopped at Bealls department store, and after sorting through designer jeans, pushing past Polo and Union Bay, he found what he was looking for: Wrangler Cowboy Cut.

He bought two pair, one blue, one black, plus some black T-shirts and a wool crew-neck sweater that didn't look like something his mother had made. *Beige*, he thought. Ecru, the tag said. Either way, he was content.

On his way back out of town on Highway 16, he stopped at Billy's Western Wear and tried on a lot of cowboy boots— Noconas, Justins, Ariats. At last, after walking around in each of them for a while, he decided on some Tony Lamas in brown bull hide. Settled, because what he really wanted was a pair of Tony Lama black ostrich boots, but he didn't have near enough money. He also bought a matching leather belt after considering and rejecting a big buckle bearing a Texas star.

"It's too much," he admitted out loud to the salesman. "Too much, too fast." He had worn a big belt buckle with a bucking bronco on it when he was a boy, and Jamie Taylor had once busted his knuckles trying to punch him in the stomach.

Jack smiled at the thought.

Maybe later.

As he walked out to the truck, he had another thought. Next door was a Home Depot. He pulled into their parking lot, wandered inside, and took a look at what they carried in their battery section. They shelved chargers and rechargeable batteries together. He picked out a package of four AA Energizers that came with a charger to show his dad and to get the product number.

Holy cow, he thought as he stood in line and looked around. It was a hardware theme park that stretched on into infinity.

This place has everything. No wonder people drove the forty-five minutes to get here.

He shook that thought out of his head. People loved his father. After all, they'd kept the Chisholm's store in business for three generations—four, counting his daughter, Alison, wherever she was.

A lot could be said for doing business with integrity in your own hometown.

The checker put Jack's batteries in a white plastic bag, and he ambled back out to the truck. He noticed an F-150 was parked next to his dad's pickup, and someone was leaning against it.

The two of them marked each other at the same time. It was hard to say which of them was more surprised.

It was Bill Hall with his gray felt cowboy hat tilted back, one finger in his belt. He was bigger—he'd developed a substantial gut, although nothing like the one on Dennis, which was truly a wonder of the world—and had some gray at his temples. But he looked hearty and healthy, and was definitely the Billy Hall he had known his whole life.

Bill stood up straight upon seeing Jack, as though he'd been caught doing something obscene.

"I thought your dad was driving," he said. "I was going to explain why I was coming here."

He touched his hat and made as if to walk past Jack.

"Bill," Jack said, putting out a hand to detain him. They both looked at that hand, and then at each other.

"Y'know, Twelve," Bill said, "I'd guess we don't have much of anything to say to each other." He brushed Jack's hand to one side and stepped past him.

"Bill," Jack called after him. He stopped a few steps off. "I just wanted to say—man, I'm sorry."

Bill didn't turn around. "I'd guess you're sorry for a whole mess of things just at the present moment. Doesn't do much for me, though."

"You're right about that," Jack said. "I am a mess, true enough. But I can be sorry too. I'm sorry that I left the way I did. I didn't think about all the people I'd be leaving behind when I walked away from my dad."

"No," Bill said. He turned to face Jack now. "You surely didn't think of us."

His face held no compassion anymore, no warmth. Once they would have run into a burning building for the other. Now they looked at each other as if they were strangers. Less than strangers, maybe.

Bill turned, took a step.

I would still run into a burning building for him, Jack thought.

"Billy," he said. "You were my best friend in the world. It was stupid, but I wanted to close the door on all this."

"You were on a rocket ride," Bill said, letting out a big sigh, "toward the future." He looked around the parking lot. "And yet here we stand today."

He pointed a finger that skewered Jack's heart. "I counted on you. Even if we were on different sides of the country, I told myself, if I need Jack, he'll come. If I really need him, he'll always come."

Bill looked at Jack now with something close to hatred, his jaw rigid as he spoke. "When my Sarah took sick, I called your office. You didn't come. When she died and I had to plan a funeral, I called your office. You didn't even call me back."

It was a punch in the gut that no belt buckle could deflect. "I didn't know," Jack said. "They screened my calls. I got so many." He shook his head, took a deep breath. "It's not an excuse. But I would have come if I'd known. I promise."

Looking into Bill's eyes, Jack knew this was the same person he'd known since they were five years old.

And that Billy, his oldest and dearest friend, wanted nothing whatsoever to do with him now.

"I buried my wife without my best friend," Bill said quietly. "I've raised up my girls without my best friend." He raised his voice enough that a few people walking an aisle over in the parking lot actually looked their direction. "I have lived for ten years without my best friend. So you know what I think, Twelve?"

He stepped closer to Jack as if to confide something, and Jack actually leaned in, awaiting it.

"What?" he asked. He leaned even closer, feeling some hope. "What do you think, Bill?"

"I think my best friend can go to hell."

If looks could kill, Jack would have been prone and smoldering on the asphalt.

Bill Hall turned on his boot heel and left Jack standing there, stunned. He wasn't sure how long he stood gaping, although it was long enough to draw some stares from people walking past.

He thought maybe Bill would come out again; maybe if they couldn't fix things, at least they might leave them on a better note.

The Bill he had known ten years ago would have listened to him, maybe tried to find a way to forgive him.

But the Bill who was driving all the way down to Kerrville to buy something he used to buy in Mayfield, the Bill he'd become since Jack had left—that Bill would outwait him, would die inside the Home Depot rather than come back out and say another word to him.

When he realized this, he crept back into the truck. He ejected Axl and Slash, pushed in the Reverend Al Green, and the sweet, sad sounds of "Tired of Being Alone" filled the cab as he backed out of his space and exited the parking lot.

On the way home, he played the conversation over in his mind.

What could he have done differently? What could he have said?

And as he pulled into his own driveway, the conclusion was clear and incontrovertible.

What should have been done differently should have been done differently years ago.

Whatever difficulties he had with his father, Jack should have been around for everyone else he loved.

But maybe I'm not too late to start making things right, he thought. Not as a man of God. He was a failure there. But maybe as a man—

He had forgotten the chicken. He backed out of the driveway, drove back into town. On the way, he passed Saint Mary's Catholic Church, catty-corner from the not-quite-Lutheran church, across the street from First Baptist, which was thriving in the midst of downturn and chaos everywhere else. They were probably rocking both a contemporary and a traditional service on Sundays.

Worshipers were coming out from the Saturday afternoon mass at Saint Mary's. Jack saw Father Frank shaking hands at the door, leaning in to talk to each of those parishioners with a smile on his face as though God had created a wonder at their births.

"Now that's one good pastor," Jack murmured.

He wished he could say hello. But he had promised to get chicken. With something that felt strangely like regret, he drove past the church, ordered twelve chicken tenders, mashed potatoes and gravy, biscuits, and sweet tea at Chicken Express. He paid for it with the last of his cash.

So much for any other crazy Saturday night plans he might have made.

"I guess it is football with the old man." He sighed.

The University of Texas beat Oregon State in the Alamo Bowl. He and his father devoured the chicken, as well as some chocolate cake Mary had dropped off. And while Jack still ached over his encounter with Bill, he knew enough to know that he'd encountered some true wisdom earlier: either Bill would forgive him, or he wouldn't.

In any case, he had said what needed to be said.

Now, perhaps, something better could happen.

After all, miracles come in all shapes and sizes.

9.

Jack was already up and dressed when he heard his father moving around in the kitchen. He had a limited window of time for what he had planned, and he wanted to be well under way before anybody could try to stop him. So, even though he knew it was going to be a long—and painful—day, he wanted to begin it as soon as he could sneak away.

Painful because he was sore from the day before. His back, his arms—he already hurt in muscles he didn't even remember he had. And it would only get worse.

He made his way down the stairs, stiffly, slowly, hoping his muscles might thaw with motion. In the kitchen, he took a couple of aspirin from the cabinet, washed them down with water, pocketed two or three more for later.

"Me, I'd sleep in if I didn't have to go to church," his dad called from the table. "You want me to make you some eggs?"

"Toast and jelly is fine," Jack said, slipping two slices into the toaster and setting two aside to make a sandwich. "Okay if I drive the truck today?"

"Of course," his father said, buttering his own toast.

"And can I borrow your store keys?"

His father looked over at him. "You have some work left to do that I don't know about?"

"Yessir," Jack said.

Tom looked at him thoughtfully. Then he slid the door key off his key ring and across the table. "There you go."

"Thanks, Dad."

"I'm going over to Mary's after church," Tom said. "You're invited."

"I'm actually going to be a little busy today," he said.

"With what?" his father asked. He looked across at him, an eyebrow arched. "Now you've got me curious. Is it your batteries? Are you going to save the world?"

"I'm pretty sure you'll hear all about it," Jack said. "No secrets in Mayfield." His toast popped up, and he turned around, snatched it out and onto a plate.

He sat down at the table as his father cut his fried eggs into tiny squares with his knife and fork.

"You know," Tom said, "I think I may have a surprise for you myself. That matter I told you I'd work on."

"What?" Jack said.

"That important matter," his father said, and he couldn't help smiling a little.

"Finding Tracy and Alison?" Jack's breath caught.

His father nodded. Jack's heart fell.

Sure, he would find them. The Internets would track them down, no problem.

"I should have news tomorrow or Tuesday," he said.

"That would be great," Jack said, not committing himself to

the possibility at all. He wondered for the first time if maybe the cancer was in Tom's brain—if maybe he wasn't all there anymore. "That would be great, Dad."

Tom sized him up. You could see from the expression on his face that he was considering whether or not to say something.

"Our lawyers filed a motion in Seattle Friday," Tom said. "They argued that you couldn't be kept away from your daughter without just cause, and certainly not without a court order, which nobody has filed. The judge issued an order for us. So our lawyers were able to find out where the church's lawyers were forwarding the checks. An address in Boston. And the private investigator thinks he has them located. He'll be able to confirm it if and when he sees Alison or Tracy."

Jack felt as though he had been hit by a brick. His mouth hung slightly open, and he knew he must look like a fish on dry land.

"Boston," he said at last. He would never have found them. Tracy had never said she wanted to go to Boston, had never come on any of his speaking trips to the Northeast. "You—you did it."

"I told you, son," Tom said gently. "The clock is ticking. I don't have a moment to waste."

"I know. But you did all this in a week? How— But—" He gave up. "I've been calling them for six weeks."

"Actually, I did all this in three days," Tom said. Again, that shrug. "People move quickly when you give them a reason to."

It dawned on Jack, and he looked up in something like horror. "Dad," he said. "How much is this costing you?"

Tom looked back at him, and he said, his voice calm, without particular emphasis, "Everything I've got."

"Dad." Jack shook his head. "But—"

"But nothing," Tom said fiercely. "I can't take it with me. Nothing can be done for me, no medical treatment, no last-minute heroics. That money will not prolong my life. My time will come, and when it comes, I will die." He pointed a finger across the table. "I talked with Mary. She agreed with me. That money needs to be used right now, used for this."

"But you've worked your whole life—" Jack began. He thought of the countless hours, of the sacrifices, of the ceaseless toil. His father was one of the hardest working men Jack had ever known. "You saved this—"

"It's my money, Jack," Tom said. "I get to spend it any way I choose." His shoulders relaxed a bit. "And I choose to spend it finding my granddaughter."

"Okay," Jack said. "Okay. I get it." Or he thought he did, anyway. He could see himself making the same choice if he were in a similar position.

Still, it was a lot to absorb before his morning cup of coffee—especially if that coffee was only Maxwell House.

"Got to go," Tom said, checking his watch. "I'm teaching Sunday School."

"I figured," Jack said. He had been waiting for this window of a couple of hours when his father and others would depart early for church. "I'll see you tonight, okay?"

His father plied him with that measuring glance again. "You're not going to get into trouble, I hope. Or get me in trouble? I don't think I have enough money left to mount a strong legal defense for either of us."

"Dad," Jack said. "You're just going to have to trust me."

Tom looked at him, his head a little to one side. Then he nodded. "I do, Jack. I do." He raised a hand. "Have a great day."

As soon as Tom was out the door, Jack made a sandwich, threw it in a sack with a bag of chips and a couple of apples, and hurried out to the truck. He checked his watch—it was a little after nine.

Church would let out at noon, if not before. There was no telling how they worked the schedule without a regular preacher, but they certainly wouldn't run longer than noon. People's Sunday dinners might be in the oven.

At the hardware store, he rushed about assembling everything he needed: a nail gun, the right nails for the job, a sturdy bucket, a rope, a claw hammer, a cat's paw to pull nails, a utility knife, a tape measure, a chalk line, a good strong ladder.

He checked his watch again. By now, everyone who was going would be at Sunday School.

He drove over to Mrs. Calhoun's house, parked in the driveway, and put the ladder against her eaves. Slowly, he made his way up the ladder, his calves and back already aching.

He pulled the thick tarp away and was pleased that while the roof under it was in particularly bad shape, he didn't see any large holes. The boards underneath appeared stable.

Then he climbed up to the crown of the roof and began pulling nails and tearing off the old shingles. At first, he winced every time he pulled a nail, but either the aspirin began to kick in or his muscles began to warm. He knew that later he was going to feel every single nail he was pulling now. But it was important to get a good start and work quickly.

If he had much of the old roof pulled off by the time Mrs.

Calhoun got home from church, she could hardly object if he started putting on her new roof, could she?

The weather was still fine—warm, sunny, a beautiful springlike December day. They weren't expecting rain all week—something he'd checked when he first got this idea. He didn't know how long it would take him to strip and roof this by himself—he'd never roofed except on a crew, and that was just one summer for extra money. It might actually be a multi-day job since he was working alone.

He remembered his short time as a roofer, had relived it before deciding to take on this project. That had been a vision of hell—the July sun beating down with tangible force, the shingles so hot beneath him that they could burn flesh. He, Bill, and Van all wishing they had never come home from their respective colleges to melt on some godforsaken rooftop.

But today was nowhere near as hot. Except for the wind, which was gusting a bit, and the fact that he was uncomfortably high off the ground, the only challenge was the work itself.

The first curious bystander showed his head during the first twenty minutes of the job. While Jack had supposed that the entire town would be at church, the truth was that some people didn't go, and many of the Catholics had gone the afternoon before. One of Mrs. Calhoun's neighbors saw Jack on the roof from his backyard, came over to the fence, and called up, "Hey, *hombre*, what are you doing up there?"

Jack looked down at him. It was Mr. Rodriguez, the highschool shop teacher. "Hey, Mr. Rodriguez," he called back. "It's me. Jack Chisholm. I'm putting on a new roof for Mrs. Calhoun."

"Jack Chisholm?" He stood there for a moment thinking, then

he nodded in recognition, and Jack's heart fell. Mr. Rodriguez was recalling his entire history, distant and recent.

"Didn't you take Home Ec?" he shouted up.

Jack pulled loose another shingle and flung it into the front yard. "You know I did," he called back. "Everybody knows that."

"Maybe I should climb up and give you a hand, then," Mr. Rodriguez said.

"I wouldn't say no," Jack said. "You got a cat's paw?"

"Oh yeah, *no problemo*," he said. Sam Rodriguez was famous for saying "No problemo."

Drive a nail into your forehead? No problemo. Go see the nurse, hombre.

He disappeared into his shop out back, and a few minutes later Mr. Rodriguez was on the roof next to Jack, pulling nails with an economy of motion that Jack could only envy.

Jack actually did pull nails like someone who had taken Home Ec.

"I heard about those guys that took Mrs. Calhoun's money," Mr. Rodriguez was saying to him now. "*Descarados*, all of them. Jerks. Who steals from an old woman?" He was a small man, fit, in his sixties now, but he moved across the roof with the grace and skill of a dancer. Unlike Jack, who lumbered. "I didn't figure she'd ever get her new roof."

"Same here," Jack said.

"I didn't even think of this," Mr. Rodriguez said, his face reddening. "To offer this."

"It's okay," Jack said. "I wouldn't have either. Not until this week."

They looked around at what needed to be done, smiled at each other, started pulling nails and shingles loose again.

They worked steadily. With two of them now, they were clearing the roof down to the plywood quickly. It wasn't long before two more workers joined them.

"I called some of my students before I came up," Mr. Rodriguez explained as two high-school boys climbed up the ladder and stood looking around. "Devon and Ricardo," Mr. Rodriguez said.

The two boys said hi, shook hands with Mr. Rodriguez and Jack. They were carrying claw hammers and wore knee pads. Both looked like they knew their way around a roof.

By the time church let out, the four of them were well on their way to having the old roof off. Mrs. Calhoun pulled up in her Lincoln at fifteen minutes after twelve to find her front yard full of gawkers, six men and boys standing on her roof, and a rain of old shingles littering her front yard.

"Jack Chisholm," she called up at him after she got out of the car and did some gawking herself for a moment. "You come down here right this instant!"

"Yes, ma'am," he called back, prying up his shingle and tossing it well away from where she stood. He got slowly to his feet—his back was hurting most of all, now, from the bending and stooping—and climbed down the ladder.

"What in the world," she said, pointing up at the roof, "is going on up there?"

"Well," he said, "some folks thought this might be a way to help you out a little bit."

"Some folks thought," she said.

"Yes, ma'am," he said.

"A little help."

"Yes'm," he said. He did an uneasy little dance under her gaze.

"Are these"—she could not hide the smile that spread across her face—"elves?"

"Yes, ma'am," he smiled in return.

"Jack, were you the angel behind this little miracle?"

"Oh no," he protested. "It was, like, spontaneous. You know how things are in a small town." He held his hands up, shrugged. "People help each other out."

Tears began to form in her eyes and her face crumpled. She raised that tiny balled fist to her mouth, and spasms ran through her as she struggled not to weep.

"Hey," Jack said gently, putting a hand on her shoulder. "Mrs. Calhoun. You've done a lot for the people of this town." He patted her shoulder, then stood uneasily. "You've done a lot for me."

She blinked rapidly, still incapable of speaking, and tried to smile.

"Jack Chisholm," Mr. Rodriguez called from the roof. "Tell Mrs. C. that you have to get your Home Ec–loving *culo* back to work."

They smiled at each other.

"Well," she said, "maybe I'd better make some coffee. And lemonade."

"That would make us very happy," Jack said. He turned to go.

She put out a hand, surprisingly strong, and grasped his arm.

"It is a miracle," she said.

He looked down at her arm, patted it, and smiled. "All shapes and sizes, Mrs. Calhoun," he said. "All shapes and sizes."

Then he climbed back up the ladder and got his Home Ec–loving butt back to work.

After lunch, seven more workers joined them. Once they'd pulled off all the old shingles, they began laying down the new felt, starting the new shingles at the edge and working back up toward the crown. By late afternoon, more people were on the roof than could comfortably fit, and Mr. Rodriguez sent down his students and some of those who'd been working the longest. He tried to send Jack down, but Jack was enjoying himself too much.

"No, hombre," he said. "I'm head elf. I gotta be up here."

Warren had gotten a call from someone after church and drove in from the ranch. He was now happily using a nail gun nearby. Father Frank heard about the roofraising and was sitting on the hood of that 1986 LeBaron, Mayfield Wildcat maroon and white, talking with some of the wives and mothers who had joined Mrs. Calhoun in bringing refreshments. Some *conjunto* music played from the open windows of one of the pickup trucks on the street. Somebody had unloaded a smoker and was smoking hamburgers and bratwursts. Somebody else had brought menudo in a big pot and started dishing it out in bowls. A bottle of red wine and then another made the rounds, and someone filled an ice chest with Lone Star beer.

He wasn't sure how many of Mayfield's citizens drove by or dropped in, but it was a lot. At one point, as they neared completion and Jack had run out of room to work, he looked down across the yard to see several couples dancing. He saw Father Frank backing Mrs. Calhoun carefully around the front yard in something approximating a two-step, heard her hooting with laughter. It sounded like maybe she had taken a sip or two of the red wine.

Jack's father was sitting in a lawn chair with some other seniors from the Lutheran church like they were watching a Mayfield ball game.

The pastor of First Baptist, Brother Raymond, was out

directing traffic on the street, along with a couple of other deacons from that church.

As for local law enforcement? Jack saw Randy parked down the block in a police cruiser, looking sourly at the goings-on and maybe wondering if they needed a permit of some sort.

As Jack looked out at the street, which had been bumper-to-bumper all afternoon with onlookers coming and going and staying, he even saw Bill Hall's red Ford truck pause for a moment to take in the scene.

From the roof, Jack raised a hand, a Texas wave.

Bill saw him.

Then the big red truck rumbled slowly away without another sign.

At last, the roof was finished. The men and boys on the roof looked at each other and let out a cheer. They clasped hands, patted each other on the back, sore but happy. People in the yard began to clear away the trash and old shingles.

It was done.

But it seemed to Jack that an occasion like this needed to be marked in some way, that people couldn't simply be allowed to drift away.

He looked around, saw Father Frank, and had an idea.

"Will you bless the roof?" he asked. That seemed like the proper thing to do—if, in fact, their common labor of love had not already blessed it beyond need.

"Would you like me to do that?" Frank asked Mrs. Calhoun, with whom he was still dancing in some fashion.

"It would be an honor," she said. "And maybe keep it from leaking."

Father Frank made his way over to the ladder, put a foot on the bottom rung, climbed slowly and carefully up until his outstretched right hand rested on the new shingles on the eaves.

"In the name of the Father, and of the Son, and of the Holy Spirit," he began. All of the Catholics present crossed themselves, as did some of the Lutherans. Jack followed suit after glancing around.

"Peace be with this house and with all who live here," Frank said in a loud outdoor priest voice, and he paused while a handful of the Catholics, including Mr. Rodriguez, right next to Jack, returned the customary, "And with thy spirit."

Father Frank made the sign of the cross over the roof. "When Christ took flesh through the Blessed Virgin Mary, he made his home with us. Let us now pray that he will enter this home and bless it with his presence." He bowed his head for a moment.

Then he stopped, slowly crept back down the ladder, made his way across the yard to Mrs. Calhoun who was watching with hands clasped. When he spoke again it was in a quiet, intimate voice that people had to strain to follow.

"May he always be here with you," he said to Mrs. Calhoun. "May he share in your joys, comfort you in your sorrows." He reached out a hand, put it on her shoulder. "Inspired by his teachings and example, seek to make your new home above all else a dwelling place of love, diffusing far and wide the goodness of Christ."

"I will," she said, blinking. "I promise."

"I know you will, Nora Calhoun," he said softly. "You always have."

Then he winked at her.

Father Frank turned to all of those gathered, workers and gawkers, all of those at the feast, Catholics and Protestants and unbelievers alike, and he raised his hand to shoulder height and gave the benediction. "And may the blessing of God—Father, Son, and Holy Spirit—be upon you this day, and remain with you forever."

"Amen," they all replied. It sent a tingle up Jack's spine, and for a moment, he found himself unable to move.

It was as if God had reached down and sparked something into being.

He wasn't the only one who felt that something holy had just happened. They all looked around, blinking as though a flash had gone off in front of their eyes. But after the blessing, they slowly departed, stopping to shake a hand, to share a hug, to finish off a Lone Star. An old Hispanic couple started dancing again to the conjunto music. Mrs. Calhoun shook the hands of every person there, some of them multiple times, as if either her memory was imperfect or she had indeed been nipping at the red wine.

She stopped finally at Jack, and at first he feared that she was going to cry again. She showed every sign of it.

"I did pray for a miracle, Jack," she said. "This morning." She smiled. "Just a small one."

He nodded. "That's exactly what you got," he said.

"What did I say to you the other day?" she asked. "In the store. About you coming back at a good time?"

He smiled. "It was a good time," he agreed. "You needed a new roof."

"I needed more than that," she said, batting at him with one hand. Her face became suddenly serious. "After what happened with those men, I needed to believe in something."

Jack nodded again. He understood that, more than she knew. "Me too," he said.

"And what are you finding to believe in?" she asked, the old Sunday School teacher poised.

"Well," he said slowly, "after a day like this? I don't know." He looked around. "Well, to start, I'm beginning to think that most people are good, deep down." He shrugged. "Where that comes from, that goodness, I don't know. But that's something to hope for, right? That maybe most people will do the right thing, given a chance?"

She looked around the yard, at the people saying good-bye, at her blessed new roof.

"Maybe," she said.

"I am sorry that someone took advantage of your trust," he said. "You're a good person. You deserve better." He shrugged. "Today you saw something better."

He suddenly yawned, stretched. "But now I'm tired. And I'm ready to get off my feet." He yawned again. "Come see me in the store?"

"I will," she said. "Thank you, Jack." She crossed her hands on her chest. "Thank you."

"You are most welcome."

He wandered the yard, gathering his tools, helping others load the final old shingles into a truck for the trash heap.

His aches had aches of their own now, but despite that, he couldn't stop smiling.

His father folded his chair and said good-bye to his peers. He looked across at Jack, clasped his hands in the air like a prizefighter claiming victory, called, "See you at the house," and departed.

Father Frank walked over to Jack. "So, Nora Calhoun was telling me that this barn raising just sort of spontaneously erupted."

"I believe it did, yes," he said.

Frank fixed him with a knowing eye. "One of my parishioners reports that it had a ringleader." He grinned. "A head elf, I believe he said."

"Well," Jack shrugged, "maybe." He resolved to remember that Mr. Rodriguez was a blabbermouth. "But then there were two people and things just started to snowball. And then nobody was the ringleader anymore."

Frank led Jack away from a knot of laughing people, took him by the arm, and looked him straight in the eye. "Did you know anybody was coming to help you when you climbed up on that roof?"

Jack hesitated. He shook his head. "I—hoped. But I knew that I needed to do something. Whether or not anybody else came. I needed to."

"Today was something," Father Frank said. "It—surprised me."

"Surprised you?"

"When the prodigal son limped home from his riotous living, his motives were mixed, at best," Frank said. "He stumbled home simply to survive. But after that, after he got home, who knows how he changed?"

He fixed him with a long, appraising look as though he could see Jack changing in front of his very eyes. "Someone did a good thing here today, Jack."

Jack looked around at the yard full of people, at the houses beyond. "I'd guess that somebody does a good thing in this town just about every day, Father Frank."

Frank nodded. "You've got that right," he said, then he held out his hand. "Well. Welcome home, boyo." Jack took his hand and shook it twice. He smiled. "Buy you a pint?"

"Rain check," Jack said, rolling his shoulders and stretching again. His body was in agony, and tomorrow would be worse. "I hear a hot bath and maybe some muscle relaxers calling my name."

"Well, it's a standing offer at Buddy's," Frank said. "Shayla and I will make you feel welcome. Or you can always come and have some wine at God's house."

Jack looked at him. "Isn't that—you know—against the rules?" Jack held up his hands. "I'm not Catholic. I'm not, you know, even very much of a Christian at the present moment."

"It's not my table, Jack," Frank said. "It's not even the Church's, God bless it. God's mercy overfloweth. It goeth where it goeth." He grinned and then he winked at him as well. "In any case, I won't tell if you don't."

Jack smiled back. "Maybe," he said. "Anyway"—he climbed into the truck—"I'll see you, Father Frank."

They waved at each other. Jack backed out carefully, watching so he didn't hit any people or fenders. Everyone was waving at him as he backed out. Everyone was waving at each other.

Someone did a good thing here today.

I'd guess that somebody does a good thing in this town just about every day.

Funny, he and Grace Cathedral had done good things for people on the other side of the world. A lot of good things. For a lot of needy people.

But he couldn't remember the last time he'd done a good thing for someone standing right in front of him.

The last time he'd helped somebody face-to-face.

And not to minimize doing good things for someone in abject poverty or someone without clean water. But he wondered if it might be easier for the rescuers to do good for someone they would never see again than to try to rescue those they see every day.

When he pulled in, his dad was sitting in the kitchen, something was baking in the oven. "Lasagna," his father said. "Mrs. Riley sent it home with me."

"Mrs. Riley used to be an amazing cook," Jack said, suddenly hungry.

"Still is."

At each of their places, Jack saw chilled mugs of what looked like beer. His dad was actually setting his mug down after taking a sip.

"I thought you didn't like having beer in the house," Jack said. That had been a hard-and-fast rule his whole life. No beer, no wine, no alcohol of any kind.

"I used to worry what people would think," his father said, waving a hand. "And that I liked it too much. Neither are a worry for me now." He smiled. "And I thought today, of all days, you deserved a cold beer."

"Father Frank thought so too," Jack said.

"He gave me the idea, actually."

Jack sat, sniffed, raised his mug, drank. It was a blond ale, smooth, with a little tang of citrus. A great beer to drink after a hard day of roofing.

"Wow," he said. He held up his mug to the light. "That is not Bud Light."

"It's called Fireman's Number Four," he said. "From a little brewery in Blanco. Won a medal this year at some big beer contest." He shrugged. "We're not Seattle. But we do make some good beers hereabouts."

"God bless the Germans," Jack said, raising his mug.

"God bless the Germans," his father agreed. They drank.

They didn't talk, but it felt comfortable, each of them looking at the mugs, appreciating how good it tasted.

"Umm, Dad," Jack said, as he remembered all the supplies he had taken from the hardware store that morning—nails and tools and probably more than he could pay for in a month of hard labor.

"Yes," Tom said, wiping his mouth with the back of his hand as he set down his Fireman's Number Four.

"I think I, uh, took out a pretty big advance on my pay today."

Tom smiled. He reached a hand across the table, patted the top of Jack's bruised and blistered hand.

"Why don't you and Mary argue about that," he said. "It looks to me like Chisholm's just opened a sideline in contracting. Anyway, I don't think we've finished our year-end inventory. Who knows what was on those shelves and what wasn't?"

"Tomorrow's the thirty-first. I guess we haven't finished yet."

"New Year's Eve," Tom mused. For a moment he seemed a thousand miles away, then he looked across at Jack. "You made any big plans?"

"Not yet," Jack said. "I'm holding my options open." Elton might call; the White House might demand his presence.

"You do that," Tom said. "Hold your options open." He got that faraway look again. "Because I'm thinking it could be an exciting day." He raised his mug, took another sip, and—because apparently this was now the thing to do—he winked at Jack.

Jack raised his mug in salute, drained it, and got to his feet. Lasagna was baking, and it smelled good, beyond good, but what he was really hungry for more than anything else right now was a long, hot bath.

10.

Jack woke suddenly at the sound of his name.

Someone was calling him. Where was he?

In his bed. In his old room.

What year was it?

He was very old, apparently. He couldn't move.

He lay there for a moment, wondering if maybe he was strapped to the bed, and then he came to a better, more informed conclusion.

He could move. It was just better if he didn't.

It was Monday morning, he remembered now. New Year's Eve, a day after he'd helped put on Mrs. Calhoun's new roof, two days after he'd loaded and unloaded three truckloads of timber and concrete and shingles.

A few years back, on the first day Jack had started lifting weights again as part of his regular workout routine, he'd started on back and biceps, and he had done way too much, gone too heavy, relived his athletic past in ways that were no longer wise or even possible. He was not the sort of person to do things halfway.

And he had awakened the next morning like this, stiff, sore, miserable.

This was worse than that time, though. This was back and shoulders, legs and neck and abs, every part of him that he could name and most he couldn't, the cumulative effect of two days of hard labor like he hadn't done since he was in college.

"Jack," his father called from downstairs.

"Uhnn," Jack answered. So that's why he woke up. He rolled to one side, somehow heaved himself upright.

"Jack," his father called again.

"What?" he said. Didn't Dad know he was dying up here? What could possibly be so important?

"How many eggs do you want?"

Jack groaned. He checked the clock—7:35. Okay. He'd slept in. Breakfast questions had some validity.

"Two," he called. "No. Three."

He was in pain, but he was also hungry—starving, actually. He hadn't eaten lasagna last night, but had gotten out of the bath, climbed into bed, and fallen asleep immediately.

Now he tried to get dressed and found that he could do nothing without it hurting. Pulling a shirt over his head hurt his rib cage, his shoulders. Pulling up his pants hurt his back, his biceps.

"This is what you get for doing good deeds," he muttered to himself.

"It's on the table," his father called up.

"Coming," he said. "I'm moving a little—ugh—slow up here."

He moved gingerly down the stairs, crept into the kitchen, eased slowly into his seat.

His father smiled at him. "You shaved that little—" He flicked below his lip to indicate a soul patch.

"And put on some Wranglers," Jack said. He groaned. "I am too sore to even think about pulling on skinny jeans."

"That's what you get for doing good deeds," Tom said.

"I know," Jack said. "Right? I never woke up bruised from a day in the pulpit."

"Speaking of stepping in the pulpit," Tom said.

"I don't like the sound of this," Jack said.

"It's just that I've heard a couple of folks might talk to you about saying a few words from the pulpit."

Jack crossed his arms and looked down at the table. "At the church."

"The Lutheran church," his father said.

"Sort of Lutheran," Jack said.

"Just so."

"I can't preach," Jack said.

"No," his father said. "Not preach, even. Just say a few words. Especially after what happened yesterday." He pushed himself back from the table, got up to refill his coffee. "This town hasn't had much to be hopeful about. And never much in that long stretch between the end of football and two-a-days." He shook his head, although he was as big a football fan as had ever breathed.

"Yesterday was something, Dad. But most of us were there. We saw what happened."

"But what did it mean? You could just say a few words about it."

"I can't, Dad. I don't have any words." He took a bite of his eggs, then another. They were perfectly cooked. "I don't know what happened yesterday. How can I get up and tell people what to believe if I don't even know myself?"

"Maybe you could skip the part about telling them what to

believe," his father said, buttering his toast. "Maybe you could just say a few words from your heart."

"I can't preach," Jack said for the last time, and a door in his heart swung shut. "I don't think I'll ever preach again."

"Gonna make it hard to get that big church back if you never preach again," his father said mildly. He picked up his spoon, stopped midway to the jar of grape jelly, pointed it at him. "Think about it."

"I never stop," Jack said. "Thinking. About any of it."

His father nodded. "It's the curse of the Chisholms. What should we have done? Why didn't we do better?"

"I got that from you," Jack said, and he realized his voice held ten years of stored-up accusations.

If he was offended, his father didn't show it; he didn't even look up from spreading his jelly. "And where do you suppose I got it from?" he asked.

Jack sat there, awareness dawning. Now he remembered those marathon Thanksgiving prayers, the admonitions in the shop to do things precisely the right way, the denunciations for even the slightest deviation from the accepted way of being.

"Grampa Joe," he said.

Tom nodded, raised his toast to his mouth, took a bite.

"And I expect he got it from his father, and he got it from his, and so on, and so on," his father said between bites. "All the way back to Adam."

"But when you came after me in Mexico," Jack said. "And since. You didn't make me feel ashamed. Haven't."

"I thought maybe," Tom said carefully, "it was time we broke that pattern. Smashed it to bits, even."

"But how did you—" Jack had wondered about the difference he'd perceived in his father since he came home, the loss of self-righteousness, the gain of what he could only call tenderness.

It was a more personal question than he had ever asked his father.

He couldn't possibly ask it.

"You seem—different."

His father took a sip of coffee, set the cup down. "I believe I am," he said.

"Then what—"

"I found out I was going to die," Tom said. He raised his hands, palms up. "Simple as that. It's a fine motivator."

Jack looked down at his Maxwell House. Was it small-town truth serum? He took a sip from his cup, climbed out on his own limb. "But surely you didn't get that diagnosis and then just decide you were going to be different. Because you are different, Dad. I hardly recognize you."

His father took another drink, and this time he set the cup down hard, sloshing coffee over the side.

He bit his lip, looked down at the mess he made. For a moment, Jack thought his father was going to cry.

"Let me—" Jack began, reaching for his cloth napkin and beginning to wipe up the spill.

"When I found out that I wasn't going to live long," his father said as he watched the damp section of the table dry, "I gave up pretending to be strong. I gave up trying to do what was right. For a while, I just gave up, period." He looked up at Jack. "I couldn't bear leaving so much undone. For a while, I climbed inside a bottle." He anticipated Jack's look of astonishment. "That's right.

Mary ran the store. I don't know who fed me. Casseroles just showed up."

"Dad, you—"

"I wasn't afraid of dying. But I was terrified of dying without seeing you again. Without seeing Alison. Without making things right." He looked down, ran his hand over the table. "Then one night I was drinking bourbon and watching Fox News and they were running the story about you. What you did. How the church threw you out." He shook his head. "Mary thought you deserved everything you got, but something didn't seem right to me. Angry as I might have been, I never stopped wishing things were different." He shrugged. "So I called Father Frank. I told him I needed help."

He laughed as he raised his cup. "And you can probably hear him now, can't you? Sitting there, right there where you are now, both of us nursing our black coffees, my head pounding from a hangover. 'The world thrives on bad news, Tom,' he said to me. 'It tells us to shape our lives around the bad news. We have to be converted from the bad news to the good news, from expecting nothing to expecting something. It's time to expect something.' He was talking about this bad news—yours, mine."

Jack could hear Frank saying that. All of it. But one thing still puzzled him. "What is the good news in this, exactly?" he asked.

"My very question," he said, pointing at Jack. "'The good news,' Frank told me, 'is that you can help your son realize he is still loved after making a mistake. Because God knows, we all make mistakes.' And he looked at me pointedly."

"So—" Even though he was looking at his father, even

though he was hearing his words, it still seemed unbelievable that a person could change so monumentally. "What, exactly? You got tired of your bad news?"

"I got tired of living it and spreading it. Because I finally realized that when we are down and on our last legs, only the good news can save us."

"But what is the good news?" Jack asked again, a little more agitated this time.

"That depends on the person," his father said.

Jack glared at him. "Dad, if you hold up your index finger and tell me that the secret of life is that 'one thing' from *City Slickers*, I will mess you up."

His father snickered. "The good news," he said, raising a calming hand, "is that you are sitting right here with me. That is plenty of miracle for now. Maybe more good news is on its way. And maybe the good news is deeper and more profound than just your sitting there. You and Frank can hash that out a lot better than I can." He finished his coffee with a slurp, set it down a little more gently than before, sat back in his chair. "But this is plenty. I never thought I'd see you again." And he spread his hands to indicate Jack sitting there in front of him.

Voilà.

Tom's cell phone rang from the hallway, and his father shot out of his chair, out of the room. Jack would not have thought him capable of moving so quickly.

"Speaking," he said. "You did? When?" He checked his watch. "I'll get us tickets on the"—he was checking something—"1:25 from Austin. Gets in at 9:40." Jack could hear him writing something down. "Yes. We will. We will. Thank you."

Tom was quiet and then said again, in a wholly different tone of voice, "Thank you."

Tom walked back into the kitchen, stood behind his chair. "Pack a bag," he told Jack. "Pack warm."

"Are we going to Boston?" Jack asked. He couldn't believe it. Didn't dare.

Tom nodded, smiled with sad eyes. "Tracy said that we could see Alison tomorrow."

Jack sat blinking. "Really? Oh, that is a cruel joke, Dad—"

"Really," Tom said.

"And Tracy? Can I talk to Tracy?"

"I'd imagine you'll have to," he said. "I'm already mostly packed. We'll need to stop by the hardware store, though, put up a sign—"

"Let me run in and do it," Jack said. "I left my coat and hat there."

"Okay," Tom said. He seemed lost in thought.

"Dad," Jack said.

"Hmm? Oh. I was just thinking. I've never seen Alison in the flesh. Only on television."

"What?"

"I thought I told you I used to watch your show," Tom said. "Watched it after church."

"I thought you didn't like my sermons," Jack said.

"I didn't watch it for your sermons."

"Well," Jack said. "Tomorrow's New Year's Day. We're going to Boston, and we're going to see my family. That's got to be a good sign."

"Jack—"

"I was an English major, Dad," he said. "I know a potent symbol when I see one."

"I just don't want you to put the cart before the horse. You and Tracy will have a lot to talk about."

"But we finally get to talk!" Jack said. "I've been trying to talk to her since—"

"I just don't want you to put the cart before the horse," his dad repeated.

"Okay, Dad," Jack said. "Fine. Whatever. The horse is in front of the cart." He got up and hurtled into the hallway, swiped up the store and truck keys from the side table. "I'll be right back."

He hoped it would be sunny when they met. It would be cold, sure. It was January in Boston. But she had always loved the outdoors. Maybe he and Alison and Tracy could go to a park. Maybe they could have dinner together afterward. He knew of a place where you picked out the food you wanted cooked, brought it up to the cooks, and they grilled it for you. Alison would love that.

She'd see. He was in such a good space. He knew what he wanted. Everything was going to be better. She couldn't help but respond to that, right?

Three blocks toward town was the Taylor house. It was an old, monumental three-story with turrets—maybe the nicest house in town. James wasn't just the mayor; he owned the bank, after all, like his father had owned the bank, and his father before him.

As Jack drove past, he saw a teenage boy out front throwing a football into a net. He must have been out there a while now—the grass around the net was littered with footballs.

The boy took a five-step drop, squared up his hips and shoulders, and threw hard into the net.

Jack stopped and rolled down the passenger window. "Nice toss," he called.

"Thanks," the boy called back without looking at him. He picked up another ball from the green plastic bin in front of him, dropped back five steps, threw strong into the net.

Jack started to roll up the window. Then he paused for a moment and called out, "You know, you're squaring up your shoulders and hips really well. But you're throwing a little heavy off the front foot. You look like Tim Tebow. Not in the good way."

The boy had another ball in his hands, looked down as if he were going to throw again, then looked at the truck for the first time.

"Tim Tebow won the Heisman," he called back.

Then he took up the ball again, prepared to drop back.

"When you start to throw," Jack shouted, and the boy froze, "you want eighty percent of your weight on the back leg. Twenty percent on the front leg. And you transition to the reverse. Right now, you're throwing with eighty percent on the front leg. It throws off your balance. Believe me, I know."

The boy had dropped back, but this time, he didn't throw the ball. He lowered it to his waist, walked across the yard, stood ten feet from the truck.

"You're Jack Chisholm," he said.

"I am," he said. "And you must be Cameron. QB 1, your dad tells me. Congratulations."

"You took Mayfield to State," Cameron said.

"Me, your dad, a whole lot of folks did."

Cameron looked over at the house, turned back to the truck, and shook his head. "Man, my dad. He can't stand you. If he sees us talking, he would lose his mind."

"Yeah." Jack cleared his throat. "Maybe. Listen. Think about what I said. If you start off that back foot, you'll have better balance, more distance, probably more accuracy."

Cameron tossed the ball in the air, caught it, tossed it, caught it. *I'm QB 1*, his expression seemed to be saying. *And who are you, exactly?*

Fair enough. Jack made a move to shift into drive.

Jack saw a movement and heard a bang from the front porch as the screen door opened, closed. *Oh God*, Jack thought. Not good news no matter who it was.

It was Darla Taylor, once Darla Scroggins, once his Darla, a lifetime ago. She looked out at the street, strained for a moment to see who it was, then raised a hand in greeting.

She looked good. Beautiful, even. She was in jeans and a sweater that accentuated every curve. She didn't look like a mother of three.

Mother of three. How was that even possible? They had broken up his senior year over— what? He couldn't even remember now. They broke up before State, and Jack's head was somewhere other than in the game in the first half. Finally, a hard hit from a player on the other team—and a good yelling from his coach— got him thinking not about what Darla was doing in the stands but what was happening on the field. By then, it was too late.

After the game, James took her on a date. Two weeks later they were an item. A year later they got married.

Jack still didn't know how all of that had happened so fast, how she'd gone from loving him to loving his archenemy.

It was like Lois Lane had dropped Superman for Lex Luthor. Something was fundamentally wrong with it.

But it happened. And then they had kids. Three of them, one of whom stood here tossing a ball in the air.

The world goes round and round, Jack thought.

That could have been my wife.

This could have been my boy.

This was not helpful, not now, not ever, especially not when he was getting ready to try to win back his own wife and child.

Darla started down the front steps, and Jack found himself being infected with something that felt like panic.

"Gotta go," he said, looking out at Cameron. "I hope Texas offers you something. God knows they need a QB."

He nodded at them both and drove off in a rush.

He did wish the kid well. It was a huge responsibility to be QB 1 in Mayfield, Texas.

And he had nothing but sympathy for anyone who had to live with James Taylor.

At the store, he grabbed his coat from the rack. His maroon and white knit hat was in the pocket. He looked around the store for something distinctly Texas that he might take to Alison as a gift. He couldn't find anything that didn't look distinctly like it came from a hardware store. They'd grab something at the airport.

Someone knocked at the front door, and Jack realized that he hadn't written up the sign yet. "We're closed," he called.

The knock came again. It was Kathy Branstetter.

"Hey," he said, opening it a crack. "Sorry. We're closed."

"I saw you come in," she said. "I wanted to tell you something. I think you'll be pleased."

"Well," he said. "Okay. But I'm in kind of a hurry."

She came in, looked at him as though they shared a secret.

"Yes?" he asked.

"The *Post* ran your picture this morning." She looked at him, her lips wavering as though she wanted to smile but wasn't sure she ought to yet.

"The *Washington Post*," he said.

"That's right," she said.

"Ran a picture of me."

"That's right."

"How'd they get a picture of me?"

Again, her lips said smile, but her brain was reading the room. "I—well, I, umm, kind of sent it to them."

He crossed his arms and frowned at her. "You what?"

"I sent them a picture of you on the roof yesterday," she said. "They ran it today. Now they want me to do a full-blown story on you. A piece on the return of the people's pastor."

He felt his stomach turn over. "You sent the *Washington Post* a picture of me fixing Mrs. Calhoun's roof?"

She nodded.

"Why would you do that?"

"Well," she shrugged. "It's a good picture, for one thing. For another—"

"And they know I'm here?" He was shaking his maroon and white cap at her.

"Everybody knows you're here," she said, stepping back. "I

ran into three print reporters and two cable news people just now at the gas station asking for directions to Mrs. Calhoun's."

"Yeah," Jack said, kicking at the floor. He really wanted to be kicking her, but that was neither kind nor chivalrous. "See, Kathy, that's not right. I didn't go up there so people could take pictures of me. So reporters would come to town and bother Nora Calhoun."

"Really?" she said. "All those pictures and tweets and YouTube videos you used to release, and the books you wrote where you went on and on about doing good in the world—"

"That's not me," he said. "I mean it was. But that was for show." He stopped worrying his hat and stuffed it in his pocket. "I climbed on that roof yesterday to help my friend. That's it. You shouldn't have been taking my picture. And you certainly shouldn't have sent it off to the national news."

"You *are* national news," she said defensively, her hands on her hips. "You know that full well—"

"I *was* news," he said. "Now I just want to be left alone."

She snorted. "Sure. Left alone. Listen, Jack, I can help you manage—"

"You're not hearing me," he said.

"I can help—"

"I think you've done enough," Jack said.

"If we could just talk—" She started to open her pad.

"I'm on my way out of town."

"You're leaving?" She blinked at him rapidly.

"I'll be sure to issue a press release when I return," he said. "You can hang out and play reporter with your friends until I get back. Be sure and give them some pictures. I think my right profile is stronger."

"You're mad. Why would you be mad?" She turned her head slightly to one side, looked at him as though she were seeking a new angle. "This isn't about a reboot?"

"A what?" He shook his head. "What are you even talking about?"

"Jack," she said. "I told you. I followed you. Was there ever a time in the last ten years when you did a good deed without a camera rolling? Ever?"

It was as though a chasm had yawned open in his chest and he was toppling into it.

She was right.

She was absolutely, 100 percent right.

"That's not me," he said again, quietly, hoping it was true.

"Jack, if I can just file a story—"

He looked pointedly at her. "We're closed," he said. "And I'm not in Mayfield for a reboot, or whatever it was you said. I'm here trying to get my act together, figure some things out, and I do not want to be bothered while I try and do that."

"Wow," she said. She was looking at him sideways again, and then she raised a hand and rubbed her chin. "I think—umm—I think I may have misread the situation."

He indicated the door again with a twitch of his head. "Well, I don't think I misread you, Kathy. I hope this gets you in good with the *Post*. Maybe you can go back and start up your old life." He ushered her toward the door now with his hand. "I don't think I have that luxury."

"I'm sorry, Jack," she said. "I completely misunderstood—"

He opened the front door, scooted her onto the sidewalk, and locked the door behind her.

She stood there for a moment, as though she had more to say, but he didn't look up at her.

When he did look up again, she was gone.

He scrawled and posted a sign: Closed until Jan. 3.

Then he crept out the back door, looking up and down the street as he emerged. A big white van with electronics on top was headed slowly his direction, as though it were checking street addresses.

He was in the truck and gone by the time it parked in front of the store.

But two cars and a couple of vans stood in front of his house, and a good dozen people were milling about his driveway and in the street.

"Wow," Jack said to himself. "Slow news day."

"Reverend Chisholm," one woman called as he got out of the truck.

"Jack," a photographer yelled out, and when he looked that direction, the man snapped a string of photos, *click click click*.

They crowded, jostled, and he let them get in, let them pull in close. He was surrounded by photographers, two TV cameras, several recorders, and a couple of microphones.

"I'd like to make a statement," Jack said.

"Finally," one reporter muttered. They leaned in a bit.

"Please leave me alone," Jack said, slowly and distinctly. "Please leave my family alone." There were murmurs of demurral. "Please leave the good people of Mayfield, Texas, alone. Go and cover some real news."

"You are real news, Jack," a female reporter said into her mic before holding it back his way.

"Please," he said. "I'm saying please. I'm trying to put my life back together. And all any of us are asking is to be left alone."

"Jack," another reporter said into his mic, "have you spoken with Sally Ramirez?"

"Have you launched your comeback here in Mayfield?" another asked.

"Is this roofing thing a way to rehabilitate your public image?"

"When are you going to preach again?"

"What's your next book gonna be called?"

Jack held up his hand. "These are important questions." He sighed. "But I'm in a big hurry, and I only have time to answer one. So. My next book," he said, beginning to push his way through them, "is going to be entitled: *If the Media Don't Get Off My Lawn, I'm Going to Be Forced to Call the Police.*"

One of them actually started writing it down. Then they all got it and began grumbling.

"Have a lovely day," he said, and he opened the front door and closed it firmly behind him.

"They're back," his dad called from the kitchen.

"Yeah," Jack said. "I . . . umm, I saw that. Sorry."

"We need to leave shortly."

"I'll be ready," Jack said. He paused in the hallway, looked at himself in the mirror. He looked different without his soul patch, different in Wranglers and a T-shirt that didn't have ironic sayings emblazoned on it.

He almost passed for a decent human being.

Almost.

"Dad," he said, "have I ever done anything good in my life without wanting people to know about it?"

He heard a chair pull back from the table, heard his father shuffle into the hallway and look over Jack's shoulder into the mirror.

He felt, then saw, the hand on his shoulder.

"I'm not going to listen to that kind of talk about my son," he said. "Come on. Pack and let's go to Boston."

11.

Jack picked up a *Post* and a *New York Times* in the Austin airport. He was in both, not front page, of course, but still, a whole lot closer to the front than he expected to be. The pictures showed him using the nail gun, Mr. Rodriguez by his side.

Mr. Rodriguez wasn't named. His good work was not, apparently, newsworthy.

"Someday," Jack murmured, once they were airborne. Jack had always been a nervous flyer, couldn't talk until after they'd taken off and clearly weren't going to crash back to earth. A part of him could never quite believe that something so big could take to the air.

"What?" Tom asked. He was opening the in-flight magazine.

"Someday nobody will care about any of this anymore. Right? I'll be able to live my life. Whatever my life is. Without a camera on me."

"And that will be a good thing?" Tom turned the page.

Jack nodded. "I've been in front of too many cameras, and for all the wrong reasons."

"You look good on camera," Tom said, reading. "You've got

those chiseled good looks. Like Grampa Joe. He was a handsome man."

"Not the point, Dad," Jack said. He discovered that he was already getting nervous, although they still had to land and go to a hotel and try to sleep before meeting with Tracy and Alison.

If they landed safely.

If Tracy came to meet them.

"I don't want to be handsome," he said, trying to shrug off those thoughts. "I want to live my life and love my family and try and be helpful to somebody."

"Good things," his father said, not raising a nose from his magazine. "But you do look good on camera."

The detective said he would meet them at the hotel. They took the subway to a Best Western that was not too far from the Back Bay, the section of Boston where Tracy was reportedly living.

"Fenway Park is only a mile away," his father said with wonder when they got into their room and looked at the tourist info.

His phone rang. Tom answered, said, "We'll be right down," and smiled at Jack.

"The detective is here," he said, as though he were announcing royalty.

"You've been waiting your whole life to utter that sentence, haven't you?"

They took the stairs down, and there they met Ronnie Romano, who was sitting outside in the driver's seat of his Cadillac Escalade.

"How you doin'?" Ronnie asked Jack as they climbed in the car. "Good to see you."

"I'm all right," Jack said.

"Mr. Chisholm," Ronnie said to Tom. "You feelin' all right?"

"Tired, Ronnie," Tom said. "And I feel a little sick. But I'll feel better in the morning."

"Your dad asked me to give you some of the rundown tonight," Ronnie said. "And take you by the place they're at, but that ain't where you're gonna meet them tomorrow."

"Where are we meeting them?"

"Prudential Center," Ronnie said. "The Shops at Prudential Center," he corrected himself. "So, you like Japanese?"

"People or food?" Jack asked.

"Ha!" Ronnie said. "You're all right. Well, your wife—Mrs. Chisholm—she said that Alison likes this place Wagamama. Japanese food. You can sit at a big table, have a little privacy to talk, you all meet in a public space." Ronnie looked over from his driving. They were getting ready to pass the Citgo sign that Jack had seen outside of Fenway in a hundred baseball broadcasts. "One thing. And this was absolutely a deal breaker for her. She said no press."

"No press?" Jack asked.

"She sees one TV camera, one reporter, and she heads for the door."

"No press," Tom agreed.

"It's just," Ronnie said, "forgive me for pushing on, I saw your picture in the *Globe* this morning."

Jack groaned, shook his head.

"And if a photographer shows up to, you know, chronicle the happy reunion—" He paused, shrugged. "You see my point."

"I haven't told anyone I was coming," Jack said. "And if I see a TV camera, I'm out of there too."

"Okay," Ronnie said. "That'll work. I'll tell her. Ease her mind a little. She seems real nervous. Funny." He gave Jack another quick glance, looked back to the road. "You don't seem like such a bad guy."

"I used to think that myself," Jack said.

"Jack," his father said from the backseat. "He's a good boy," he told Ronnie in the rearview.

They turned off a major street and onto a side street with brownstones on either side. "Up ahead," Ronnie said. "The corner of Newbury and Hereford." They pulled over, double-parked.

"What," Jack said. "That castle?"

"They must have gotten a ton of money for what you did," Ronnie said. He reconsidered. "Sorry. Maybe I shouldn't ought to have said it like that."

The brownstone was turreted limestone with a green roof. All it lacked was banners from the parapets. Maybe a moat.

"This a safe neighborhood?" Jack asked.

"Two blocks from the Convention Center," Ronnie said. "A ton of foot traffic, restaurants, stores, bars. As safe as anywhere."

"Is there a school around here?"

"That I don't know," Ronnie said, raising his hands apologetically.

Jack looked up at the building. The windows were lit up, most of them. Behind one of them was his wife. His child. To be this close and not be able to see them—

"What time are we meeting them tomorrow?" he asked.

"Eleven o'clock," Tom said softly. "Then I got tickets for an afternoon flight out."

"So soon," Jack said. His shoulders slumped. Ronnie shifted

uncomfortably in his seat, and they started off down the street, leaving the castle in the rearview.

"If some marvelous reconciliation happens," Tom said, "or shows a promise of happening, of course you should stay longer."

"She asked that we not stay," Jack said, suddenly realizing.

"She says it's too much, too soon," Ronnie said. "She understands you should get to see your kid. But she says that doesn't mean she wants to see you." He raised his hands from the wheel, apologetic again.

"Drive," Jack said.

Ronnie nodded and drove on.

Jack spent the night troubled. He dreamed of the Japanese restaurant, table empty, waiters raising their hands like Ronnie. *Sorry. We don't know where they are.*

But Tracy was waiting at the table with Alison at Wagamama when they arrived a little before eleven. She was dressed in a skirt and nice blouse, very professional, knee-high black boots. She looked beautiful. He saw her before she saw him. She was pushing at her hair, the way she did when she was uncomfortable.

Then they both looked up and saw him. Alison's face broke open with a smile. Tracy's was guarded, neutral, as Alison ran from the table to embrace Jack.

"Al," Jack said, kneeling and breathing her in. She was still a skinny thing, small for her age. Tenth percentile in height and weight, the doctors kept telling them. Tracy was tiny herself, came from a long line of tiny people. "Al. Oh, I've missed you, princess."

"I missed you too, Daddy," she said, letting him go and leaning back to look at him. "Where have you been?"

"I've been staying with your grampa," he said, and stood up. "Alison, this is your Grampa Tom."

"I've seen your picture," Alison said. "But I don't remember you." She shook his hand politely, returned her attention to Jack. "We're living in a castle now," she said. "My room is in a tower."

"Just right for a princess," Jack said. They had walked to Tracy's table now, where she sat waiting. "Tracy."

"You shaved," she said.

She pushed at her hair, then bit her lip when she caught herself doing it. Jack didn't know what she'd do to compensate for biting her lip. He didn't have the tics down past that.

"Thank you for meeting us," he said. "It's nice—"

"Mom said you sent a detective to look for us," Alison said. "Like in a movie."

"Your Grampa Tom did," Jack said. "It never occurred to me." He looked at Tracy, tried to get her to meet his eye. "A lot of things never occurred to me. Like I was saying, I'm really glad—"

"The lawyers say we need to talk about visitation," Tracy said. "And I understand that. But it's such a long way to Seattle—"

"I'm not living in Seattle," Jack said.

"I know, you're with Tom at this moment, but—"

"I don't know that I'm going back to Seattle," Jack said.

"That would be a lot to live down," Tracy said in a low voice. *Bam.* Jack didn't know how to respond. "I—"

"There's a direct flight from Boston to Austin," Tom cut in. "I'd be happy to buy tickets. Maybe she could come for a few days before school starts?"

"That's—that's so sudden," Tracy said, raising a hand. Her face flushed red. "I'd have to think—"

"You must have known that sooner or later I'd want to see Alison," Jack said. He didn't mean to, but he was pushing. Time was a factor here, whether Tracy knew it or not.

"I didn't know that you'd want that," she said. "I didn't know what you'd want. I don't even know who you are anymore."

He looked at Alison, happily coloring on the paper tablecloth. How does one even respond? He dropped his head, looked at the tabletop.

At that moment their server stepped to the table, introduced himself as Jeffrey, wrote it on the tablecloth directly in front of Jack. "Can I start you off—"

"We need a second," Tracy told him. "Iced teas, maybe." She looked at Tom, who nodded.

"Apple juice for me," Alison volunteered without looking up from her coloring. She was paying more attention to them than she let on.

"Are you planning on staying in Boston?" Tom asked gently.

Tracy looked at Tom, then down at the menu, then at Jack, then down again. "I don't know," she said. "I'm taking voice at Berkley this spring. I've got Alison placed in a good school." She sighed. "Nobody knows my name here. Nobody makes jokes or points fingers. And at least the church is taking good care of us."

Jack felt each word like a knife. He put his hand on his chest, took a deep breath. "I am so sorry," he said. "I can't tell you—"

"No," she said, her voice rising. The people at the adjoining table looked over, then turned quickly away. "You can't tell me, Jack. You'll never know what it's like to be humiliated by the one you love."

155

"I think actually I'm getting a pretty good idea," Jack said, as the people at the next table sized him up.

"We didn't think we'd be able to solve things today," Tom said, holding his hands up as if to separate two fighters. "That'll take time. I know that. We just came to ask if Jack can have Alison soon. I'm—" He paused, looked down, looked back at Tracy. "I'd love for her to visit."

"Tom," she said, reaching across the table to him and managing to simultaneously glare at Jack. "I am sorry that you don't know your granddaughter. That was never my decision. I don't know that she wants—"

"I want to go to Texas," Alison said, again without looking up. Tracy glared at her without effect. They had apparently discussed a different strategy.

"I don't know, Tom," Tracy said, leaning back in her chair. "I just don't know."

"Can I talk to you for a second?" Jack asked her. This was no good. He needed a moment alone with her without the onlookers. He looked out at the indoor pedestrian mall. "Just for a second."

"That wasn't our deal," she said. "Nobody said anything about being alone with you."

"Wow," he said. He looked across the table at her, watched her push at her hair, then angrily drop her hands under the table. "You hate me that much."

"We don't say 'hate,'" Alison said. "It's not a nice word."

"Right," Jack said. He'd actually been the one who taught her that.

"I have some right to be angry with you, Jack," Tracy said,

her jaw clenched. "I think even a supreme narcissist would be able to acknowledge that I have some right."

"And that's me?" Jack said. "That's really what you think?"

"Don't raise your voice in front of our daughter," Tracy said. She put her menu on the table, made as if to stand up. "Oh, I knew it was a mistake to meet you. You've got everything, the power, the lawyers and detectives—"

"I've got nothing, Tracy," Jack shouted. "I've got no money, I've got no friends, I've got no place to go—"

"You've got Tom," she said, begging him with her eyes to be quieter, to not make a scene.

"Tom will be dead by this time next year," Jack said. The words broke him open. He raised a hand to his lips as if to call them back.

Tracy's mouth fell open. She looked at Tom. "You're—sick?"

He nodded, solemn, uncomfortable. He clearly did not want to be used as a bargaining chip in these negotiations. "I am not going to get better," he said, "if that is what you're asking."

"Tracy," Jack said, leaning across the table toward her. "I am sorry to have embarrassed you. I was. I am. What I did—I made a mistake, I regret it, I can make it all better. With you. With Alison. If you'll only—"

"Don't," she said.

"—give me a chance," he finished.

She looked at him, shook her head.

"Don't," she whispered.

Jeffrey came back to the table, began parceling out iced teas and apple juice in a kid's cup with a straw.

"Will you ever forgive me?" Jack asked.

"I will," Alison said. She grinned up at Jack for a life-giving moment before devoting her attention to sipping her apple juice.

The server looked expectantly around the table. "Are we all ready to order?"

"We need just another minute," Tom told him.

"Okeydoke," he said, smiled tightly, and backed away.

"I'll talk to the lawyers in Seattle," she said, resignation in her voice. "I know you've got a right to see Alison. We'll talk it over. Set it up. I'll have them contact your lawyers."

"Tom's lawyers," Jack said. "Actually."

The table fell silent, broken only by Alison setting down a blue crayon and picking up a green one.

"I'm sorry, Tom," Tracy said at last, looking across the table at him. "Sorry for everything. If I'd known, I would have done things differently. It's not fair—"

"I'm happy to be sitting here right now," Tom said, and he certainly seemed to be. Despite the tension, he had been smiling since the moment he sat down across from his granddaughter.

"And—" She paused for a moment and looked over her shoulder to make sure the server wasn't returning. "Jack. I guess I'm wondering. What do you want, actually? Why are you here after all this time?"

Jack took a big breath. Go big or go home.

"I want you back," he said. "I want us to be a family again."

Tracy looked at him like some interesting species of bug that had crawled out from beneath a rock.

"Just think about it," he said. "Please, Tray. I'd like another chance."

"I'm sure you would," she said.

And then the server was back, looking hopeful and, now, a little desperate. The lunch rush was getting ready to start, and they had yet to order.

"We'll have the duck gyoza for a starter," Tracy said. "I'll have the mandarin sesame salad." She smiled at Alison, who was looking up at her with a grin, and Jack saw that her eyes still crinkled when she did this. "Mini ramen with shrimp for the chimp."

"And more apple juice," Alison said.

"One more apple juice," Tracy agreed.

"Gentlemen?" the server asked.

"Nothing," Jack said sourly.

"No dessert for you," Alison said.

"You can eat some of the duck dumplings," Tracy said. "You should eat something."

"Yakisoba," Tom said brightly. He had clearly been thinking about this. "Extra shrimp. Extra spicy."

"Are you—" Their server looked at him dubiously, this pale, skinny old man. "Are you sure, sir? That will be very spicy indeed."

Tom looked at him—just looked at him—and smiled. "Young man," he said, "I am a citizen of the great state of Texas. The day you can out-spice me—"

He stopped, smiled again, and chuckled.

"Well," he said, looking across the table at his grand-daughter. "That day ain't here yet."

They ate. If Tom was overwhelmed by the spice, he gave no indication. And at last, they all pushed back from the table. The dining room had grown crowded, their server's frequent visits suggested that they were beginning to overstay their welcome. And while Jack felt like he could sit and watch Alison color expertly all afternoon, he doubted that Tracy shared that sentiment.

They got up from the table, walked out into the now-crowded pedestrian walkway, and Alison looked up at Jack and then to Tom. "Thanks for sending detectives to find us," she told him. "That was cool."

"You're welcome," Tom said.

"Anytime," Jack said. "I'll see you really soon, okay?"

Alison looked up to her mom, who gave her an imperceptible nod.

"Okay," she said. She leaned across and hugged him around the waist. He closed his eyes, didn't dare breathe. And then she stepped away.

Jack didn't know the protocol for departing your estranged wife. A hug or kiss was clearly out. And while a handshake seemed ridiculously perfunctory, Tracy didn't seem to want any contact with him, so that was probably impossible as well.

"I missed you," Jack told her.

Nothing.

"I called you every day."

Her lips pursed. Almost against her will she formed a sad smile. "I know you did," she said. "It took forever to delete them all."

"Just think about what I said." Jack seemed to be asking that of a lot of people lately. He wondered for a moment if Tracy was also passing off her front foot.

"I missed you too," Tom said to her, but unlike with Jack, she seemed to be more than willing to hug him.

"I'll be praying for you, Tom," she said when their hug ended. "I'm sorry for your pain."

"I'll be praying for you," he returned. "Take good care of my granddaughter."

They stepped back from each other.

"Good-bye, Tom," Tracy told him.

He nodded. "Good-bye, Tracy," he said. "Come and see us real soon," he told Alison, who shook his hand formally.

"I will most certainly do that," she said.

Jack checked his watch. "We gotta get to the airport."

Tom glanced at the time. "So we do."

Jack raised a hand. A Texas wave.

Tracy did the same.

Alison waved wildly for a moment, returning to her mother's side.

Tom and Jack turned away, stepping into the rush of people passing through Prudential Center. It was like getting swept into rapids. When Jack turned for a moment to look back, he couldn't see either one of them. They were just gone. Vanished.

12.

I hate this new year," Jack said once they had landed safely in Austin and were taxiing to the gate. Tom had been sleeping—had slept even through the bump of their landing—and for a moment Jack was filled with the fear that his dad might not wake up. But he opened a bleary eye now, and Jack could see how tired he was, how the trip had drained what little strength he had. "I want another one."

"What's that?" he said. "Hate what?"

"I thought this New Year's Day would be the start of something big," Jack said. "Not the beginning of the end."

"Now, now," Tom said, raising a hand and sounding like the old man he actually was. "We don't know what will be. And Tracy said that Alison could come."

"I know," Jack said as they pulled to the gate and people got to their feet. "I know."

The flight home had been a long one, not helped by the flight attendant who recognized Jack—and seemed a little put out that the people's pastor insisted on a Jack and Coke. Or that his elderly father was paying for it.

When they landed, Jack turned on his phone—force of habit, he knew perfectly well he'd have no messages—and his message light beeped.

"What the—" he began. He checked the first number. Seattle. Danny.

He should have waited until they were off the plane, at least listened to the message first.

But he couldn't.

"Hey," he said as soon as Danny picked up. "What's wrong?"

"Did you find them?" Danny asked.

"Yeah," Jack said. "We talked to them today."

"How did it go?"

Jack looked around, gauged the attention level of his father, the proximity of his neighbors. "It could have been—better. But great to see Alison." He checked his watch. It was late here, not quite as late in Seattle, but still later than he ever stayed in the office. "Are you still at work?"

"I have to preach this weekend," Danny said. "It's—what is it called?—Epiphany. The wise men." He paused—Jack guessed he was drinking from his ever-present cup of coffee. "The elders voted to start following the liturgical calendar this year. I've never preached this before. I don't even know what it means."

"Epiphany," Jack said, thinking and watching people a couple of rows up step into the aisle. "Well. That's Greek. It means 'showing forth.' When we see things revealed as they truly are." He'd learned that in a literature course on James Joyce, not in a class on the Bible or preaching or Greek, none of which he had ever taken anyway. "The wise men are seeing the thing they sought, after their long journey. That'll preach."

"I just don't know how you did this week after week," he said. "Everybody wants it to be so good. They want to laugh and cry and who knows what all. You spoiled things for me."

Jack looked out at the runway, into the dark, dark Texas night. *You spoiled things.*

"Are you okay? What's going on?" Jack asked.

Silence. Taking a drink of coffee. But the pause went on too long. At last, Danny's voice came, subdued. "We're down three thousand in Sunday attendance since you left."

"Wow. And contributions?"

"Down by almost half."

Jack whistled. *"Lieber Gott,"* he whispered. He knew what Grace Cathedral needed to take in just to keep the lights on, let alone to do any good in the world, and it was a lot more than that.

"I can't do this on my own," Danny whispered back. "I keep telling them they've got to bring you back. And that's what they're hearing from a lot of the folks who've left. He made a mistake. Big deal. Bring him back."

"Why are you whispering?" Jack asked.

Danny didn't respond.

"Are you calling from an elders' meeting? Because you really shouldn't oughta do that."

Danny snickered. "Nah. I just—it feels like a lot of people are watching me all the time now."

"You're a terrific pastor, Danny," Jack said. "Things will calm down. You can make this work." He stood up.

"The elders are terrified," Danny whispered again. "But not half as much as me. You've got to come back. Just apologize, do whatever they tell you, and come back. Please, Jack."

"Hey," Jack said. It was their turn to step into the aisle, and he needed to reach up and pull down both their carry-ons. "It's going to be okay. I'll call you later."

"Soon," Danny said. "Please, Jack."

"Wow," Jack said after he disconnected. He manhandled their bags down from the overhead, began carrying them both off the plane.

Tom was a little wobbly—he put out a hand to steady himself as they walked up the aisle—but they made it out to the car. After Jack loaded the bags and headed out of the parking lot, he checked his other messages.

Three of them, all from the 325 area code. Mayfield.

"It's those reporters," he said. "Calling from their posh Mayfield hotels."

Which would be the Nite Inn, a line of sad little motel rooms on the highway headed south out of town. Or the Redbud B and B, a three-suite establishment run by Philip and Eric, whom Mayfield suspected of being too friendly, but loved too much to find out for sure.

He listened to the first message—Nora Calhoun. Reporters had been all over her place, trampled her grass, asked her a bunch of questions. She hadn't told them a thing.

"Pretended I was deaf," she said, and she was laughing like she'd been at the red wine again.

The next one was from Mr. Rodriguez, of all people. "Hey," he said. "Home Ec boy." Jack could almost see him grinning wickedly through the phone. "You know, that was a pretty good thing we did on Sunday. Father Frank asked me to look into building a ramp for Alice Gutierrez. She's in that wheelchair now, you know, hombre, and she needs some help. Are you in?"

"Oh yeah," he muttered. They were leaving the Austin

airport, pulling onto 290 headed west toward the Hill Country. He checked traffic and merged before listening to the last message.

The third and final call was from Bill Hall. He sounded as stiff and uncomfortable as if he'd been tied head to toe with new rope. "The board of deacons asked me to call," he said in a low voice, "and see if you'd be willing to say a few words on Sunday. I told them I didn't believe you would. So there's your out. But I told them I'd call, and now I've done it." He didn't say good-bye.

"Crazy, Dad," Jack said, setting the phone on the dashboard. "I haven't had that many messages in seven weeks. Unless you count calls from the media. Which I don't." He looked over at Tom and found him gently snoring.

Jack shook his head. "Dad, you shouldn't have made this trip." He reached across, patted him gently on the shoulder so as not to wake him, let his hand linger there.

When they got home two hours later, Jack got his father up and into the house, unloaded the car, then paused for a bit in the driveway to look up at the stars. He was not used to seeing them, and especially not so many and so close. The moon was a waning full moon, and the stars were so numerous it was as if someone had taken a brush full of white paint and spattered a black canvas.

"Never saw anything like this in Seattle," he muttered, settling into a chair on the front porch and looking up.

"Ah," came a familiar voice. "But you did have the coffee, at least."

"Father Frank," Jack said. "A voice from the darkness."

"I was actually hoping to catch you," he said from the yard.

"Was milling about and trying not to be mistaken for a burglar." He came up to the front steps. "May I?"

"Come on up." Jack indicated the chair next to him.

"How's your father?" he asked, likewise leaning over the railing and looking up at the stars. "I was a wee bit concerned for him."

"Tired," Jack said. "Exhausted might be more true. I hope this trip—"

"It is the trip he hoped to make," Frank said. "He saw your daughter?"

"Alison," Jack said. "Yes. I don't remember the last time I saw him so happy."

Frank nodded. "Good. And you?"

"Ah. Well." He looked at those low-hanging stars. "It had high points and low points."

"Give me the high. I've had a long day."

"I got to tell my wife I'm sorry. I think. I'm not sure she heard me." He shrugged. "I'm not sure if she knew what I was apologizing for. But I felt better for it."

"Step Five," Father Frank said.

"What?" He looked across at him. Frank was still looking up at the stars.

"Ah," Frank said. "I sometimes forget we're not all formally in recovery. 'Admitted to God, to ourselves, and to another human being the exact nature of our wrongs.' From Twelve Step spirituality."

"Oh," Jack said. "Right. Serenity and all that."

"And all that. So, did you confess to God and to yourself as well?"

Jack looked over at him again. "You know, you're a monumental pain. Why do you care what I do or don't do?" He was surprised at the heat in his voice, but it had been a long, hard day for him too. Week. Month.

But Frank took no notice of his tone. "I can never find the North Star," he said, still looking upward. "I would dearly love to know where it is. Then I would never be lost again."

"Seriously, Father Frank," Jack said. "You're loitering around my house. I thought you were a reporter."

"The news media are all at the bar," Frank said. "Which is actually why I left, went for a stroll. All of them here covering a religion story, and yet not a decently religious person amongst them."

Jack put out a hand, patted Frank on the shoulder to shut him up. "Seriously. Why. Do. You. Care?"

Frank raised his hands. "To answer that, I have to tell a story."

"Of course you do," Jack said. "Wait. Did I just say that out loud?"

"About eight years ago, I suffered what became known in Mayfield as one of my most famous relapses. The way people talk about storms: The Blizzard of '61. Father Frank's Drunk of 2004. I couldn't remember why I stopped drinking." He shook his head. "I couldn't even remember why I'd become a priest. My whole life, all I'd given up. What was it for? So I drank more and more. I became a nuisance to others and a danger to myself, and my calling was in danger of being lost forevermore."

"I never heard—" Jack began, before remembering that he'd not been home in ten years.

"And then," Frank said, and he paused for a moment before he could go on, "I had a visit from a man I barely knew, could barely tolerate. And what he said to me turned me around."

"Who was it?" Jack said. "Tell me it was the mayor."

Frank chuckled, shook his head. "The mayor and I have never engaged in much dialogue. Or fisticuffs, unlike some people. No." He grew serious again. "Late one night someone knocked on the pastorage door. I staggered over and opened it. It was John Heinrich."

"No," Jack said.

Frank nodded.

"Pastor John, the modern-day Martin Luther?"

"The very same. I invited him in, offered him a drink. He said I'd already had enough for both of us. I thought I might punch him in the nose, then and there. Then he said it, and I felt sure I was going to."

"Said what?"

"He leaned forward across the table and he said, 'Francis, I do believe you have lost your call.'" Frank did a very credible Pastor John, German-tinged accent and all. "Have" came out as "haff."

"Wow," Jack said.

"'Francis,' he says to me, 'I'm just back from Fredericksburg hospital. Two dead babies. I am tired to *mein* very bones, but when I saw your light on, I knew I had to talk to you.' Pastor John looked down at the table, then back at me. 'You and me, we don't see eye-to-eye on everything.'

"'On anything,' I told him. Not completely true, but I was in no shape for civil discourse.

"He kind of worried with his hands a little bit, and then I

realized that he really didn't want to be there. Didn't want to be saying any of this. 'God will not let me sit idly by and watch. You will not know this, but I went through this very same thing nine years ago.' He smiled at my bottle, and it was a knowing smile, boyo. He went on.

"'Schnapps unstead of Bushmills, but the very same thing. I had forgotten why I became a pastor. I had forgotten the joy. I had lost my way.'"

"Wow," Jack repeated. He couldn't imagine Pastor John saying this. Any of it.

Couldn't imagine what it would feel like to have it said to you.

Father Frank was looking down at his hands. "He was right. I hated to even admit it. But he was right." He smiled. "I still wanted to punch him. But then he said the second thing that caught me in my tracks." He looked over at Jack, smile growing.

"Okay," Jack said. "What, what, tell me, please."

Frank laughed, and it was with real joy. "He told me that in every faithful life, there comes a second call when the first one is no longer sufficient, a call to deeper faith, hope, joy. John Heinrich told me that, and he was right."

Then he looked pointedly at Jack. "I care, Jack Chisholm, because I have been where you are. Because I believe what is happening in your life as we speak, is that second call, the one that will define who you are from now on."

"Wouldn't it be pretty to think so?" Jack whispered. Hemingway. That English major continued to pay dividends.

Frank continued to look at him.

"Pastor John said all that?" Jack was not yet willing to take on Frank's conclusion. "It seems a little—advanced for him."

"He was not a well-educated man," Frank said. "And even now that I am sober, I believe he got some things badly wrong. For a so-called Lutheran, he did not understand grace so well. But, Jack, he pastored those people for forty years, rain and snow." He blinked rapidly a few times. "And he came to my door in my darkest hour. When all he really wanted to do was go home and rest in peace."

The wind moved around in the tree branches. Down the street, a dog was barking.

"I'm not saying that you're right or wrong," Jack said at last. "But I'm just back from a trip where my wife didn't even look me in the eye. My church tossed me to the curb like yesterday's garbage. My greatest hope is that I'll get to see my daughter again soon. And other than that, I have nothing. Nothing."

He couldn't help the fear he felt gnawing at him. "I don't see a call to anything good. A call to anything at all."

They sat quietly again. And still the stars shone, still the wind blew.

After a bit, Frank said, "Can I tell you another story?"

Jack let out a slow sigh. "What could possibly stop you?"

"Not a blessed thing," Frank said. He leaned forward in his chair toward Jack. "So here it is: A few years ago I went home to Jersey to visit my sister. One night I went for a walk, and I passed a reception hall, lit up as for a party. As I passed, a hundred people or more were filing in the front door. They were all dressed up, just come from a wedding it looked, and they were going to the reception, already in full swing." He smiled at the memory.

"I could hear the music and laughter, Jack, the drinking and the dancing. And the looks on their faces! They were bursting with impatience, so sure they would be welcomed, so sure of a beautiful evening."

He stopped, spread his hands as if to say he was finished, looked at Jack meaningfully, inviting him to get it.

"What?" Jack said. All he was getting was irritated. The last thing he wanted to think about at the moment was weddings and receptions. He remembered the small wedding he and Tracy had, their reception on a budget, in the days before he became the people's pastor.

Those had been good days, he realized now. They were poor—and happy.

And they used to laugh.

He shook his head. "I don't—"

"That reception is the second half of your life," Frank told him. "Like most of us, Jack, you are standing outside looking in, unwilling to believe that a banquet is waiting, doubting that something could ever be worth celebrating again. We'd all like to go in, but God help us! What if we're wrong? What if there is no banquet? What if it's just some sick joke?"

Jack nodded slowly. He wanted to believe. He wanted to know joy again. But where would it come from? "And you think somewhere in this"—he indicated himself, the porch, the town beyond—"is a second call?" He took a deep breath, let it out.

He couldn't see it.

"Yes. A second call to faith. To hope. To service." He appraised Jack. "I think parts of it are getting through. You're doing little pieces of the dance."

"I don't think I'm even on the dance floor, Father Frank." He leaned back in his chair, closed his eyes.

"No. I see something happening. But something else is calling you. And it's not what you did wrong the first time. That's not what the second call is about."

Jack snickered involuntarily. "Then I guess that lets me off preaching this Sunday."

Father Frank looked at him sharply. "What?"

"Nothing. Saint Paul's asked me to say a few words on Sunday."

"You should," Frank said. "You absolutely should."

"Don't be such a priest," Jack said, opening his eyes and leaning toward him. "I'm not a preacher anymore. I don't have anything to say. To them or to anybody else."

"You absolutely should," Father Frank repeated.

"You are not my priest," Jack said, a flush rising up the back of his neck. "Or my father."

"No," Frank agreed, raising a placating hand. "I'm your friend, and only your friend." Jack looked over at him. Frank nodded. "Today and tomorrow, boyo. I'll be here."

Jack sat back in his chair and looked out at the yard. "That's— thanks. That's nice. But, Frank, I still don't have anything to say. Today or tomorrow or the next day."

Father Frank thought for a moment. "It's Epiphany this Sunday," he said.

"So I've heard."

"The wise men from the East, seeing the baby Jesus?"

"So? That doesn't give me anything, Frank. Seeing the baby Jesus is not my current difficulty."

Frank sighed. "Epiphany is about revelation, Jack. It's about seeing what is right in front of you. I wrote my sermon this morning."

"Seeing what is right in front of you," Jack repeated.

Father Frank nodded. "Read the story again. Think about it. If you want, we could meet tomorrow night at Buddy's and talk about it."

"Bible study at the bar," Jack said.

"Where better?" Frank said. "'It is not the healthy who need the doctor, but the sick. I came to call not the upright, but sinners.'"

"Gospel of Mark," Jack said. He smiled. "Hey! Maybe Brother Raymond will let out Wednesday services early and come join us."

"When pigs fly," Father Frank said. "He likes to meet at the donut shop, when he deigns to meet at all. You come alone."

"Maybe," Jack said. He stood up, leaving the chair rocking behind him. "You go on home now."

Frank shook his head slowly. "I think I'll check in on the media," he said. "Give them the latest."

"I believe all of this is covered in the privacy of the confessional," Jack said. "Isn't that doctrine?"

Frank got to his feet, looked one last time at the stars, took a deep breath.

"I will never sell you for thirty pieces of silver, Jack," he said. Then he smiled. "But if someone offers a new organ—"

"Git," Jack said, shooing him off the porch.

Frank walked out onto the sidewalk. Jack turned to go inside.

Was he really thinking about this?

Bible study at Buddy's?

Taking the pulpit at Saint Paul's not-quite-Lutheran Church?

A second call?

He smiled, shook his head, went up to bed.

13.

The next morning at the store, he cleared off the oldest batteries to make shelf space for recyclables, which were on their way in the next delivery. That left him with more than a handful of ancient batteries, some of which he doubted would so much as momentarily power up a penlight.

"I hate to donate these," Jack said. "They're worthless."

"Throw them away," Tom said from behind a new old *Reader's Digest.*

"I can't do that," Jack said. "Chemicals in the landfill. Leaching into the aquifer. All that."

"I'll take them," Mrs. Calhoun said. "I can use them for my smoke alarm."

"But they don't work," Jack said.

"Neither does my smoke alarm," she said.

They looked at each other.

"I'll get you a bag," he said.

"So, Jack," Nora Calhoun said as he slid the batteries into a plastic bag for her. "I hear Brother Bill asked you to mount the pulpit for us."

Tom looked up to see Jack's reaction.

"Like you didn't know," Jack said to him. He looked across the counter at Mrs. Calhoun. "I believe I might come and say a few words this Sunday," he said.

She nodded. "It's Epiphany," she said.

"Like I don't know that."

"Sorr-ee," she said. "It's just you were at one of those stompy, clappy sort of churches."

"I know what Epiphany is," Jack said. "I'll try to say something fitting."

"Thank you, Jack," she said. She softened, and her smile became beatific. "My new roof is lovely. I look at it every morning."

"I'm glad." And he was. Her words gave him a glow of satisfaction.

The bell *ting-ting*ed as she left. Tom raised an eyebrow.

"Don't start," Jack said.

"It's just I don't recall your mentioning—"

"Don't start," Jack said.

Somewhere back in the shelves, Manny was whistling an old song. "Besame Mucho," Jack thought it was. Outside, three panel trucks were hoping to catch sight of Jack on the sidewalk, and three reporters were standing on the sidewalk ready to file live reports.

"Who is it today?" Jack asked.

"A San Antonio station, a Dallas station, and CNN," Tom said. "And I've talked to five more on the phone." He smiled. "I asked them politely not to tie up our business line."

Jack turned to the front window. The female reporter on the other side, Cynthia Someone he recognized from CNN, waved at him, beckoned him to come out. He raised his palm in a Texas wave, turned back around.

"Should I do something about them?" Jack asked.

"They should leave you alone," Tom said, turning the page. "When something more interesting comes along, I reckon they will."

The morning was slow. Mary came in at lunch with meat loaf and scalloped potatoes. Leftovers from New Year's Day. She'd baked yeast rolls fresh that morning.

"No wonder Dennis is the size of a spaceship," Jack said.

"You hush," she said. "He was big before I started cooking for him, let me assure you."

She listened to their report of the trip, brightening only when she heard that Alison might be coming soon. "Oh, I need to get her something."

"You are already guaranteed to be her favorite aunt," Jack said.

She beamed at that for a moment before remembering. "I'm her only aunt."

"Exactly," Jack said.

"No meat loaf for you," she said. She yanked the food from in front of him, then set it back down. "I want to take her to the zoo," she said. "In San Antonio."

"We'll talk about it," Jack said. "First we have to get her here."

The reporters crowded around Mary when she headed back to work. It appeared that she might be threatening them with physical violence. In any case, they retreated from her with some speed.

"Some things never change," Jack said to his father, who was reading "Laughter Is the Best Medicine" in *Reader's Digest* and occasionally chuckling.

"No, they don't," Tom said. He chuckled again, turned the page.

In late afternoon, the door jangled, a murmur of low voices followed, and then Tom called out into the shelves where Jack was stocking paint. "Jack. Front and center, please."

"Just like an intercom," Jack muttered as he emerged from the aisle where he was working. He stopped in his tracks.

Darla Scroggins Taylor and her son, Cameron, were standing in front of the counter. She was smiling; he was scowling. That averaged to no expression at all, which was what Jack was struggling to maintain as he stepped closer.

"Hey," he said to Cameron. He nodded to Darla.

"I think Cameron has something to say to you, Jack," she said.

Jack looked more closely, waited.

Cameron didn't seem to have anything particular he wanted to say. He was examining the tiles on the floor. Yellowish, in serious need of replacement.

"Cam," Darla said, and her voice took on an ominous hitch Jack remembered.

"Hey," Cameron said, his words as halting as if speech had been granted to a Great Dane. He looked up at Jack. "I–I tried out what you said."

Jack nodded. *Go on.*

"I added like five yards to my max," he said.

Jack nodded again. *Okay.*

"I guess I just wanted to say thanks."

"You're welcome," Jack said. "I hear a lot of good things about you. I just want you to be your best. Mayfield needs a great quarterback."

"Jack was a great quarterback," Darla said softly.

"You were supposed to play for Texas," Cameron said. He looked at his mom. "Right?"

Wow. It still stung to think about, even after all these years. Jack nodded, let out a slow breath. "I tore my ACL in the state finals," Jack told him. "You saw what happened to Robert Griffin?"

Cameron looked simultaneously awestruck and repulsed. "Yeah. I saw that. It was awful."

"That was me. Halfway through the second quarter. Didn't even see him coming."

He hadn't been thinking about the rush. All he could think about was Darla standing over with the other cheerleaders, about why she had broken up with him. It was not a recipe for a focused performance, and at last it had caught up to him. He had felt his knee go sideways, bend in a direction knees are not supposed to, and then he was at the bottom of the pile writhing in pain so horrible he thought he would not survive. Somebody was shouting "Ball! Ball!" and his friend Bill Hall was bent over him trying to pull bodies off the pile and yelling, "Twelve! Are you all right?"

He was not all right.

Three surgeries later, he was still not all right. He never played football again. The University of Texas was generous. They honored their scholarship offer, and he actually went there for three years before feeling the call to ministry. But he never took another snap.

Another thing he lost.

"I knew it was bad when he didn't get right up," Darla was saying. "I never saw him get hit so hard he didn't just bounce to his feet."

"It was bad." Jack sighed again, deeply this time. "I thought it was the end of the world."

"But you got the offer," Cameron said, talking to his oversized teenage feet again. "You were that good." He looked up through a screen of bangs. "I wondered if maybe—maybe you could watch me throw. Maybe give me some more pointers."

Cameron was asking him, but Jack looked at Darla, spoke directly to her. "That is a monumentally bad idea." If James Taylor found out Jack was talking to his son behind his back, James would charge him, throw him in a headlock, try to beat him senseless.

Or throw him in jail for something.

Corruption of a minor. Drinking without a license.

Darla stood her ground though. He had always admired that about her. "Jack, he's been to two quarterback camps now. James hired a coach to work with him on Sundays, and nothing much came out of it. Cameron said you watched him throw for all of thirty seconds—"

Jack shook his head. "Darla, all I saw was myself. I used to throw off my front foot. That's all."

"Well," she said, looking up at him with those pleading eyes he could never resist. "I just thought maybe—"

"I want to go to Texas," Cameron interjected. "That's been my dream forever. And I know I've still got a lot to learn."

"Don't you want the Mayfield Wildcats to win?" Darla asked him innocently, in that voice that used to make him crazy.

Jack looked at Tom, who assiduously avoided meeting his gaze. He looked at Cameron, who was staring down at his shoes. He looked back at Darla, and she met his eyes with eyebrows raised. He motioned her impatiently away from the others. She followed him into the nearest aisle.

"D, if I so much as walk onto a practice field and watch him throw, the entire town is going to know about it."

She shrugged. "So what?"

"I don't want to make trouble at your house," Jack said, his voice low. "Please, Darla. I've got all the trouble I can possibly deal with now." He looked out the window at the TV trucks.

"Jack," she said. "Just watch him throw. Give him some pointers if you see something. It doesn't have to be formal."

"I'll know," Jack insisted. "You'll know." He sighed. "Cameron will know."

"I won't tell," Cameron said from the front of the store.

"Great." He led Darla back from the aisle to the front desk.

Jack stood in front of Cameron and shook his head. "No. Not unless your dad says it's okay. A man doesn't coach another man's boy without telling him. It'd be like sleeping with his wife." He flushed. "Or something."

Darla shot him an amused glance, and he shook his head. "Sorry."

Cameron bit his lip. He didn't show a lot of emotion, but what he was showing looked an awful lot like disappointment.

Was Jack afraid of James? Or was he afraid to fail?

Why didn't he want to do this?

"Listen," Jack told him. "I'll talk to your dad." That should be pleasant. "You keep throwing off that back foot."

Cameron looked up, nodded. "Okay. Yeah."

The boy pushed the door open and walked out. Darla lingered for a moment.

"D," Jack said. "What are you doing?"

"Not a thing, Jack Chisholm," she said airily. "Just taking advantage of an old friendship."

"More like taking advantage of an old friend," he said with a smile.

"I'm glad you're home," she said. "I'll try and get James to be reasonable."

"Good luck with that," he said.

When she left, the reporters on the sidewalk approached, retreated.

He turned to his father, who still avoided looking up. "That article you're reading had better be about how to turn lead into gold," Jack said.

Tom could not maintain his deadpan expression. "If you thought I was going to get in the middle of that," he said, closing his magazine, "you are crazy." He checked his watch. "It's five. Want to go out and meet the press?"

"Oh yes," Jack said. He did a quick check of the store while his dad paid Manny, counted down his drawer, and shrugged on his jacket.

"Jack!" came the shouts when they emerged onto the sidewalk. "Reverend Chisholm!"

Jack waved. He didn't smile. While Tom locked the door, he turned to the proffered mics, to the cameras, and simply said, "Happy New Year."

Then he and Tom walked to the car.

They shouted after him. He heard one of the reporters cursing, although whether she was angry at him or the universe was difficult to say.

In the car, he told his father that he was meeting Father Frank at seven. "We're talking about my sermon," Jack said.

"At Buddy's?" his father said.

"Exactly," Jack said. "No one will suspect."

"You want me to come with?" Tom asked.

"How do you feel?"

Tom took a self-inventory. "Tired," he said. "Trip took a lot out of me." That much was true. Jack had to wake his father that morning, and fix a less than satisfactory pan of eggs while Tom dressed.

"You get some rest," Jack said. "I'll go over after dinner."

"Have you called Bill back to tell him you're going to preach?"

"Wow," Jack said. "No. I guess I thought maybe you—or Mrs. Calhoun—"

"You should call him," Tom said. "That's only right."

"Ugh," Jack said. But once they got home he did, while his father heated up some of the casserole from Sunday.

The phone rang four times, then someone picked up. "Bill Hall."

"Bill," Jack said. "It's Jack."

Dead silence.

"Jack Chisholm."

And more of it.

"I, uh, I was just calling to tell you I could say a few words Sunday. If that's what you want."

"It's not what I want," Bill said, finally entering the conversation.

"Okay," Jack said.

"Just so we're clear," Bill said.

"Okay."

"I was asked to call you. That's the only reason I did."

"Well," Jack said. "I think you have made that abundantly clear."

And—silence.

Was Bill thinking about all the times Jack had failed him? Was he remembering their deer hunts, their swimming hole? Was he remembering pulling people off of him as Jack rolled in agony in the state finals? "I'll see you Sunday," Jack said finally. He had already said "I'm sorry," and there were too many other things to say to even know where to start.

The other line went dead, and Jack stood still, the phone keening in his ear.

"Everything okay?" Tom asked after a moment.

"Nah," Jack said. "It's not." He set his phone down. "Maybe it won't ever be."

Tom shrugged. "And maybe it will. Come on. Dinner's warm."

At the table, Jack asked Tom if he could take some time on Thursday and Friday afternoons to think about what he was going to say on Sunday. "I'll make deliveries Saturday," he said. "Talk Sunday."

After church, he was already planning to work with Mr. Gonzalez and whoever else might be led to show up and build a wheelchair ramp for Mrs. Gutierrez. But before Sunday, he needed some time to pray, to reflect, to sit with the reading from Matthew—the wise men, old bad King Herod.

What on earth did he have to say to anyone, let alone about this particular thing?

As the week went on, he still wasn't calling it preaching, was sticking with the "a few words" model that seemed to take the pressure off everyone. He wasn't a preacher anymore. That had gone sour. He would say a few words. That's all.

"Are you afraid to preach, boyo?" Father Frank asked him at Buddy's as they looked at the readings together—Frank sipping his ginger ale, Jack drinking an icy mug of Shiner Bock. "Is that what it comes down to?"

Jack nodded, first slowly, then vigorously. "I am terrified down to my very boots."

Frank looked longingly at Jack's beer, shook his head. "Then why, pray tell, are you getting up there?"

That was the question. Jack started ticking things off on his fingers. "My father loves that church. My mother loved it, although I could not tell you why. The songs, I think. The old hymns." He finished his beer.

"You want another, Jack?" Shayla asked. She was polishing a lot of glasses these days. Five members of the press sat at the bar, three in the booths, all of them shooting daggers at Jack for refusing to talk to them during the day—and coming into their only safe place at night.

"No thanks, Shayla," he said. "I'm making an early night of it."

Frank pressed on. "Your parents are not a sufficient reason to take this on," Frank said. "Why are you really preaching Sunday?"

"Hey," a cameraman said. He was about three sheets to the wind, but still capable of overhearing much. "Are you preaching Sunday, Jack Chisholm?" He weaved a little on his stool. "In a church?"

"Jack is preaching at Saint Paul's Lutheran Church this coming Sunday," Father Frank said. "Tell your friends."

The cameraman leaned over and told his reporter. His reporter slid off her stool and went over to the booths filled with newsies. All of them took out their phones and started making calls.

Jack watched this with growing horror.

"Hey," Jack said, turning on Father Frank. "You—you are a big fat blabbermouth man of God." He raised a hand in the air, resisted the urge to slap Frank with it. "Why would you do that?"

Father Frank set down his glass. "Do you imagine you can do this thing casually, Jack? Just say a few words. No one will know or care?" He shook his head. "There is nothing casual about preaching." He smiled ruefully. "Unless you rely on a catchphrase."

"I didn't want CNN to know about it," Jack said. "I'm just trying to make amends. To—"

"It is an awesome responsibility to speak on behalf of God," Father Frank said. "To bring the good news to a world full of pain. I want to know that you remember what you're signing up for."

"Frank, I have preached to more people—"

"You haven't preached to these people," Frank said. "Most of them are older, most of them are barely getting by, most of them are scared of the future. Not hopeful. Scared." It sounded like he was getting into a preaching mood himself.

"I know," Jack said. "Things around here haven't changed that much—"

Frank laid a hand on Jack's arm to silence him. He fixed Jack with a gaze that burned. "I'm begging you, Jack. Make them feel better. Not worse." He took his hand away, patted the bar in front of him, and Shayla began pouring him another ginger ale. "Preach the good news, Jack. Not that we are unloved and unlovable. Jesus sat down to dinner with everyone who wanted to be there. It is amazing grace, not universal disgrace."

"I don't know what I'm going to preach," Jack said hotly. "Especially now that CNN is coming." He tried to glare at Frank, but couldn't seem to make it stick.

They had talked about the gospel reading, about Herod and the wise men, about the moment Jesus was revealed to those who sought him through a torturous journey.

Jack had preached from this passage before—to talk about Herod, about sin, about power misplaced. He was sure he had that sermon somewhere on his iPad.

But Frank was saying that he needed to preach something new, something fresh, something that would be true in this place.

"I don't know what I'm going to preach," he repeated. "But I am going to preach."

"All right, then," Father Frank said. "I don't suppose you'd mind if I came and listened?"

"Right," Jack said. "Because my stress level won't already be sky-high? Maybe Brother Raymond can bring his folks over." He dropped his head to the bar. A little too hard. It hurt. "What am I going to do?" he muttered.

"Find the good news," Frank said. "And tell the truth."

"Can those things even sit in the same room?" Jack asked. He raised his head. Rubbed it. "Listen—Frank. I'm grateful for your time." He looked around the room, made sure nobody was listening. "And we've got a construction party Sunday after church. I'm going to miss the Seattle game."

"This will be more fun," Frank said. "Better for your soul."

Jack shrugged. The last one had turned out pretty well.

Jack worked at the store Thursday and Friday mornings. In the afternoons, he got in the truck and drove down to the old swimming hole, where Live Oak Creek was five or six feet deep in spots. The water was clear and green and surrounded by tall trees. This time of year, the branches were bare except for the gray pompoms growing on the branches, feeding on the tree. Club moss, Jack thought they were.

Friday was sunny and windy, with the temperature climbing up into the seventies. It was just about as perfect a January day as one could ask for in Texas. The water rippled as the wind blew, and the sun pierced down to the bottom of the pool. Jack opened his journal, took off his boots and white socks, sat on the bank. When he began to sweat, he dropped his feet experimentally into the water.

"Arrggh," Jack shouted. Ice-cold needles seemed to pierce his feet. He yanked them from the water, began drying them off, although it didn't help.

"It did get down to thirty-three last night," a female voice said from behind him.

Maybe if he didn't turn around, she would go away. "Are you always going to just appear out of thin air, Kathy?" he asked.

"I'm like Batman that way," she said. "It's a useful trait for a reporter."

"Batman disappears," Jack said. "See how that works for you."

"Hey," she said. "This isn't just your spot. I spent my teenage years hiding here while the good-looking girls were floating the river in teensy bikinis or whatever it was they did for fun."

He turned and looked at her with a suspicious eye. Anything to take his attention off his tingling feet. "You didn't follow me down here?"

"Dude," she said. "I'm really kind of upset that *you're* here." She settled herself onto the limestone shelf that people jumped off into the water, a respectful distance away. Two blue herons flapped their long wings, gliding low over the water and landing on the opposite side of the river, about twenty yards away. They could hear traffic on the river road, the whir of tires, and the rush of the wind in the cedar trees.

It was perfect. Had been perfect.

"Forget this," Jack said, getting to his feet and gathering his journal and pen.

"What?" Kathy asked.

"Enjoy," he said, bending into an expansive mockery of a bow. He turned to make for the truck, but she called his name.

"I'll go," she said. "You were here first. And I can see you're still mad at me." She shook her head. "At the very least, I owe you a little peace and quiet." She got to her feet, walked purposefully toward her car, a tiny red Honda.

Against his will, he called out her name. She turned. "They let you get away with driving one of them there Jap cars in the heart of Texas?"

"I think it was built in Tennessee," she said. She opened the door. "I'll see you around, Jack."

"Hey," he called before she could get in the car. He took a step in her direction. "I am still mad at you." He looked around, looked up at the big blue cloudless sky. "But there's enough sky for both of us. I'm not even getting anything done. I just thought maybe some good thought would come to me here."

"Really?" she said. She paused, her hand still on the car door. "You sure?"

"Come on," he said. "Before I change my mind."

She shut the door, began walking slowly back. "When I first got here," she said, "I thought you were praying. Then, when you dipped your feet in, I thought you were cussing."

"A man can pray and cuss at the same time," he said.

She walked back over, considered how far away she needed to sit. He thought he'd make it easier. "Can I ask you something?"

She settled within conversation distance on the bank. "I guess," she said, crossing her legs.

"Are you staying or leaving?"

She looked up through the branches of the tree above them. "What are those things?" she said. "They look like tribbles."

He didn't say anything.

"From the old *Star Trek* show," she explained.

"I know what tribbles are." He looked up at the branches with her. "I think those are club moss. They're parasites."

"Parasites," she repeated. "Ugh." The tree was covered with them.

They sat for a moment, the sun warm on his shoulders, the water lapping against the bank. Jack closed his eyes.

"It feels like I should be getting on with my life," Kathy said. "Keeping this paper going—what is that about? Nobody buys papers anymore. It's like releasing an album on eight-track tapes. It's not even cool and retro. It's just stupid." She looked back up through the branches.

"Are you doing it for your father?"

She looked across the river at the herons, who were spreading their long wings in preparation for flight. "How would I know?" she said. She shrugged. "Maybe."

The herons flapped a few times, separately, then in unison. Then they took flight, following the river. One arced away in a slow, lazy loop, then followed the other down and around the bend, out of sight.

"I think maybe it's the people," she said. "In some weird way it feels like I'm needed here." She dipped a hand into the creek, shivered, pulled it back out, and shook it dry. "Even if what I'm doing is ridiculous, a hundred times less important than what I was doing."

"I thought what I was doing was important," Jack said.

"Jack," she said. "You had an audience of millions." She made it sound as though he had owned a horse-drawn carriage made of pure gold and equipped with a chocolate fountain. "And now—"

She broke off, took a quick glance to see his reaction.

"And now?" he said. He was interested.

She let it fly. "And now you're going to preach to fifty people, half of whom won't be able to turn up their hearing aids loud enough to hear you."

"I'll e-nun-ci-ate," Jack said. He looked sideways at her. "So you heard."

"Everybody heard," she said.

"Everybody? Oh, I don't like the sound of that."

She sighed. "I am sorry, Jack. I thought—well, let's just say it would be a good thing if you didn't google yourself just now."

"I got out of that habit three days into this adventure," Jack said. He laughed. "I used to preach about how we didn't feel bad enough about ourselves. I felt bad enough about myself in about thirty-five seconds on the Interwebs."

"Saint Paul's may have more than fifty people attending on Sunday."

"No cameras," he growled, looking at her.

"They'll have to stay outside," she said. "But I'd guess some press will be there. This is an angle. A story. The resurrection of the people's pastor."

"Oh, for—" He got to his feet, turned in a circle, glared down at her. "Don't call me that. I'm not that. If I ever was. A pastor—"

It was like Father Frank was in his head.

"A pastor watches over his sheep," he said quietly. "I was—" He shook his head, dropped gracelessly back to the ground. "I don't know what I was."

"I hear they're having a little social after. To welcome you."

"Well, they're going to have to relocate it," Jack said. "We're doing another building thing. Sam Rodriguez tells me we're putting up a ramp."

"For Alice," Kathy said.

"That's it," he said. "I can't lollygag around church. We have work to do."

She smiled, looked around, leaned back on her hands. "I think maybe this is why I'm still here."

"The creek?" Jack said.

She spread her hands. "It's a small world," she said. "After all."

She got to her feet. He got to his.

She held out her hand, tentatively.

He looked at it.

Then he took it.

"What are you preaching Sunday?" she asked.

"Come and see," he said.

She nodded, smiled. "Maybe I will."

14.

On Sunday, a number of people came to see. The parking lot was full, cars were parked along the street, and Jack suspected that First Baptist had caught some of their overflow. Someone at Saint Paul's would hear about that from Brother Raymond on Monday. Media were out on the lawn filing reports, and when Jack arrived, they descended on him in a rush.

"What are you doing—"

"Is this a new start—"

"Was that construction project—"

"Have you been asked to return to—"

He raised a hand, cut off their questions. "I've got to go preach," he said. "Thanks for your interest."

"What is your sermon about?" they asked. "What is—"

He raised a hand again. "Come and see."

He pulled the heavy wooden door open and stepped into the narthex, the church's foyer.

Bill Hall was waiting inside in a gray suit and a yellow tie. He looked as if he had been waiting for a while. He did not extend a hand when Jack approached.

"For a second," he said, "I thought you weren't coming." He looked grimly at Jack. "Since that's what you usually do."

Jack bit down a reply. "I'm here," he said.

"Is that what you're wearing?" He looked Jack up and down. "Pastor John used to wear one of those robes."

"I'm not your pastor," Jack said. He was wearing Wranglers, boots, and a button-down blue oxford open at the neck. Frankly, he felt dressed up. "I'm just a guy come from the hardware store to say a few words."

He held the front door open for a family that goggled at him when they recognized him. They passed on into the church, found a spot near the back. Someone—Bill and the deacons, he guessed—had put out extra chairs, and all the same the church was full.

Jack walked down the bedraggled red carpet toward the carpeted dais, where on the left Nora Calhoun was playing one of the old hymns on the organ. A lot of vibrato. On the right, one of the Bates sisters was playing piano; he wasn't sure which one. They all looked alike—had their whole lives.

"Softly and Tenderly." He hadn't heard that song in years.

"Ye who are weary, come home."

He noted unexpected but familiar faces. Father Frank sat with Tom on the aisle, third row back, and Jack nodded at them, took his father's hand.

Jack himself took a seat on the front pew. A big wooden seat was on the dais in front of the choir, but Jack did not want to sit in the preacher's chair, to feel all those eyes on him throughout the service. It was going to take a measure of bravery just to stand up. It didn't need to be any harder.

He looked back over the order of service. It was simple. Bill would welcome the congregation and lead the singing. Someone would read the Bible lessons. Jack would preach, and afterward, the deacons would distribute bread and wine at the front of the church. They had not asked Jack to preside over the blessing of communion at the altar. This wasn't communion, per se. It was just fresh-baked bread and good Hill Country wine laced with good intentions, holy in its own way.

They finished the song and took up "Blessed Assurance," a hymn by Fanny Crosby. Mrs. Calhoun loved Fanny Crosby; she had told Jack when he was a boy that Fanny Crosby was a blind woman who wrote eight thousand hymns.

"Blessed Assurance" was one of his mom's favorites. He could still remember her singing, "This is my story. This is my song." They used to slow the words of the chorus almost to a halt, a caesura over each note, "This . . . is . . . my . . . ," before launching like a drunk careening downhill on a bicycle into "story, this is my song."

Bill mounted to the pulpit. He spoke over the chords, expressed no surprise at the full house, simply invited all those present to turn in their hymnbooks to number 331. Everyone stood and began to sing.

Jack opened his book, although he scarcely needed it. He had sung through this hymnbook as a kid, still could sing most of these songs by heart. His mother had sung in the choir. Jack looked up at the choir now—four old women, one old man, a teenage boy. They were singing with big smiles on their faces— the expression he remembered on his mother's face as she sang.

After "Blessed Assurance" they sang, "Oh, How I Love

Jesus." Jack checked that his notes were in his pocket. He had decided against preaching from his iPad—it seemed inappropriate, somehow—and anyway, he didn't have anything close to a finished sermon.

This was not a place for PowerPoint.

What he had were some words, scribbled down during the week. Some had arrows linking them.

He felt sure he had never been less prepared to give a sermon.

A teenage girl read the Old Testament lesson and the Psalm. Tom himself climbed the steps to read the New Testament lesson. Then he said, "Would you stand, please, for the gospel reading." Everyone lumbered to their feet. It was like thunder after the relative silence. Tom read the story from Matthew of how the wise men had sought Jesus, how they had asked King Herod where the newborn king was to be found, how they had arrived and found the baby Jesus and worshiped him and given him their precious gifts.

Then everyone sat.

Tom ambled back down the steps.

And Jack passed him, ascending one step at a time. They nodded at each other.

Then Jack stood at the pulpit, looking out over the roomful of people. He saw people who had been at the block party at Mrs. Calhoun's. He saw some of the newsfolk in the very back and up in the balcony. He saw men and women who had grown up in this church, who would be buried in it.

He saw his onetime best friend, seated in the second row, his father in the third row, Mary behind him, Kathy three rows behind her.

He looked out at them all, and it grew silent, and he thought about how he used to proceed.

Begin with a prayer, he thought. *Let's at least do that.*

But he hadn't written a prayer, hadn't stage-managed the connection to his sermon.

Nor had he engineered connections between the hymns and the reading and his sermon, all of which he used to obsess about in Seattle. The hymns Mrs. Calhoun had picked probably didn't fit with the readings at all, except that they were songs about Jesus.

And this prayer—it wouldn't be fluid, wouldn't be eloquent. His prayers these days were less like conversation and more like a drowning man yelling for help.

It would have to do.

"Let us pray," he said, and he closed his eyes, squeezed them shut.

"God," he said, and he took a deep breath. He knew what his prayer had to be: "Give me words to say that will be worth hearing."

He opened his eyes. Their heads were still bowed. They clearly expected more.

"Amen," he added.

Slowly they looked up.

He looked down at his notes.

He took a deep breath.

"Today," he said, "is the day we celebrate the Feast of the Epiphany. You heard in our gospel lesson about the wise men who came from the East, how they sought the new king who would be born, how they found him."

He looked down at his notes again, found that he couldn't

look up from them. He needed to at least make some eye contact for a sermon about seeing. "Epiphany is about seeing things as they are, seeing things we have been longing to see, seeing things for real.

"Epiphany," he said, forcing himself to look up from his page, "is about the truth."

They looked on, parishioners and curiosity-seekers and members of the media, all of them wanting to hear something true.

Okay, he told himself. Okay.

"I haven't told the truth for a long time," he said quietly. "I haven't even preached the truth for a long time. Not the whole truth. Not really.

"Some of you have known me my whole life. Some of you are here this morning just because it's me standing here this Sunday. You're all wondering what I'm here to say.

"Well, I'm here to tell the truth." He looked down at his notes. He was a long way off of them now. He folded them up, stuck them in the pocket of his jeans, put both hands on the pulpit for support.

"I'm here to talk about how seeing what is right in front of us might be a good thing, even if it's hard, even if we don't understand where it might lead us."

They were all watching, listening. Even some of the newspeople had put down their pads.

Kathy Branstetter was nodding at him. *Go on*, her eyes were saying. *I want to hear this.*

"I came back to town a week ago," he said. "And I'd been gone a good long time. A lot has changed." He looked out at them, tried to make eye contact with those he knew from town.

"Places where friends used to live are boarded up. The yards are grown up with weeds. Buildings I used to know downtown are closed, empty shells with no reason to still be standing."

He took a deep breath. "The truth is, that's how I feel here in front of you this morning. Like there's no reason for me to still be standing. I messed up in a big way. I hurt the people who trusted me, the people who depended on me."

He shook his head. "Right now, I feel like one of those vacant buildings, standing up but hollow inside. No reason to still be here."

He looked out at them; some were watching intently, others were looking away but still listening. "I'm not telling you this because I want you to feel sorry for me," he said. "I don't want that. I'm telling you this because I hope that maybe my story can be of use to you in some way." He shrugged. "I've lost everything in the last two months. My family, my job, my money, my reputation, my self-respect." He looked around the congregation. "Maybe some of you know what it feels like to lose something and not know how you're going to go on. I'm guessing most of you do."

Some nodded—mainly older members of the church. And a few others.

Tom.

Mary.

Kathy.

"I thought that was how I would feel from now on," he said. "Lost. Abandoned. Empty. But last week, I remember looking at something brand new, something filled with hope, something that was built with love." He turned and looked at the organ, where Nora Calhoun was sitting, leaned forward, listening. "Some of you were at Mrs. Calhoun's house where we pushed back together against the wreck and the loss and the ruin. Together, we did what one person could not have done alone. Together, we made someone's life a little bit better, showed her that she was loved and appreciated, reminded ourselves that we were capable of so much more than the tiny selfish lives we've been living."

Jack blinked back tears; he was not the only one. Mrs. Calhoun was sniffling and someone in the back of the church was sobbing openly.

He raised his hands. He had not come to make people weep, but to tell them the good news.

Somewhere in all of this was good news.

"A friend of mine told me this week that it is an awesome responsibility to stand in front of a church and try to speak for God." He nodded at Frank, who sat looking steadfastly up at him. "He challenged me to remind you that in the midst of all our bad news, in the midst of the vacant lots and the boarded-up buildings, the ruined roofs and the ruined lives, there is good news."

He nodded. "There is good news."

"Look around you," he said. "Look and see." He held up his hands and some of them turned their necks like owls to take in the people on all sides of them, those above them in the balcony.

Jack nodded. "Good people are here. Love is here. And hope should be here.

"Look around," he repeated. "See what is right in front of you. Don't just see the boarded-up buildings, the boarded-up lives. See the possibilities."

He was rounding third. Headed for home. He suddenly saw it all fall together—the Bible story, the lives of his listeners.

His life.

"Today is the Feast of the Epiphany," he said, speaking softly but with growing strength. "It's the day we remember how the story of Jesus intersects with those who came looking for him." He paused, looked around the room. Every person was following with rapt attention. He moved to his conclusion.

"The story of Jesus, the Jesus who was revealed in the flesh to those wise men, the Jesus who is revealed to us, does not say that life is easy." He shook his head. "In fact, it says the opposite. That hope can be broken. It can be battered. It can even be nailed to a cross and left for dead."

He shook his head again. "But don't believe it. Don't you believe it for a second. The love of God, the irresistible grace of God, washes through this world like a river. It cannot be stopped. It cannot be contained.

"And hope can be battered, but it is never dead.

"That's what I am telling myself this morning. It's what I think I was supposed to tell you. And that," he said, "is the truth."

Silence.

Just silence.

But it was a silence full of something, something he had invited to be present, but something far bigger than himself or his words.

He looked out at Father Frank, remembered the blessing of the roof, and he raised his hands to the congregation.

"In the name of the Father, and the Son, and the Holy Spirit," he said.

"Amen," they said.

He made his way slowly down to the front pew. Bill Hall and

the other deacons made their way up in the silence to take the bread and wine, the chalices from the altar.

"We invite you," Bill said, then stopped to clear his throat, "to take communion with us." He looked out at the church, packed to overflowing, looked up to the balcony. "All of you are welcome at the table of Christ."

Two lines formed in each aisle, on either side of Jack, who sat leaning forward, his eyes on the floor. He had no idea if his sermon had been an abject failure or a success, had no idea what either of those things even looked like anymore. It used to be he knew—the congregations would stand, they'd applaud, social media would explode after the service.

He knew it was the shortest sermon he'd ever preached, maybe the least eloquent, and he couldn't care less.

He felt that something had happened at the end. Something real.

He hoped so.

In front of him, Bill Hall stood with the bread, tearing a tiny piece and placing it in the hands of each person in line. "This is the body of Christ," he said to each of them. "Broken for you."

In front of Jack and a little to his left stood a man he did not know with the chalice. Young. Maybe new in town since Jack left. He was offering the chalice to each person, and they dipped their bread or took a sip. To each person he said, "This is the blood of Christ, shed for you."

In the other aisle, Mrs. Calhoun took bread from Archie Sandstrunk, sipped from the chalice that Corinne O'Neal offered her, ascended back to the organ where she started playing another hymn.

"I Surrender All." It was almost like they were at First Baptist doing an altar call. Because the crowd came forward; they kept coming. Bill had to retreat to the altar for more bread, and the chalice-bearers had to replenish their supply as well.

At last the lines died down and those men on Jack's left went up to the altar. Bill Hall moved directly in front of Jack, and Jack looked up to see what he was doing.

Bill was offering him bread, and he had tears in his eyes.

Jack stood up. He held out his hands.

"This is the body of Christ," Bill said, tearing a substantial piece and putting it into his hands. "Broken for you."

Bill wiped his face with the back of his hand and stepped away.

"Amen," Jack managed to say. The bread was homemade. He had never tasted anything so good.

"This is the blood of Christ," the young man said, stepping forward and offering Jack the chalice as if it were his most precious possession. "Shed for you."

Jack took it from him. He drank. He handed it back just as carefully.

"Amen," he said.

The three of them stood there for a moment. Everyone was standing, the music was playing, something was supposed to happen next.

Bill took a step toward the center, still holding his plate of bread. The organ became quiet, and he raised his voice. "We've come to the end of our service. Thank you for coming. Go with God." He stood still, the air expectant. "The deacons will stand at the back door to greet you." Then Bill looked at Jack and took a step toward him before he asked, "And, Brother Chisholm? Will you come back and say a few words again next Sunday?"

Jack looked at Bill.

Jack looked back to his father and Father Frank.

And then he nodded.

"Absolutely," he said.

"Good," Bill said. "Good."

He took a step back to the center and spoke again as the people began to leave.

"Go with God," he repeated. "Go with God."

And so they did.

15.

The Mayfield City Hall is on the square across from the court-house, which is old, limestone, neoclassical, domed, and has stairs you aren't supposed to use to look out over the countryside.

You also aren't supposed to make out with your girlfriend or drink Coors Light up there.

These were all things Jack learned in his youth.

The City Hall had no such sterling memories attached to it. It had, for forty years at least, been in the storefront of an old general store, columns flanking a big plate glass window, and inside, a reception area, the city offices, and in back, the three cells of the municipal jail.

Jack had not been in the City Hall for—well, he couldn't remember the last time.

Carlene Petsch was the city secretary. Carlene had been called "Petshop" in their youth, if only rarely to her face. It made her cry, got people sent to the office. She had grown into a hard, hefty woman, the kind of *hausfrau* who could bake an apple pie and then beat you to death with her rolling pin. Jack felt his already considerable anxiety ramp itself up as he closed the front door behind him on the Monday morning following his sermon at Saint Paul's.

"Hey," he said, his voice calm. "Carlene."

She looked up at him, waited for him to state the purpose of his presence. Jack supposed that she might have absorbed some of her boss's animosity by osmosis.

Jack stuck his hands in his pockets, looked around the office. "Is, uh, James in?"

She looked back down at her desk at something considerably more important than him.

He wondered if it was the *People* with Katie Whatshername on the cover.

"The mayor is with someone," she said finally.

She didn't offer a seat, but he took one. He looked at the magazines on the side table—*Hill Country Reporter, Texas Highways*. He picked up a *TIME*, recognized it as the one that covered his scandal, put it back on the table.

He heard voices from the hallway, got to his feet.

A reporter and her cameraman preceded James into the reception area.

"Hey, Jack," the reporter said when she saw him. "You get summoned too?"

"Hey," he said back. "Summoned?"

"Speak of the Devil," James said. "And he shall appear."

"Thanks," the reporter said to James. What was her name? Kathy? Cathy? Cathleen?

"My pleasure," James said.

"You ready to talk to us?" she asked Jack.

"Not today," he said.

"You may want to," she said. "Before long." She gave him a look he could not decipher, and then was gone.

James watched them exit, then he looked across at Jack with undisguised disapproval. Carlene was likewise unhappy at Jack's presence, although her disapproval came off as a smirk.

"Thanks for saving Randy a trip," James said.

"What are you talking about?" Jack said.

"I trust you saw Randy at your little enterprise yesterday."

Randy had been sitting in his cruiser down the street from Mrs. Gutierrez's house. Jack remembered that every time he looked that way, Randy was glowering and shaking his head.

But Jack hadn't had much time to spare for Randy. Dozens of people had showed up. They had run a ramp from the sidewalk to the front porch—sunk posts, built rails, the whole thing. It was beautiful. Mr. Rodriguez had been their leader, but Jack supervised the unloading of cement, the mixing, the sawing, and did his share of hammering. Boys from various youth groups came—including Cameron Taylor, who had dug postholes. Men came from each of the churches—and some from no church at all. Mary's boyfriend, Dennis, had pushed a wheelbarrow. Warren Koenig had brought two ranch hands—and smoked lamb chops.

Again, a block party of generous proportions grew—larger than the week before with more food, more drink, more people—and at the center of it sat Mrs. Gutierrez in her new wheelchair, nodding happily and talking nonstop to anyone who would listen.

"They are good boys," she kept saying. "Such good boys."

Randy apparently didn't think so.

Nor, clearly, did James.

"Carlene," James was saying, "are you finished with it?"

She smiled up at him, pulled something off the desk in front of her. She handed him an envelope. "All done, Mr. Mayor."

He took it, extended it to Jack with a smile growing into malevolent glee.

"What is it?" Jack said without accepting it.

James's hand did not waver.

"Mr. Mayor?" Jack said.

"Jack," James said, "please find enclosed a cease and desist order from the city of Mayfield."

Jack snatched it out of his hand, tore open the envelope. His eyes ran across the phrases: "Contractor operating without a license—without proper permits—disturbing the peace—health and safety issue—endangering the community."

"What is this?" Jack said.

"I would think that even a person who didn't finish college should be capable of reading a letter," James said.

Carlene snickered, put her head down so she didn't have to meet Jack's eyes.

"I'm not a contractor," Jack said. "Wait. Are you trying to shut down—"

"I am ordering you," James said, "on behalf of the City of Mayfield, to stop your unlawful construction enterprise."

Jack had never punched someone in City Hall. He paused to reflect on whether the proximity to the city jail should deter him, decided that maybe it should.

"That enterprise is a spontaneous attempt by the people of your town to help each other," Jack said in a low voice. "A spontaneous eruption of charity."

"It is anarchy," James said. "It is unlawful."

"It is the best thing that's happened to this town in twenty years," Jack said. "And you didn't think of it. That's what you hate about it."

"Carlene," James said, turning to go, "send my next appointment back."

"We won't stop," Jack said.

"You have been warned," James said without even looking at him. "Go ahead. See what happens if you continue." He turned to go back to his office, but Jack stood stock still, looking after him. "Was there something else?" he said, without turning.

"I came to talk to you about Cameron," Jack said in a voice barely above a whisper.

James turned back around, faced him, took two strides forward. "What on earth could we—you and me—possibly have to say about my son?"

Two feet. That was the physical distance separating them.

The metaphysical distance was something more.

Jack let it fly. "I thought maybe I could help Cameron a little bit with his accuracy. His footwork. Maybe talk to him about reading defenses."

Each word spoken seemed to heighten James's shade of red. His hands formed into fists.

"Stay away from my boy," he ground out between clenched teeth.

"I—" Jack began.

"No!" James shouted. "Do you think I don't know you? Don't know what you're doing?" He stepped even closer, and his voice dropped. "You're doing what you always do. Well, it won't work. If you come near my son, I'll see that you're run out of this town."

He shook his head. "You're not going to alienate my son from me. Or my wife."

He took one step back without dropping his gaze. *Are we understood?*

Jack smiled, although it was not a happy one. "It doesn't take a college degree," he said steadily, "to know you don't need my help doing that."

James closed the difference between them in a fraction of a second. He grabbed Jack's collar—he was wearing jeans and a T-shirt beneath his jacket—and it's unclear what may have happened had the front door not opened at that precise moment.

James released Jack and took a step backward. A subtle smile snaked onto his face.

"Kathy," he said.

Jack turned. Kathy Branstetter.

"Mr. Mayor," she said. "Jack. Were you summoned too?"

"I was," Jack said, taking a step away from James. "And now I'm leaving. Jamie." Jack nodded to him. *Are we understood?*

Then he stepped through the front door, let it close behind him. His heart was pounding. He looked down. The letter was still in his hand.

He walked the three blocks back to the store, breezed past the media on the sidewalk—four more people than last week, he noted with dismay—and into the store, where his father sat talking with Charlie Gobel.

"Jack," he said, "you remember Mr. Gobel."

"Yessir," he said. "How's Molly?"

"All right, son. Bless you for asking."

Tom turned to Jack. "Mr. Gobel was wondering if our contracting unit had any interest in carports."

Jack looked blankly at his father. "What?"

"Could you get a team together to tear down his old carport, build one that would stand up straight?"

"A team?"

"Yes, son. A team of workers." Tom looked at his son with his brow slightly furrowed.

Jack looked down at the letter in his hand.

He looked out the window at the media, who didn't know it, but who were sitting on a much bigger story than they had ever imagined.

Jack looked back at his father.

And he decided.

"I believe we could work on it this Sunday after church," he said. "If that works for you, Mr. Gobel."

"Thank you," Mr. Gobel said to Jack. He shook his hand. His grip was feeble, like a child's.

"Thanks, Tom." Mr. Gobel turned and inched his way toward the door.

"It's our pleasure," Tom said. Jack nodded after him.

"I thought it was about time someone from First Baptist got a little help," Tom explained after the door closed. "I don't want anyone accusing you of favoritism."

"No," Jack said. "That is the last thing we want." He looked down at the letter in his hand.

"What's that?" Tom asked.

"Nothing," Jack said. He stuffed it in his coat. "Not a thing."

"I've—we've—got good news," Tom said. He stepped forward and hugged Jack.

The action was so strange—so out of character—that Jack almost stepped away before catching himself. He raised one arm, patted his father gently on the back. "Hey. What good news is that?"

"Alison is coming to visit."

Jack pushed his father back and looked him in the face. "Really?"

His father was beaming, nodding. Jack knew that he was too. "I just heard from the lawyers."

"The lawyers? Not—not Tracy?" That seemed—clinical. Distant.

His father didn't take his meaning. "Her lawyers called our lawyers in Seattle. Alison is flying in on January 18."

"Next Friday," Jack breathed. "Really?"

His father nodded. "Just for the weekend. She starts her new school on Monday. But, Jack—" He couldn't go on. He raised a hand to cover his eyes.

"I know," Jack said. He stepped forward and hugged his father again. "Thank you. Oh, and I'll pay you back—"

Tom's expression said that this was the stupidest thing he had heard all day. Jack put his hand in his pocket and found the letter. "Listen—"

He decided against it.

"That's great. Everything's great."

Jack sat down behind the counter and got out the phone book, looked up James's home number, dialed it.

He was not going to live in fear.

He was going to do the right thing. Whatever it cost.

Darla answered the phone. "Hey," he said.

"Jack?" she said.

"The same," he said. "Hey, I—"

"I know why you're calling," she said. "He called just now. I know you can't   "

"I'll be at the practice field this week," Jack said. "Every afternoon after school." He smiled. "Just watching. That's all."

Darla didn't speak.

"Okay," she said at last.

"If it'll cause you problems—"

"No," she said. "Thank you. It's—very generous. I just—"

"Cameron is a good boy," Jack said. He thought back to his work at Mrs. Gutierrez's house. "And he could be a great quarterback. You tell me if it becomes a problem for you. That's the last thing I want."

"Jack," she said, "there are things I love about James." She sighed. "And things I cannot stand. Pease believe me when I tell you I have had to learn to stand up for myself."

"You tell me, D," he repeated. "I'd never want to cause you any pain."

"I'll tell Cam," she said. "And I'll let Coach Miller know you're coming."

"Whoa. Nuclear option?" Jack asked. The one person higher on the ladder than the mayor in a small Texas town is the football coach.

"He's my only son," she said. "And you're right. He could be a great quarterback. A great person. He just needs the right nudge."

"All right," Jack said. "I'll talk to you, D."

"You know it, Twelve," she said, and she hung up.

Tom raised an eyebrow.

"I'm doing a little coaching," Jack said.

The eyebrow arched higher.

"Quarterback coaching."

If that eyebrow went any higher, it was going to hit his hairline.

"Of my archenemy's son."

"Ahh," Tom said. "If it's only that."

Jack snorted. "You mean Darla? Dad, that train left the station a long time ago." He shook his head. "No. It's just—you should see this kid throw. Reminds me of me. He could go all the way. Be something."

"Just watch yourself," Tom said.

"That, sir, is sage advice." Jack patted his father's shoulder. "Let me put a call in to Mr. Rodriguez about Sunday, and I'll be ready to get to work."

That afternoon at the football field, those few members of the team who were not playing basketball showed up for light practice. Cameron Taylor was one of them—and he had two receivers and a running back to throw to. They did calisthenics, some drills, and then Coach Miller set up Cameron at midfield and he and QB 2 began throwing routes.

Jack was sitting about halfway up the stands, the concrete cold underneath him. It was an overcast day, a little chilly. He had a Dr Pepper on one side, his journal on the other. It was open, whether to take inspiration for Sunday's sermon or notes on Cameron's QB play remained to be seen.

After Coach Miller got his linemen set up with the blocking sled, he walked over to the stands and waved Jack down to talk to him.

"Sir," Jack said.

"You can call me Mark," Coach Miller said. "You're a grown man now." He was in his sixties, iron-gray hair in a Marine Corps crew cut, an old-time football coach in an Internet world.

"Yessir," Jack said.

"You here to watch the boy, I understand," Coach Miller said.

"Yessir," Jack repeated. "To see if I can—"

"I know what you're here to see," Coach Miller said. "I'm glad of the help. That loser James brought in from Houston—" He shook his head, rubbed his hands together. "Well, I like to killed him."

"It's a brave new world, Coach."

"Ain't that the truth, Twelve." He looked down at his clipboard. "Quarterback coaches and no-huddle offenses." He sighed. "We put in a modified Oregon offense last fall," he said. "Spread offense is perfect for this boy, though. I swear, he is almost as good as you."

Jack smiled, but his brain was working overtime. A spread offense spreads out the offense—but also spreads the defense, makes it declare what it is doing so that the blockers—and the QB—can see it. It opens up passes, but also rushing plays, since defenders are no longer jammed in the middle of the field. If the safeties drop back into deep coverage, it actually means the rush is the smartest play, five blockers against five defenders. A good QB has to read that defense, see where the percentages lie, pass, run, or hand off. A rifle for an arm doesn't make a quarterback—it's what's above the shoulders.

"How are his reads?" Jack asked.

"Good. Not great. If the defense changes things on him, he's still learning how to adjust at the line."

"You running mostly out of the shotgun? I watched him doing drop-backs the other day."

"We mixed up some zone read options with the shotgun, some traditional play action, some deep drops."

"Seven steps would let him see things a little better on pass plays."

Coach Miller nodded. "He could be an inch or two taller, I think he'd have the world by the tail. But he's got all the tools." He looked back at the field. "Good to see you, Twelve. You're welcome on my field anytime."

"Thank you, Coach." Jack went back up to his seat and watched.

Just watched.

A couple of other locals dropped in. Nothing was bigger in Mayfield than Wildcat football. Even before formal spring practice people were already interested in next fall.

On Tuesday afternoon, Jack again sat and watched. Cameron had plenty of gifts—he threw well and accurately, if not always in the tiny window that would be required. Sometimes he threw behind his receivers. Sometimes he didn't lead them enough on deep routes. All of that could be fixed with time and practice. He had good mechanics.

Jack's phone buzzed during practice. He didn't answer it. Later, when he checked messages, he saw that it was from Martin Fox.

He didn't listen to it.

On Wednesday afternoon, Jack was sitting in the stands at the end of practice making some notes to share with Coach Miller. Down on the field, the players were running their last sprints before heading into the field house.

"What are you doing here, Chisholm?" came a voice he knew too well.

Two shoes stopped in the aisle next to him.

Somehow James had pulled a reverse-Batman on him.

Jack finished his note. The worst that could happen was James would get the opening punch in. It wouldn't be the first time.

"I told you to stay away from my boy," James said. His voice was uneven, his breathing shallow. Jack wondered if someone had told James that Jack was watching practice. He must have sprinted over from downtown.

"They look good," Jack said without looking up. "Especially that QB 1. I think they could win a few this fall."

"I want you out of here!" James was yelling now, and Jack could hear in his voice that he was readying himself for something besides words. "I want you out of here right now!"

"Taylor!" That voice still sent a chill through Jack, and probably through every other young man who had gone to Mayfield High. Jack looked down, and Coach Miller was poised at the edge of the stands pointing a finger up at them. "What is your damage?"

James looked down at the coach and back at Jack. "Coach, I told him—"

"Chisholm has my express permission to be at my practice in my stands," Coach Miller said, marching up the stairs, red-faced. "He is trying to help me turn your boy into a quarterback."

Even though Coach Miller stopped three steps below them, it was clear where the power was.

"I don't want him near my boy," James said, his voice low. He refused to even look at the coach.

"That ain't your call in this place, Taylor," Coach Miller said. "Why don't you walk away before I have to ban you from my practices?"

James dared a glare at Coach Miller, couldn't sustain it, shifted it to Jack.

"I'll get you," he said. "Don't you doubt it for a minute. This is not over."

"Sweet Baby James," Jack said. "I'll see you around."

If Coach Miller hadn't been present, blood would have been spilled.

James walked away.

Jack sat back down.

Coach Miller settled next to him.

"I'd watch my step off this field, Twelve," the coach told him. "That man would as soon kill you as look at you."

"He won't kill me," Jack said. "That's not his style. He'd rather humiliate me. And how can he humiliate me any worse than I've already done to myself?"

"All the same, son," Coach Miller said. "You take care." He looked meaningfully at him. "That man hates you. Always has. Always will."

Jack sighed. "I know, Coach. If you'd just made him QB 1—"

"Then we would never have made State." Coach Miller shook his head. "And don't think he doesn't think about that every day of his life. Anyway. What's done is done."

"Truer words were never spoken, Coach," Jack said. He opened his journal. "Here's what I saw this week."

16.

He did what?" Mary asked that night at Tom's. Dennis had grilled sirloins, Mary brought baked potatoes and brussels sprouts, and Jack and Tom provided dessert—a Sara Lee cheesecake from the freezer section of the supermart. "Bachelors!" Mary sniffed.

"Coach ordered Jamie out of the stadium," Tom said. Jack glared at him. "I'm not violating your confidence, if that's what you're thinking, son. I got three calls at the store before you'd even left practice."

"Glad you're helping out, Twelve," Dennis said. "But that's a big steaming pile of crap to step in."

"I didn't step in anything I didn't already have on my shoes," Jack said, handing Dennis a Shiner.

"True enough," Dennis said. "How do they look this year?"

Jack nodded. "I see a lot of talent. And Cam Taylor is the real thing. He's got an arm, and if he can develop a head to go with it, they can go all the way."

Dennis pumped his fist as though the championship was already won.

"What are we going to do when Alison gets here?" Mary asked.

"Whatever she wants," Tom said, unboxing the cheesecake and taking a good look at it. "Is this supposed to still be frozen?"

"You all!" Mary grunted. "I'm not going to have my only niece starve to death while she's here."

"She likes pizza," Jack said. "And hamburgers."

"I'll grill for her," Dennis said.

"And something green," Mary said. "She's not going to eat like you three if I can help it."

"How did you get her here?" Dennis asked.

"The lawyers in Seattle made the arrangements," Tom said.

"Seattle," Jack said. That set off a nagging thought. What was it about Seattle?

"Jack?" Mary said. "Are you okay?"

Jack dropped the hand that had been cupping his chin. "I got a message from Seattle," he said. "I didn't listen to it."

"Well, are you going to?" Tom asked.

"Nah," he said. The room went silent.

Jack looked around the group. "I can't just erase it?" he said.

"Do you run from things now?" Mary asked. "I thought we were past that."

"What a pain," Jack muttered, but he took his phone out, slid it on, flipped to his voicemail. It was still there.

Martin Fox. 57 seconds.

"Do it already," Mary said.

"Okay," Jack said. "Unbelievable."

Jack had not heard Martin's voice since the day he lost his job. And it certainly had not sounded so . . . breezy. Cheery, even.

"Jack," Martin said, "I'm calling with good news. The board of elders met and it was almost unanimous to invite you to come back."

Jack almost hung up then, but the others were watching him, so he made himself listen to the rest of the message.

"I won't lie to you, Jack. We have some work that needs to be done. On you. On the church. But our attendance is down a third. Giving is down by half. You know we can't move forward with those figures. So come back. We'll make it work. I think we can match what you're getting in Mayfield, don't you?"

He chuckled. Then hung up.

Jack blinked a couple of times, rapidly.

"What is it?" Tom asked. "What did they say?"

Jack dropped his hand, put his phone in his pocket, turned away from them all. "They want me to come back."

"Oh," Mary said. "Grace?"

"That's—that's good, right, Twelve?" Dennis said. "I knew they'd come around."

"They think I'm the best person to fix the problem I left them," Jack said, without turning around. "I'm not sure that's true. What do— Dad, what do you think?"

Tom didn't answer. Jack turned around.

Tom was looking down at the cheesecake as though it held the secrets of the universe.

"Dad?"

Tom shook his head. Mary took his arm, led him over to the table, set him in his chair at the head.

"Let's eat," she said. "Who wants brussels sprouts?"

That evening at Buddy's, Jack told Father Frank about the phone call, about his family's reaction, about how his father wouldn't even speak to him.

"How did you feel when you heard the message?" Frank asked.

"I felt—I can't tell you," Jack said. "I was excited. Relieved. And angry. Martin acted like they'd never cut me loose."

"Do you want to go back?"

Jack looked down at his beer. "A part of me does. The part that knows the drill. That could step right back into that place like I never left."

Frank studied Jack's face. "But the other part?"

Jack took a drink. "The other part knows it would be the easy way out. And that I'm not the same person I was before." He shook his head. "But it would be easy. And maybe it would be like erasing—"

"What happened happened," Frank told him. "You know it. Everyone knows it." He drank some of his ginger ale, looking as if he wished it was something stronger. "If you go or if you stay, Jack, that's your decision. But—"

"I know," Jack said.

Frank looked down at his Bible. They had been studying the passage about the baptism of Christ—the lectionary reading for Sunday. He suddenly looked off at the media sitting in the booths, and he sighed.

"Have they forgiven you?" he asked.

"What?"

"They're asking you to come home. Grace Cathedral. Like in the blessed story of the Prodigal Son. Have they forgiven you?"

"No," Jack said. "I seriously doubt it. It's a financial decision. But it makes sense—"

"When your father asked you to come home," Frank said, "had he forgiven you?"

"Yes," Jack said. "You know he had. Before I even asked him."

"'When he was still a long way off,'" Frank quoted, "'his father saw him and was moved with pity. He ran to the boy and clasped him in his arms and kissed him.'" Frank closed his Bible and turned to Jack. "His father didn't cross-examine the prodigal, bully him, lecture him on ingratitude. He was just so overjoyed at the return of his son that he welcomed him home. The father took him back just as he was."

"I know," Jack said, "but—"

"But nothing, boyo," Frank spat. "Either they love you and they forgive you, or they don't. If you return to them knowing that they don't, it's your decision. But it will be a poor decision, mark my words."

Jack looked at Frank. "You wouldn't do it? To maybe save your marriage. To get back your self-esteem. To earn a real paycheck?"

Frank refused to look at him. "It's your decision. But what happened happened. You know it. Everyone knows it. Don't pretend." He actually looked in the opposite direction of Jack—in the direction of all the drinking media. "Don't pretend."

They didn't even finish talking about the baptism of Christ. Frank was angry and didn't have much else to say. Jack got up from the bar a few minutes later. He walked out to Tom's car, leaned against it, and looked up at the heavens. The stars were clear and bright and close enough to touch.

Jack didn't call Martin back on Thursday. He went to the store, went down to the creek after lunch, dropped by practice at four o'clock. He wanted to talk to Danny, see what was what. He'd left a half dozen messages. None of them were returned.

On Friday after lunch—a week until Alison came—he drove back to the swimming hole with his Bible and his journal. He was working through the baptism passage again. What to say? It had been so easy the first week—he had just told the truth.

No. It hadn't been easy at all. Telling the truth was hard as hell. He hadn't even been sure what he was going to say until he was standing in the pulpit, and it hadn't all fallen together until he was already under way.

He couldn't just stand up in front of them again this week and confess that he was a sinful wretch. That was going to get old fast.

Tell the truth.

Preach the good news.

Where was the good news in someone being immersed in water as a sign of forgiveness?

What's good about needing forgiveness? Doesn't that mean you did something wrong?

Jack dipped his hand in the clear green water—still cold, but not quite so frigid as last time.

He let the water trickle out between his fingers. It felt good.

A vehicle drove up behind him, parked, idled for a moment, then turned off. A car door opened and steps moved in his direction.

"What do you want, Kathy?" he said without looking up from his Bible.

"How did you know it was me?"

He smiled, shook his head. "When is it not?"

"Okay," she said. "I just thought I might find you here."

"You knew you would," he corrected.

"Okay," she admitted. She came a little closer, was not growled at, so sat nearby on the ledge. She crossed her legs beneath her and took a deep breath. "I have an idea. I think you need to google yourself."

"Correct me if I'm wrong," Jack said, taking another palmful of water and letting it run through his fingers. "But didn't you tell me not to google myself?"

"I think there's a lot of stuff about you circulating right now you ought to know," she said.

"How much of this news originated with you?"

"Not the first bit of it," she said. "Scout's honor. It looks to me like a whole bunch of people are trying to get you to do what they want."

"Well, that's funny then," Jack said. "Because I haven't paid a lick of attention to the news." He looked at her. "Is it that bad?"

"Some of it," she said. She scrunched her face, shook her head. "You don't deserve it, that's for sure."

Okay, it must be pretty bad. He took out his iPhone. He had two bars—probably enough to browse online.

He looked over at her. "You decided yet?"

"What?"

"About leaving?"

"Oh," she said. She stared at the ground between them.

"You know—that talk we had last week. About why you were still here? I'd love to know your answer."

"No, you wouldn't," she said, without looking up.

Jack sighed and closed his Bible. "Tell me about honoring your father," he said. "What does that mean to you?"

She peered out at the water, arms hooked around her knees. "It's not that we got along," she said. "One of the reasons I left was because it was so hard being around him."

"Okay," Jack said. "Would you have come back if he hadn't been sick? Would you stay if he hadn't—you know."

"Died?" she said. She turned her head, looked over at him, then back out at the water. "You can say it, Jack. It's not a secret." She turned back out to the far bank. The wind was blowing downstream, rippling the water. "I know I have to live my own life," she said. "And I'm considering—I'm considering more than one option. But the truth?"

She raised her hands in front of her face as though she were praying. Maybe she was.

"Everything I am or will ever be is because of my father," she said. "What I love about myself. What I struggle with. The writer and editor. The perfectionist. The person afraid to love. And then—to come home to him before he died. To know he loved the person I've become." She laughed shakily. "As screwed up as that person may be sometimes."

She took a deep breath. "You know, Jack, I think there's nothing as powerful as knowing your father loves you."

He nodded. "You're not far wrong there."

She glanced at him almost shyly, looked away. "Are you preaching this Sunday?"

"Yup."

"You're not—going away yet?"

"Ah," he said. He picked up his phone, typed his name into a search box, was not surprised to find that of the 1,336,000 items, the top news was that he was returning to Grace Cathedral.

"Can Disgraced Seattle Pastor Be Forgiven?" one headline read.

"Cheating Jack to Return to Pulpit?" another wondered.

"A lot of question marks in those headlines," Jack said. "What's this piece? I see a video. 'Christian Charity or Photo Ops?' Is that Cathy? Cathleen? What is her name?"

"Ah," she said. "That is a smear job courtesy of our good mayor. It's the story I refused to run."

"Do I want to see it?" His thumb hovered over the link.

"Do you enjoy seeing yourself accused of everything short of necrophilia in your bid to return to the national spotlight?"

"Wow." Jack breathed. He put his phone back in his jacket. "Coach really should have started him at quarterback."

"Then we would never have gone to State," she said. She pushed herself to her feet, dusted herself off, watched the water for a few seconds. "What are you preaching Sunday?"

"It's the First Sunday of Epiphany, the baptism of Christ," Jack said. "So—no idea."

"I liked your sermon last week," she said. "It made me feel—" She paused, kicked at an invisible rock or twig.

"What?" he said.

"Like I wasn't alone." She blushed, a slow flush that spread up her neck and all the way across her cheeks.

"That's nothing to be embarrassed about," he said. He checked his watch. "Crap on a hat. I'm late for practice." He gathered his stuff quickly, patted her on the shoulder as he passed, and dashed to his car.

"Jack," she called after him. "What are you going to do?"

He laughed and shook his head. "You'll just have to check the news," he said.

17.

Tom felt poorly Saturday and went to bed early, which left Jack, Mary, and Dennis sitting around the table and enjoying one of Mary's lemon meringue pies—homemade, not store-bought, as she so loudly proclaimed. Right out of the Fannie Farmer cookbook.

"I hope it's not the flu," she said. "That's going around."

"Or that intestinal bug," Jack said. "Three of the reporters are out with it." He smiled. "So far."

"Hey, Twelve," Dennis said. "I was—well . . ." His voice trailed off. Then he recoiled a little, as if someone had kicked him under the table.

"Did you just kick Dennis?" Jack asked Mary.

"I'll never tell," she said airily. "But I believe Dennis has a question for you."

"Can—could—" He looked up at the ceiling, as though the answer might be up there somewhere.

"Just spit it out, Seventy-eight," Jack said, "spit it out."

"Well," he said, "I've never been much for church—"

"Has not darkened the door of a church in his life," Mary

said, and Jack suddenly realized that maybe it wasn't just somebody's failure to commit that held this relationship back from
heading to the altar.

"But I was thinking maybe I'd come Sunday. Hear you
preach."

Jack nodded. "And you're wondering if I'll make you feel
bad?" Dennis didn't exactly nod, but he didn't shake his head
either. "If you'll feel out of place?"

"I think he wants to know if it's okay," Mary said. "Honestly!"

"Dennis," Jack said, "you are more welcome than you know."

"I'm not exactly the world's best person," Dennis said.

"I don't think you committed adultery on 123 channels,"
Jack said.

"Unlike some people I know," Mary said.

"Dennis," Jack said, and he bounced a hand off Dennis's
massive forearm—it was like a tree trunk. "I'm just going to tell
the truth. I'm going to talk about the good news." He suddenly
felt Frank's absence like something physical; he couldn't believe
Frank was still angry at him, didn't understand why.

Or did he?

"We'll go to church Sunday," Mary said. "You can sit with
me. And afterward, we have another project, don't we, Jack?"

Jack took a deep breath. "We do indeed," he said. "Hey," he
said. "Did you see the piece on CNN?"

They both chose that moment to study the ceiling.

"Wow. That bad?"

Dennis nodded grimly. "I ought to—"

"Not in front of the pastor," Mary warned. She turned to
Jack. "It was pretty bad. I'm your sister, and Jamie even had me

believing some of it." She swallowed once, and then she asked, "Jack, are you leaving?"

"They've made an offer," Jack said. "You know that. I haven't accepted it."

She wanted to ask more, but thought better of it.

They talked about taking Alison to the San Antonio Zoo and down on the Riverwalk for dinner. They talked about buying her a pair of boots in Kerrville.

After Mary and Dennis left, Jack crept up to Tom's room, opened the door quietly, and looked in.

Tom was in a fitful sleep, but he was resting. *That's got to be a good thing,* he thought.

But Sunday morning Tom seemed worse. He was in the bathroom three times before they left for church. Jack felt his dad's forehead and thought he was running a temperature, went for a thermometer, which Tom refused. "I am already dying, Jack. I am going to hear you preach." How could Jack deny his logic?

The church was even fuller than the week before, and the media crush was like nothing Jack had ever seen. All four networks had sent reporters and a crowd of media stood in back. The deacons were having to keep them to one side just so people could get into the church.

"I'll make y'all a deal," Jack shouted, as they saw him and moved forward across the church lawn like a centipede. "Behave yourselves. I'll give you one camera in the back of the balcony. You decide who does the feed, and you all share it. And I'll say a few words to you after. Right here."

He left them to argue the details. He had a sermon to preach, a church to meet.

Bill was standing at the door, and he greeted Jack with a smile, shook his hand. "Jack," he said. "Welcome."

"Thank you," he said. "Your family okay?"

Bill nodded. "Thanks for asking." Then he turned to welcome other visitors.

The service had the same shape. Gospel hymns, welcome by the chairman of the deacons, the readings. Tom was again tasked with reading the gospel lesson, and he was visibly weakened. He took the steps one at a time, coughed for an interminable stretch before beginning to read about John baptizing Jesus.

And then Jack was standing in the pulpit, looking out at the throng. Every pew filled to overflowing, every additional chair full, people standing in the back of the sanctuary and the back of the balcony, even people standing in the narthex. The camera was set up in the balcony, and untold numbers of people would see this now or later. Jack smiled.

"Good morning," he said.

"Good morning," came the thunderous reply.

"It's nice to see you this morning," he said. He smiled at Dennis, whose massive bulk was pinned in on either side by Mary and a young woman he didn't know. "Welcome to Saint Paul's."

He went on to talk about the story of the baptism of Jesus. Who was this John the Baptist? Why did Jesus want to be baptized?

He noticed that Father Frank had slipped in and was standing in the back, a defiant tilt to his chin. *I'm here, but I'm still angry.*

"I was talking to a friend this week," Jack said, "and she said something that I'm sure will resonate with a lot of us. She said, 'There's nothing as powerful as knowing your father loves you.'

"Mothers have to love us. They gave us life, nurtured us,

fed us, sometimes from their very bodies. And, women, please believe me when I say we are grateful. I loved my mother and I know she loved me up to her dying day."

He blinked, looked down at his notes for a moment, looked back up.

"But knowing your father loves you is different. Your father doesn't have to love you. He didn't give birth to us. The father has traditionally been outside the home working, hunting, farming, doing tax audits. We are separate from our fathers in ways we aren't from our mothers."

He looked down at Tom, who was coughing quietly into a handkerchief. "Dad," he said. "I'd like to tell a story about you. Can I have your permission?"

Tom looked up, lowered the handkerchief. "Does this story make me look good?" he asked.

Jack nodded.

"Then by all means," Tom said, to a ripple of laughter.

Jack looked out at them, picked out familiar faces.

"Those of you who live in Mayfield know that my father and I didn't speak for many years. Maybe all of you know that. It has been widely reported," he said, looking the news camera in its one eye. "I did something that disappointed my father, and in my anger and rebellion, I walked away from him for a decade. He was not a part of my life in any way, although he dearly wanted to be. He continued to reach out, even after I had pushed him to the side.

"And then one day not so long ago, I was at the end of my rope. I had made the very public mistakes that all of you know, and I thought I was done for. You know, like in the movies: 'You guys go on without me.'"

Jack smiled, although this wasn't very funny.

"Without even asking forgiveness—I don't think I've ever asked forgiveness," he said suddenly, surprised by the revelation. He turned to Tom. "Dad, I am truly sorry. But without my even asking him for forgiveness, my father forgave me. When I had done nothing to deserve his love, he loved me."

Tom was nodding. It was true. Jack looked down at his notes again. He got his voice under control.

"And when I thought I had no reason to go on, my father loved me enough to tell me that I was at the beginning of something, not at the end."

The church was quiet again, many people leaning forward in their seats.

"And I thought to myself, if my earthly father shows this kind of love and forgiveness to his son, won't God's love and forgiveness be that much more amazing?

"In this story of Jesus's baptism, Jesus is not being baptized because he needs his sins forgiven—we believe that he was the one blameless and perfect human being. But he's doing it on our behalf—on behalf of all of us whose humanity he shares. And he's doing it so we too can understand that God loves us. Sinful, sad, broken as we may be, God loves us beyond reckoning."

He looked out at them, left, right, up into the balcony, and he knew they were ready for his conclusion. "When Jesus comes up out of the waters, his Father says to him, 'This is my beloved son, and I am so pleased with him.' My brothers and sisters, we should know that God is uttering the same words about each and every one of us. 'This is my beloved child, and I love him, I love her, without reservation. No matter what.'"

He raised his hand in blessing, and without his bidding them, they stood to their feet. He smiled out at them, and in that moment, he felt something he had never felt in Seattle—not pride, not excitement, but something deeper, something richer: an intense love for every person in that building.

An intense sense of their holy connectedness.

"Walk out those doors and into your life, secure in the knowledge that your Father loves you. And may the blessing of God—Father, Son, and Holy Spirit—be upon you this day and forevermore. Amen."

"Amen," the congregation said in unison.

Bill had asked Jack to serve communion. This Sunday, he and Bill dispensed the bread, and for what seemed a never-ending stream of people—Mary, his father, Dennis, Mrs. Calhoun, and finally, Father Frank—Jack tore a piece of the homemade bread, placed it in their hands, and told them, "This is the body of Christ, broken for you."

He was surprised at first how many people had tears in their eyes, but when he thought about it, it made sense. Is there a more tangible symbol of how much the Father loves us than the broken body of Christ?

After church, he stood at the doors and greeted parishioners and visitors—mostly visitors. He was almost crushed by Dennis's bear hug, and Father Frank shook his hand and told him it was a lovely sermon, "and true as well."

He seemed to have been forgiven, without even asking.

The press conference was a short one. It was mostly Jack telling the media he was in Mayfield, he had work to do here, and they should probably go cover some other story. Surely some other priest or pastor had screwed up in the past week or so.

"But, Jack, are you going back to Seattle?" was the question that came from every quarter, and many of those exiting the church or rubbernecking at the media circus leaned in to hear his answer.

"I had a call from Seattle," Jack said. "I have no immediate plans beyond tearing down somebody's garage as soon as I can change out of my church clothes. And I'll be welcoming my daughter for her first visit to Texas next week. That's all I have to report."

The questions didn't stop when he reached the Gobels' house. Although they stood tearing shingles off a rickety carport that threatened to collapse beneath them at any moment, Sam Rodriguez would not stop asking, "We've got a good thing started here, hombre, you know?"

"I know," Jack kept saying. Out in the street, on the other side of the pile of building materials people had brought, on the other side of the growing block party, he could see that Randy Fields was seated in the police cruiser, his jaw clenched, shaking his head.

"We've got a good thing started here, hombre."

Jack nodded. "I hope we get to keep on doing it."

The crowd was even bigger today—more folks from First Baptist had come. Although James Taylor was not one of them, Cameron was one of the high-school boys taking joy in swinging a sledgehammer to bring the old carport down, and Darla was dispensing what Jack assumed was good sweet iced tea over amongst the food and beverages. Someone had set up tables and chairs.

"Looks like some excellent food from the First Baptist ladies," Warren Koenig told Jack, wiping his brow.

The old carport came down with a roar like the death of a dinosaur to the cheers of the high-school boys who now had advanced degrees in demolition. One group of workers began framing the walls, another worked to secure base timber into the concrete, a third began unloading material for the new roof. Jack and Mr. Gonzalez had decided that as long as they had the labor—and they certainly did—and as long as the material was there—and people had brought more than enough—they would build the Gobels a proper garage with walls and everything.

Too many men and boys had showed up for all of them to work at once, so Jack and Mr. Rodriguez kept teams at their tasks, cycled people on and off, supervised to make sure that the volunteers drove the nails straight and measured angles correctly.

Jack kept one eye on Randy, who seemed eternally angry about this situation and just sat in his cop car, his lips perpetually pursed.

When the walls went up and they started securing the roof supports, Jack noticed Randy on the phone. He was nodding, his jaw still clenched, and he seemed even angrier than before.

People were shaking Jack's hand, patting him on the back, but he sensed that many regarded him with a degree of either curiosity or suspicion. Jack's remedy for that was to work as hard, or harder, than every man there. To carry the heaviest, to hammer the most—

"This is not an Olympic event, boyo," came the voice of Father Frank from behind as Jack stepped away to take a swig of Shiner and rest his aching muscles.

"I know," he said. "I know."

"You don't have to prove anything to anyone."

Jack turned around. "I think I do. To myself. To them. Maybe even to you."

"Did you even listen to the sermon you preached this morning?" Frank said. For the first time in days, he was smiling.

"I'm not trying to earn something," Jack said. He stopped. "That's not why—"

"I know," Frank said, holding up his hand. "You're doing this because it's a good thing. The right thing." He put his hands in the pockets of his jeans, kicked at something on the ground. "And I'm sorry, Jack. For my anger. If you choose to go, I think you'll leave here a different person. But I hope you don't go at all."

"Well," Jack said, downing the last of his beer. "You've invested a lot of time and energy in this poor Protestant."

"Not nearly enough," Frank said. "But I have hopes."

"Ouch," Jack said. He looked around the yard—around the block. The walls were up, the roof spans going up, and the plywood, felt, and shingles for the roof would follow. It was amazing—the work of days done in an afternoon, just because everyone came together and pitched in.

It was a community effort. He didn't see his father—he'd probably gone home to rest—but many members of Saint Paul's remained. He saw familiar faces from Saint Mary's. Brother Raymond was enjoying what looked like a good Lutheran casserole, and for the first time, the largest group of workers here were from First Baptist, largely thanks to the teenage demolition engineers.

Then Jack saw the one person from First Baptist he did not want here. James. He had parked down the block, was walking across a yard toward Darla with a grim expression on his face. Jack looked off to his right—Cameron had seen him too. His face had gone ashen.

James came up behind Darla, who was laughing with three other women as they poured iced tea into red plastic cups. He took her elbow and turned her around, iced tea went everywhere, and although Jack couldn't hear the words, he knew exactly what was happening.

He had known James long enough not to be surprised by anything he did anymore.

Come on. We're going home.

Let go of my arm.

How can you embarrass me like this? Is that Cameron? James had looked across the yard, and Cameron appeared as though he wanted to melt into the earth.

Jack took a step toward James and Darla. That's as far as he got.

Randy Fields had climbed out of his car and crossed the street. Now he was standing in front of Jack with one hand on his belt, where, Jack noticed with surprise, he wore an actual gun.

"Jack Chisholm?" Randy said, and if his jaw had been tight before, it was white now.

"You know it is, Randy," Jack said. He got ready to step around him. James still had Darla by the arm, and she wrenched it from his grasp. Both of them were red-faced. One of the women was trying to step between them.

"Jack, you're under arrest."

"On what charge?" Father Frank demanded, and a panic seemed to rise from some folks nearby.

"Disturbing the peace, assembly without a license, construction without a proper permit, unlicensed contractor," he said, as though ticking off items on a list. Randy surveyed the yard—and he and Jack could both feel that the mood had become very ugly all of a sudden.

"He's not doing anything wrong," Mr. Rodriguez said.

"Nobody is, Randy." He said the name "Randy" as though he were releasing a fart.

Others stepped forward, gesturing, yelling, and Randy dropped his hand onto his gun.

Jack raised his hands. "Please," he said. "Please."

They stopped yelling, made a space for him to speak.

"People get nervous when other people with hammers and power tools start waving them around." Jack's eyes pleaded with the ones nearby. "Please. Finish the job. We can work this out. I'll go with you, Randy. The rest of you, stay and finish the Gobels' carport."

"The rest of you need to disperse," Randy said, although clearly his heart was not in it. He would take what he could get.

"I'll go with you," Jack said to Randy. "Don't push your luck."

Jack looked across the lawn. Darla and James were gone, although Cameron was in the angry mob still shadowing them at a distance. Jack turned to shoo them back to work. "We can work this out. You all—"

The media had gotten wind of what was happening. They'd been lounging in their trucks—or eating casserole and tamales on the lawn.

Now there were cameras everywhere as Jack was getting hauled off to jail.

He shook his head. Public shame. Again. Fine. Whatever.

"Y'all finish that job," he called.

"We'll be right behind you, Twelve," shouted Dennis, waving a hammer, and it scared even Jack. No wonder Randy thought he might have to shoot someone.

"Finish the job," Jack said. "That's all that matters."

He turned to Randy. "All right," he said. "Let's go."

And with head held high, looking the media and everyone else right in the eyes, Jack performed his very first perp-walk to the Mayfield police cruiser.

"I'll bet I really don't want to google myself now," he muttered, as the door slammed next to him with a sound like the crack of doom.

18.

A jail cell is not the worst place in the world, Jack thought as he inspected his cell. *Especially if you've got the place to yourself.* The jail had three cells back here, but it was a Sunday afternoon, and no one else had done anything even remotely noteworthy.

"Thank goodness some kids didn't try to build an illegal tree house," Jack shouted through the bars in the direction of the police office, but Randy offered no response.

Jack was fine. Most of the comforts of home. He had a bed and a wooden chair, and in the corner were a toilet and sink. *Like a Motel 6 without ESPN,* he thought. Too bad about ESPN, actually. Another Sunday evening and he was missing the playoffs again.

Randy had told him he had to process some paperwork and then he'd give him his phone call. That had been awhile ago. Jack was going to call his father, although he had some serious doubts that Tom would have enough money left in the family coffers to make bail. Operating as an illegal contractor? That could be a hanging offense.

"Randy," Jack called after half an hour or so. He heard a flush from the bathroom down the hall, and called again when the door opened.

"What?" Randy yelled back.

"How about my phone call?"

He heard Randy groan, then footsteps coming back into the jail. "You are making my life a nightmare, Jack. I am dealing with a public relations disaster out here."

"And I would be filled with sympathy for you, Randy," Jack said. "If I weren't in jail."

Randy actually snickered at that. "Okay. I'll let you out to make your call. But nobody is on the desk today, and I've got what looks like a full-scale protest out here."

He opened the cell and indicated a desk nearby with a phone. "One call. And not to the *New York Times*."

"Oh, Randy," Jack said. "You know me so well." He sat down, realized he didn't know Tom's cell, dialed the home number.

The phone rang four times and went to message. "That's weird," Jack said. He hung up.

"Hey, Randy," he said. "My dad didn't answer. I'm calling my sister."

"I said one call," Randy shouted from the front office.

"La la la," Jack said. "I can't hear you."

He called Mary's number. No answer there, either. Maybe she was still at the building site.

In any case, Jack was not going anywhere.

The noise in the front office was getting louder—Jack could hear voices, thought he recognized some of them. Was that Dennis? Hoo boy. He walked out to the duty officer's desk, where Randy had stationed himself.

"Hey," Randy said. "What are you doing?"

"I'm escaping," Jack said. He looked around the room. Thirty people from the Gobels' were in the room, shouting at Randy. All that would fit. A sample of broadcast media, cameras, and reporters was also present. Jack raised his hands, and they quieted down a bit.

"I thought I said to finish up the garage," Jack said.

"Built without a proper permit," Randy muttered.

"They're finishing up," Warren Koenig answered. Jack saw that his brother Van, the state senator, was standing next to him and nodded a hello. "We came down because Father Frank said we had to get you out."

Father Frank was at the front of the mob. He and Brother Raymond were counting through a stack of checks and bills.

"What are you doing, Frank?" Jack said. "Nobody can afford this. I can just sit back there. If somebody could get me ESPN—"

Frank passed the money across the desk to Randy, who began counting it reluctantly.

"We've got to get you out, boyo," he said. "It's your father."

Jack felt his stomach lurch, and he leaned into the desktop. "What happened?" he asked, and he started to come around the counter.

"You're still in jail, Jack," Randy said, not taking his attention away from his counting. "Until I say you're not."

Jack stopped, leaned across the counter again. "Frank. Brother Raymond. What's happening?"

"Mary found Tom unconscious at the house," Frank said. "High fever. Difficulty breathing."

"They took him by ambulance to Kerrville," Raymond said. "They'll know something by the time we get there."

"Oh my God," Jack said. He looked at Randy, making tidy little stacks of fives, tens, twenties. "Can you hurry up?"

"Officially," Randy said, now tallying the checks, "we're not allowed to take personal checks. And I'm not supposed to release you before you go in front of a judge."

That brought an outcry from the assembled, although Randy did not look up from his counting.

"But unofficially," he said, "I do not want you here. Any of you." He laid down the last check with a flourish. "That's it. Five thousand dollars bail." He put the money and checks into an envelope, wrote Jack's name and the amount on the outside, and put it into a metal box that resembled the tackle box Jack had owned as a kid.

"Are you kidding me?" Jack asked. "Five thousand dollars?" He didn't know whether to be offended or to laugh. "Am I a flight risk?"

"Not my idea, Jack," Randy said, locking the box with a padlock and putting it into a desk drawer. "I think you were supposed to sit in jail for a long time. But like I said, I'd just as soon not have you around." He closed the drawer and locked it with a key.

Randy slid a manila envelope down the desktop to him. His personal effects. Wallet, change, cell phone, keys. Jack saw that he had seven messages on his phone, most from Mary's cell.

"Your hearing is scheduled for Thursday afternoon at three," Randy said. "Municipal court. I'd bring an attorney."

Jack barely heard him. "Where's my dad?" he asked. He had somehow forgotten, but wherever it was, he needed to get there in a hurry.

"Kerrville," Raymond said.

"I'll drive you," Father Frank said. "I don't mind speeding. In fact—"

"I'll come with you," Raymond said, and he and Frank nodded at each other. "If we get pulled over, two pastors—"

"Three," Frank said gently. He took Jack by the arm, led him through the throng, down the hall, and out to Frank's old Chrysler. Jack got in the passenger side. Brother Raymond climbed in back, moved Frank's box of cassette tapes. Irish reels. Seventies rock.

"What is all of this?" Raymond asked, as though he were being asked to sit next to a pig carcass.

"Pure gold," Frank said, throwing the car into reverse. And off they went.

They made the drive in short time, and didn't encounter a single officer of the law. "What're the odds?" Frank asked. He seemed a little disappointed.

Tom was at Peterson Medical Center, across the Guadalupe River on the south side of town. Mary had told Jack that they were in Emergency.

Frank pulled into the clergy space in the parking lot with practiced ease. He and Raymond had done more than their share of hospital visits. They hurried into the ER reception area. "Tom Chisholm?" Jack asked the nurse on duty.

"Relation?" she asked, looking up at him.

"He's my father," Jack said.

"And to these gentlemen?" she asked, making a note in the computer.

"Clergy," Brother Raymond said.

The nurse nodded, impressed, and buzzed them back. "Number eight, straight back past the nurse's station."

They walked back. The nurse's station was on the right; a paramedic crew was wheeling somebody into a bay on the left, his shirt bloody, his head bandaged. Father Frank stopped and made the sign of the cross before joining them in bay eight.

Tom was hooked up to a ventilator. Jack felt tears come to his eyes, and then Mary was in his arms, and she was weeping. "Thank God," she said. "Thank God you're here."

A doctor was bent over Tom and entering data into his tablet PC. He turned and saw the new visitors. "Jack, is it?" he asked. He was about Jack's age, short graying hair, dressed in pale green scrubs with a white jacket thrown over them. "I'm Dr. Powell. Glad you're here. Really glad. You're medical power of attorney."

"What?" Jack said.

Mary nodded. "Always have been, it turns out."

"Well," Jack said. "That's just—dumb. I didn't even come back here until—"

"We lost him on the way over here," the doctor said. "And you were unavailable. So the paramedics intubated him. Maybe you wouldn't have wanted that."

"Of course I want that," Jack said, trying not to shout. "Why wouldn't I—"

"It's just that he's got a DNR on file," Dr. Powell said. "Do Not Resuscitate. We found it when he checked in. But this isn't the cancer." He showed Jack an X-ray of lungs, cloudy white. "The cancer has weakened him, sure, and that might have made this infection opportunistic. It's viral pneumonia."

Frank and Brother Raymond had already gone over to the bed. Frank had taken Tom's hand, the one without the IV and sensors. Raymond had taken out his pocket Bible and put one hand on Tom's sweaty head.

"Is he—" Jack looked back at the doctor. "Is he going to be okay?"

"He could be," the doctor said.

"My daughter—his granddaughter—is coming on Friday," Jack said. "This is her first visit." Mary nodded, took his arm.

"Even if he gets better," the doctor said, choosing his words carefully, "I think he's probably still going to be hospitalized." He shook his head. "His age, his condition—it means every illness is much more serious." He took a step closer, put his hand on Jack's shoulder, and spoke gently. "He shouldn't even be here."

"In the hospital?" Jack asked, baffled.

"On the planet," the doctor said.

"Well," Jack said, nodding slowly. "I guess he had a few things he was living for."

"I hope he still does," Dr. Powell said. "I've got a bed in ICU where we can monitor him around the clock." He checked his watch, made a notation, looked up at them. "We'll give him the very best care we can. He's going to need a lot of rest. But I'll okay family visitors in ICU for the first night." He made one final notation, closed the cover of his tablet.

"Thank you, Dr. Powell," Jack said. They shook hands, Mary thanked him, and the doctor went out into the hall, where Jack heard him asking the paramedics, "Okay, what do we have?"

The slow and steady *beep beep beep* coming from the monitor could have been heart rate or something else—Jack had not done enough time in hospitals to know—but it was a comfort. It meant Tom was alive, was going to keep on living at least for a while.

"I was worried," Mary said. "About him. About you."

Jack looked over at the bed, at the two clergymen praying. "I had good friends," he said. "Have," he corrected, a note of wonder in his voice.

"How was jail?" she asked, digging an elbow into his side.

"Not as great as they make it out to be," he said. "I'm glad you were here. I'm glad you've always been here."

She nodded. "Me too." She sighed. "I guess that's the way it's supposed to be."

Tom was moved up to ICU an hour and a half later, and Frank and Raymond took the opportunity to depart, promising they'd be back. Mary and Jack took turns sitting by Tom's bed during the night. Dennis sat with whoever was in the ICU waiting area—he had arrived shortly after Jack and couldn't convince the nurse he was of sufficient relation to be allowed back. They had little room left for anyone else as it was.

"I told them Tom was my future father-in-law," Dennis said around three a.m., after he and Jack had drunk their third Dr Peppers from the vending machine downstairs. "Does that mean I'm, you know, going to hell or whatever?"

"Is Tom your future father-in-law?" Jack asked.

"I hope so," Dennis said. "I've asked her, you know. To marry me."

Jack shook his head. "She never told me. What did she say?"

Dennis shrugged his wide shoulders. "She told me that she loved me," he said. "And she said she was tabling that motion for the current fiscal year."

"Ah yes," Jack said. "That MBA is doing everyone a world of good."

Mary sent Jack home around five to get an hour or two of sleep and to open—or close—the store.

On the drive back to Mayfield, Jack listened to his messages— the ones from Mary, in ascending panic, one from Father Frank telling him they were on their way—and then realizing he probably wouldn't get the message, "you being in jail and all"—and one from Danny Pierce.

"Jack," he said. "Why haven't we heard an answer from you? Martin told me he called you. We want you to come back. I want you to come back. I don't know what you're playing at down there, but we're in a world of hurt and all people can talk about is bringing you home." There was a long silence, and Jack prepared to delete the message, and then Danny said, "I can't do this job, Jack. I thought maybe I could. I had a good teacher. But I can't. Please come home."

Jack put the phone on the dashboard, took a deep breath, put his hands at ten and two. There were a lot of curves coming his way.

His sleep when he got home was anything but restful. In his dream, someone was shooting at him. *Bang bang bang*. He was ducking behind a bus or some kind of big machine, and zombies roamed about. He was supposed to save a woman or maybe she was going to save him. It was all unclear up to the point when he awoke and realized that someone was banging on the door.

"*¡Déjame en paz!*" Jack shouted, before realizing that he was not in Isla Mujeres, and it was probably fruitless to ask someone in Mayfield to leave him alone, in Spanish no less.

He padded barefoot downstairs, still in his clothes from the work site, jail, and hospital, and he opened the door.

A uniformed sheriff's deputy stood on the front porch. It

was one of Shayla Pierce's ex-husbands. Buddy. No. That was the name of the bar. Barry?

"Jack Chisholm?" he asked.

"You know it is," Jack said. "You were three years behind me. What is it now? The jail want me back already?"

Buddy/Barry looked at Jack as though he were speaking—well—Spanish. Then he handed Jack an envelope.

"You are hereby served," he said. "Have a nice day."

Jack opened the envelope. Being served is never a nice thing. He expected—what? A summons to a hearing? A lawsuit from the Gobels because they didn't like their garage?

What he found was this:

Superior Court of Washington
County of King
In re the Marriage of:
Tracy Rainhold Chisholm, Petitioner,
And Jack Joseph Chisholm, Respondent.
No. 924A2013
Petition for Dissolution of Marriage

Jack raised a hand to his face and slumped against the door frame. He couldn't breathe. His vision got fuzzy, but somehow he read on.

Tracy was suing him for divorce. They were the parents of one dependent child, Alison Martha Chisholm, age eight. And the reason for the petition: "This marriage is irretrievably broken."

He staggered back inside, picked up his phone off the hallway table, called Tracy.

She didn't answer.

"Tracy," he said. "Please. Please."

But still the words read in undeniable black and white.

Irretrievably broken.

It was almost noon—he had slept much longer than he planned.

And it was still too early.

Buddy's wouldn't open until four.

But the Buy-n-Buy was selling beer at this hour.

He put shoes on. Didn't bother to tie them. Got in the car. Bought a twelve-pack of Miller Lite on sale, which made him feel a certain sense of thriftiness. Then he drove to the creek, took five beers down to the water, sank four in a plastic sack he tied to a cypress root, drank the other without stopping to breathe.

On the third beer his phone rang, and he pulled it from his pocket. "Yes," he said. "Tracy?"

"Jack," Mary said. "Where are you? Why haven't you been to the store? Someone just called me—"

"Doesn't matter," he said. "Nothing matters anymore."

Mary didn't speak for a long time. He checked to see if they were still connected, then put it back to his ear.

"Jack," she said at last. "Where are you? What's wrong?"

He finished the third beer, dropped the empty can to the ground. "I was wrong, sis. I was wrong about everything. But I can get her back. I know I can."

"Jack," she said. "Dad's awake. He's asking for you."

"Tell him I'm going away," Jack said. "I'm going back to my old job. I'm going to get her back. I'm going to fix everything."

He hung up and opened the fourth beer. Then the fifth. He

needed to sink a few more, but he wasn't ready to stand up. He would make this one last a few minutes.

The car didn't surprise him. "Do you have a homing device on me, Batman?" he asked Kathy Branstetter.

"How's your father?"

"Peachy," Jack said, taking a long drink of the fifth beer. "Couldn't be better."

She drew near, assessed the wreckage, sat down next to him. "Wow," she said. "I thought Father Frank was just your pastoral model."

"He is a reliable guide to all of life," Jack said. "Sometimes a man just wants to drink."

"I can see that," she said. "Can I ask—"

"Divorce papers," Jack said. "I just got served. By Barry. Buddy. One of those guys."

Her eyes got big, and then she dropped her chin to her chest. "Wow," she said. "I'm—well, I guess I'm sorry?"

"That was a question mark."

"I'm sorry," she said. She stared at him. "Clearly you're really upset."

"Upset?" Jack said. "I was upset when you sent off my picture to the national media. I was upset when James told CNN that I was a fake and a phony. This is beyond upset. This is—overset. Aboveset." He paused, took another drink, looked at her. "Those are not even words, are they?"

She shook her head, although truth to tell, she looked overset. "Can I have a beer, Jack?"

"In the car," he said. "Bring an armload."

"I think I will," she said.

She clomped back with four more beers—Jack sank two, opened two, handed her one of them.

"You still haven't told me what you're gonna do," Jack said. "I keep asking. And you keep not telling me."

"What are you going to do?" she said.

"I asked you first." He checked his watch. "Hey. Buddy's is open."

"I'm still trying to decide," she said. "And your decision would help me make my decision."

"Same here," Jack said. "Same here. Hey, beer number six. I'm going. Is the answer to your question."

"No," she said.

"Yuh-huh," he said. "I'm going to get my old job back and fix everything and she will come back to me."

"And if wishes were horses, beggars would ride," she said.

He looked at her. "What?"

"I'm sorry," she said. "That was—rude." She took a long swig of her beer.

"That's right," he said. "This beggar will ride." He nodded. "I will not have my horses sitting around doing nothing."

She wiped her mouth with the back of her hand. "It's just that—" She shook her head. "Forget it."

"No," he said. "No, no, no forgetting. Forget what?"

She set her beer down, her face had gone very red. "I just don't know," she said, "if she knows you anymore." She became even quieter. "If she even knows how wonderful you are."

"Of course she—" Jack stopped. He looked closely at Kathy, who was still blushing, who was still staring stolidly at the ground. "Why do you always want to know if I'm going or staying?"

She was blushing more fiercely than ever, but she looked at him now—and shook her head.

"Sometimes," she said, "you really are an idiot."

"An idiot!" he said. "An idiot? Why am I—"

Then he saw into those adoring eyes, and realized that he was indeed an idiot for not seeing it all along.

"Oh," he said. "Oh. I—Kathy, I can't—"

"I only wanted to know if you were staying or leaving," Kathy said, scrambling to her feet. "You're leaving? Okay. Great. That makes things easier. I guess I'll go too. Who wants to stay in this two-bit town? Not me. That's for sure." She said this last part as she fast-walked back toward her car, spilling some of her beer in her wake.

"Kathy," he called. "I—I didn't know. I—"

She was in the car. She was backing up. She was gone.

"Wow," he said. "One walks out the door. Another tries to walk in."

He took another drink.

And another.

He went on drinking once he got to Buddy's. Finally, that evening, Shayla refused to serve him any more. "Go home, Jack," she said. "Get some rest. Eat something, please." She looked around the room at the media filing in. "You're going to make their jobs way too easy."

"You're a good girl, Shayla," he said. "Say. Say. Tell me something. You're like the woman at the well, right? How many people have you served with dissolution of marriage papers? How many times has your marriage been irreparably—irreparably? Irretrievably. Irretrievably broken?"

She blinked at him, fast.

"Okay, then. How many times have you fallen in love with a married man? Maybe the man's marriage was—was irretrievably broken. But all the same, you fell in love with a married man?"

Shayla's eyes showed distress. "Jack," she said. "Please don't."

"I have him," Father Frank said, stepping up to the bar. "We wondered where you were. Now we know." He sat next to Jack, put a hand on Jack's forearm to steady him, nodded to Shayla for a ginger ale. "What's all this about married men and irrevocable somethings?"

Jack reached into his interior jacket pocket, pulled out the envelope, slid it across the bar to Father Frank. Frank opened it, and immediately he closed his eyes, hung his head.

"Ain't that a kick in the head?" he said. Frank took a deep breath, let it out, looked over at Jack. "I'm sorry, boyo," he said. "That's got the stench of both unfairness and bad timing just emanating from it." He folded the letter gently back, put it in the envelope, placed it back in Jack's hands. "But I am here to tell you there are better ways to handle it."

"You are," Jack said. "You are here to tell me that crawling into a bottle is not the be-all and end-all solution?" It was not a question. His voice was rising, and people were beginning to watch them.

"This isn't how to handle it, Jack," Frank said. "People will always fail you. Your father has failed you, your mother failed you, and I will fail you, if I haven't already. Everyone at some time or other will be irrevocably human and they will hurt you. But God will never fail you."

"He has failed me," Jack said. He leaned his head into his

hand. "He's abandoned me. You said I was called to something. Something new. And this? This is my reward? Jail? My father dying? My family broken? God has failed me." He dropped his head heavily onto both hands, too angry even to weep.

"Has he?" Father Frank said. "Has he, boyo?"

"Say something wise," Jack snapped, turning to Frank. "Go ahead. Make it all better. Tell me how I should go on a journey of love and forgiveness or something." He dropped his head onto the bar with a painful clunk. "It's over."

"You're still thinking of him as the God of Justice," Frank said. "The judge who is handing out your punishment for what you did wrong."

"He is," Jack said. "I know he is. Or else maybe it isn't God. It's just random bad juju. And that's even worse."

"Justice says, 'I don't owe you anything because you broke the terms of our contract.' But where justice ends, love begins."

Jack groaned. "Here it comes."

Frank smiled and went on after a sip of his ginger ale. "God is not some customs officer rifling through our moral suitcases to sort out our deeds. He sees through the smoke screen, through the deeds good and bad, to our deepest selves."

"But I deserve this," Jack said. It sounded familiar. "That is my deepest self. I brought shame on my family. I hurt my wife, my church. Myself. I deserve—"

"Thank God that God doesn't deal with us as we deserve," Frank said. "On the final day, when Jesus calls me by my name— 'Come, Francis, blessed of my Father'—it will not be because the Father is just, but because God is merciful."

Jack was resting his head on the bar now—if the word

"resting" had any meaning anymore. His head hurt. His entire life hurt. "Stop it," he whispered. "Stop talking."

Frank put a hand on his shoulder. "It's not me talking," he said.

Jack felt them come then—the big, racking sobs. They shook his body—and, drunk as he was—threatened his equilibrium.

Tracy was going to divorce him. He would never live with Alison again. They would never be a family again. He had failed them—and she was leaving him because of what he had done in a moment of weakness.

It was all his fault.

Frank's hand had moved square to the middle of his back, holding him in place, an anchor. "There there," he kept saying. "There there." It was like being comforted by a wise and gentle leprechaun.

"What am I going to do?" Jack whispered. "What am I going to do?" He had tears running down his face, he could use a tissue, and he needed to keep his head down so nobody from CNN saw his breakdown.

Frank's hand was still steady on his back, but he heard Frank take a deep breath, let it out. "I think," he said, "that you are going to have a cup of strong black coffee. Then quite possibly another one. After that, I am going to take you to see your father. And after that—"

Jack could hear him laugh then, more sniff than guffaw. It wasn't really funny. "Then after that is after that."

"One day at a time, Father?" Jack asked. He raised his head. It weighed somewhere in the neighborhood of tons.

"That's about the way of it," Frank said. "For all of us ragamuffins."

Shayla poured Jack some coffee while Frank called Mary at the hospital to tell her that Jack would be coming soon to spell her. Although first he might need to throw up once or twice.

"I'll explain," Frank said. "Or he will. But he's coming."

"There," he told Jack upon hanging up. "I give you now slightly better than even odds that she won't kill you upon your arrival."

Shayla's coffee was hot and black—bitter as sin, strong as death.

"Are you trying to help me?" Jack asked. "Or kill me?"

She smiled sweetly as she poured him a little more. "I'm trying to bring you back to life," she said. She had poured a lot of coffee for a lot of sad drunks, Jack realized.

He didn't want to be a sad drunk.

"That'll roll the stone away, sure enough," Father Frank said. "I hope you're planning to be up for a while. The rest of the week, say."

"My father," Jack said. "How—"

"Very sick," Frank said. "But his fever is down, and they're keeping him hydrated. I believe he'll win this bout."

Jack looked down at the coffee, knew he needed to drink more, raised it to his lips. "And here I am. I can't believe I'm sitting here—"

Frank shook his head, and when he took Jack's arm to silence him, it was not a gentle squeeze. "We'll not speak of that again," he said. And they didn't.

19.

Jack hung his head out the window most of the way to the hospital. He directed Frank to pull over twice so he could throw up on the side of the road. Frank stood beside him, that hand square in the middle of his back, as Jack retched up all the brokenness and bile inside him.

"I think I threw up on your shoes," Jack admitted the second time, as they climbed back in the car.

"It doesn't matter. These aren't exactly the pope's red Italian shoes," Frank said.

"I didn't think they were," Jack said. Frank was wearing beat-up cordovan loafers. "I think I got vomit on your tassels, though."

Dennis and Mary were in the waiting room when Jack and Frank arrived. Jack had brushed his teeth, gargled, washed his face. He looked pale but presentable.

Frank had wiped off his shoe.

Mary, for once, did not demand details. She took one look at Jack, her face fell, and she got up to take him in her arms. "Oh, Jackie," she said. "What has happened to you?"

"It's been a bad day," Jack said. "Please don't take a picture." That was a song by R.E.M., which Dennis recognized.

"Hey," he said, pointing his finger. "I got that."

Mary pulled back, and Jack could see she had been crying. "For Dad?" he asked.

"You can be such an idiot," she said.

He laughed. "So I hear."

"What's wrong?"

He passed over the envelope wordlessly. She and Dennis opened it as though they were Oscar presenters. *And the loser is . . .*

Her face flushed with anger. "She is making a huge mistake," Mary said. If Tracy had walked into the room at that moment, Jack would not have liked her chances.

"Bless you," Jack said. "But I think she knows what she's doing."

"You are a find," Mary said. "A catch. A wonderful man." She elbowed Dennis in the general locality of his ribs. "Isn't he, Dennis?"

"Yeah, Twelve," he said. "I'm, um, sure you are."

Jack nodded. "Thanks, Seventy-eight, for that unvarnished show of support."

Mary handed the envelope back to him between finger and thumb, as though it might be coated with anthrax. "Maybe she'll change her mind. If she doesn't, she's the one giving up. Not you."

They sat down, and everyone was quiet for a moment. They were all looking at him as though he were going to throw up again.

"What are you going to do?" Mary asked.

"I don't know. I was—I was thinking that maybe I should go back to Seattle," Jack said, looking at Frank to see if it would set off an explosion. "That maybe she would come back to me if she saw things were the way they used to be."

Mary shook her head. "You were an English major, weren't you? Even us accounting majors read that Frost poem about the road less taken. 'But knowing how way goes on from way, I doubted that I would ever be back.' Something like that."

"Something like that," Jack acknowledged.

Jack had introduced something into the room that nobody wanted to look at but you couldn't ignore. A big black farting dog.

They shared furtive glances. Jack saw Mary and Dennis share a look. She nodded at him. He nodded back, leaned toward Jack, cleared his throat.

"I, uh, I hope you don't go," Dennis said.

Jack looked at him. Dennis was fidgeting. "Why is that, Seventy-eight?"

He shrugged, those huge shoulders rolling. "I used to be really proud of you," he said. "When you were in Seattle. All those people. All that attention. But—" He dropped his massive head, and Jack noted with affection that he was blushing. Dennis focused on something across the room, instead of Jack. "I've been prouder of you these last three weeks than any of that time." He looked back at Jack. "Than since you took us to State."

"Dennis," Jack began.

"No," he said. "What you've been doing—what you did Sunday—yesterday—" He was struggling for the words.

"It's not a big deal," Jack said.

"I never heard anybody from a church say anything that sounded like they were telling the truth," Dennis said. "Not before yesterday."

Jack couldn't resist peeking at Frank, who was looking at the ceiling and trying not to gloat.

"Tell the truth," Jack muttered. "Preach the good news."

"I just think I could actually get *that* God," Dennis said. He shrugged again. "That's all."

"That God is still here," Jack said. "Whether I am or not."

The charge nurse opened the door. It was unexpected—visiting hours had ended, and their special privileges had evaporated somehow after the first night.

"He's awake," she said. "He's asking for Jack." Her gaze fell on him. She recognized him and blushed. "I guess that would be you."

Jack nodded. "Tell him I'll be right back." He looked at Mary, at Dennis, at Father Frank, and he found that despite his core-deep sadness, his heart was also filled with something that warmed it like Shayla's hot coffee.

Love.

"I've got this tonight," he said. "You should all go home." He smiled, despite himself. "Thank you."

"Twelve," Dennis said, holding out his hand.

"We'll talk tomorrow, okay?" Mary said, hugging him. "We've got to make plans for Alison. She's still coming, right?"

Jack nodded. "I don't think that's changed. I'll make sure. But—yeah. Thanks."

"I hate to leave you stranded, boyo," Frank said, after they'd stepped back.

Jack extended his hand. "You're not leaving me stranded," he said. "Actually, I think you rescued me."

Frank shook his head, but he took Jack's hand. "It's what

God put us here to do," he said. "Rescue each other." He inclined his head toward the ICU. "Go rescue him."

"Done," Jack said.

The nurse led him back to Tom's room. Tom was elevated so he could breathe better, but at least he was breathing on his own. They had taken the tube out. That was a positive sign.

"Dad," Jack said. He stepped across the room and took Tom's free hand.

"Where you been?" Tom asked. He was a little groggy, but his eyes were alert.

Jack squeezed his hand. "I'm sorry," he said. "I got some bad news, and I—" He blinked back tears, rubbed the corners of his eyes angrily with his fingers. He needed to be strong now. "It kind of threw me," he said. "I–It threw me."

"Tracy," Tom said with a raspy voice. "It was Tracy."

Jack nodded. "How did you know?"

Tom smacked his lips once or twice—they were dry. Jack found his water, put the straw up to his mouth. Tom sipped, nodded his thanks.

"I think I knew," he said. "Knew it in Boston. She wouldn't look at you." He moved his lips soundlessly for a moment, continued. "Knew she'd decided."

"Why didn't you tell me then?" Jack said. It was a flash of anger, and then it was gone. "It staggered me. It was like lightning out of a clear sky. I thought—" He stopped, realized. "I thought."

"Maybe I should have told you," Tom said. "But you were so excited. So hopeful."

"I was the only one who thought this could be fixed," Jack said. "Wasn't I?"

Tom looked at him with sad eyes. Jack sat down next to the bed.

"People will either forgive you, Jack," Tom said. "Or they won't." He squeezed Jack's hand, closed his eyes.

Tom was slumbering when the nurse came back. "I'm sorry—" she began.

"I know," Jack said. "Visiting hours." He waved off her regret. "Thanks for letting me see him. I'll catch a nap in the waiting room. You call if he needs me for anything."

"Of course," she said. "I will absolutely do that."

Jack went back out to the ICU waiting room. Another family slept at the far end, draped like cats over their chairs, but they were far enough away to not intrude on his thoughts.

He slumped down in a chair, rested his feet on a coffee table, closed his eyes.

He imagined meeting Alison at the plane in Austin, watching her come up the gangway, run into his arms.

He imagined their drive home, swooping up and down the hills of the Hill Country back to Mayfield, back to the big old house where he grew up.

He imagined them visiting Tom—in his mind's eye, Tom was sitting up and laughing. In his hospital room were balloons. Like a party.

He saw her at the zoo with Mary and Dennis, laughing at monkeys. Orangutans? Sure. Why not.

He was falling asleep.

He saw them all at church together on Sunday—Alison in the pew with Mary and Dennis, maybe Father Frank, why not put him in there. Big happy family. What was he preaching?

He was preaching on how God is always faithful. And God

always forgives. He thought maybe he was using a PowerPoint presentation.

That's when he knew he was dreaming.

Tom remained in the ICU Tuesday and Wednesday. He was still very sick, the rounds doctor told them Wednesday morning, although they hoped to move him to a regular chronic-care room by the end of the week.

A steady flow of visitors came from Mayfield even though they knew they wouldn't be able to see Tom himself. It was as though they wanted to be there—just be there—for the family. Brother Raymond came with his wife, Sarah, and their grown daughters, Evangeline and GennyBell. "Genevieve" is what the teachers used to call her when they took roll.

Bill Hall came without his daughters, since they were back in school, and he and Jack sat quietly but not uncomfortably for an hour on Tuesday afternoon. Jack asked a few questions about the girls and the shop; Bill answered in a few words. But then, he had always answered in few words.

Darla Taylor came up Wednesday morning with a bouquet from the gift shop. "Can he have flowers?" she asked, a pained expression on her face as she handed them to Mary. "I didn't think."

"No worries," Mary said. She had never liked Darla—or at least not since she left Jack back in high school. So, just the majority of their lives. But you wouldn't have known it from their hug. *Maybe things could change,* Jack thought.

"How's Cameron?" Jack asked, after they had updated Darla on Tom's condition, after they'd settled in their little corner of the waiting room.

"He's working off your notes. From last week. He said to tell you he was throwing off his back foot. Or something like that." She glanced away. "Listen—I'm sorry about Sunday. About"— she laughed nervously—"about your going to jail."

Jack laughed. "Hey," he said. "It happens. And I'm sorry Jamie dragged you off. It looked like you were having a good time." He looked closely at her. "He didn't—hurt you, did he?"

Darla cast her eyes on something across the room, then back at Mary and Jack. "We're, umm, actually, we're taking a little break." She shook her head. "Okay, maybe a long break."

"Did you move out?" Mary asked, eyes wide.

"Are you kidding?" she said. "Girl, I kicked him out!"

"Kicked him out," Mary said, breathless.

"Of his family's house," Darla said. She actually giggled. But then she got serious. "Which means he's going to be a terror at your hearing, Jack," she said. "I'm sorry for that."

Jack's hearing was still Thursday at municipal court, and although Randy had suggested he get legal representation, they had no money for something like that. Their Seattle lawyers didn't seem likely to fly in to defend him. They were snippy enough when Jack had called just to confirm that Alison was still coming for her visit.

They thought he was still in jail. It had been on all the channels.

"Nah," he told them. "I got sprung." He thought that's what tough guys said.

"If you'd read the petition," one of the lawyers had said, "you'd know that the court-mandated visitation is already in place. Starting with this first visit."

"Okay," he said. "That's cool. If Tracy would answer her phone, I could have just confirmed this with her."

"I'd imagine that Mrs. Chisholm retained counsel so that she wouldn't have to coordinate with you," the lawyer said briskly.

In a movie, Jack would prepare to defend himself with eloquence and grit, but this was real life. He had nothing to prepare. He was going to show up in municipal court where an angry mayor was waiting to ambush him. He figured it would be the two of them arguing, maybe yelling, the municipal judge to mediate, maybe Randy giving evidence.

Whoever showed up, Jack did not expect things to go well. But what was the worst they could do? Fine him?

He was broke.

Throw him in jail again?

Randy didn't want to feed him. Jack suspected he'd smuggle him a file.

Embarrass him?

Jack thought it was entirely possible after all he'd been through of late he would never blush again.

They were going to throw the book at him. Maybe several books. Heavy ones.

"So be it," Jack said as he dressed for court: Wranglers, boots, his blue oxford button-down, an ancient navy blazer of his father's with mammoth golden buttons, which Mary insisted he wear.

"No tie," he said to Mary, whose lip was protruding. Mary thought he should dress like an old IBM executive.

Jack couldn't find a parking place on Main Street for his own hearing. More media vans were in town than the previous

Sunday. "Why does anybody care about this?" he wondered aloud as he found a spot two blocks away.

As he got out of the car, his phone started ringing. He answered as he closed the car door.

"Jack," said Martin Fox. "Just calling to wish you luck in your hearing. And to let you know that we've sent a little legal help your way."

"Get out," Jack said.

"No, really," Martin said. "We want to manage this and get you back to Seattle as soon as possible."

"No, really," Jack said. "Get out. I didn't ask for your help. I'm a—what was it you called me?—a laughingstock. A cliché."

"No, no," Martin assured him. "We are not embarrassed by this at all. This is a social justice issue. You're on the side of the angels. We'll get this little matter resolved, and—"

"I don't need your help, Martin," Jack said. "And I don't want it."

Martin was silent. Jack imagined his brain running through rapid calculations like one of those 1950s computer banks before it spit out a conclusion.

"Think of them as advisors, then," he said. "Consultants. There if you need them. We're with you, Jack. We're always with you."

"Sure you are," Jack said.

More silent calculation. "We just needed a little time, you see—"

"I'm at the hearing now," Jack said.

"We'll talk soon—" Martin was saying when Jack hung up. He was swimming through media as soon as they saw him. What were all these people doing? One might think he drowned his children in a bathtub, killed and dismembered a coed. America's insatiable appetite for somebody else's drama was drowning him.

"Let him through," said the outsized voice of Dennis Mays. "Let him through, or so help me God—" And suddenly a path opened where there had been none. Once again, Dennis was running interference. Jack found the hole, followed him into the building.

"You didn't have to come—" Jack began.

"We all wanted to be here," Dennis said.

They were walking down the long tiled hallway to the municipal courtroom.

"We," Jack said.

Dennis nodded.

"All," Jack said.

Dennis nodded again, and a smile grew across his face. He pushed open the doors to the courtroom, and Jack heard before he saw that it was packed with people, with parishioners from the churches, with patrons of the hardware store, with domino buddies of his father's. More than a hundred people were packed into a room intended for fifty—they were sitting, they were standing, they were talking and gesturing wildly, Lutheran with Baptist, Catholic with heathen.

There sat Warren and Van Koenig. And Shayla Pierce. There was Betty from The Lunch Counter. Darla Scroggins Taylor, waving from her spot at the back of the courtroom. Nora Calhoun was seated with who he assumed was her granddaughter Lyndi. Even Manny, for crying out loud, was sitting and laughing with Mrs. Gutierrez. Maybe they were swapping stories about Pancho Villa.

He was stunned. He stood frozen in his steps. He thought

about the back porch of his hotel room in Isla Mujeres, remembered how just a few weeks ago he had been alone and abandoned and at the point of death.

"Come on, Twelve," Dennis said. "You didn't think your friends would let you go through this alone, did you?"

"Wow," Jack said. He looked up at Dennis. "How much did you pay them to show up?"

Dennis let out a whoop that brought the attention of all in their direction. "It's on the house," Dennis said and then gave him a slap on the shoulder that like to have knocked off one of his arms.

They walked down to the front and took their places at the defendant's table, where three strangers were already situated. Lawyers, Jack guessed, by their elegant suits and disdain.

"Reverend Chisholm," the oldest and most distinguished of them said, standing. "We're here on behalf—"

"You'll need to scoot on down a ways," Jack said, indicating the prodigious bulk of Dennis Mays, "to make room for my lead counsel."

"Gentlemen," Dennis said, as a giant might say "Fee fi fo fum." An unseemly and fearful shuffle ensued to get out of the way, so that the youngest counsel was actually sitting three feet past the table by the time all were settled.

"All rise," the court clerk called. The courtroom rose with the sound of thunder. It was like the congregation at Saint Paul's coming to their feet to pray or sing, and the same again when they settled back in.

"In the matter of City of Mayfield versus Jack Chisholm," the clerk read. "How do you plead?" He looked at the big-city attorneys. The eldest indicated Dennis with a sideways swipe of his head.

"Your Honor," Dennis said, getting to his feet and tucking his shirt back in, "we are absolutely not to be blamed in this travesty of justice."

The clerk blinked. Dennis crashed back into his chair.

"Let the record indicate," Judge Leonard Clark drawled, "that the defendant pleads not guilty." He looked down at his paperwork. "Mayor," the judge said to James Taylor, who sat at the other table with the city attorney, "I understand you brought this cause forward?"

"Yes, Your Honor," James said, getting to his feet. "I did indeed. A matter of public health and safety. Mr. Chisholm has organized—if one can dignify these gatherings with the word—three build-for-alls in which no permits have been filed. He has employed the most amateur of carpenters, including high-school boys with sledgehammers."

"Like your own son," came a quiet but clear male voice from the gallery.

"We will have no interruptions from the gallery," the judge said. "This is a hearing, not a city council meeting." He looked down at the papers in front of him. "This is a—creative—list of offenses."

The city attorney stood. "The city didn't choose the offenses, Your Honor. The defendant did. His actions are a danger to the health and welfare—"

"Call your witness," the judge said.

Randy Fields walked up to the stand. His jaw was set, and he appeared angry. Very angry. He looked at Jack, at James, shook his head. Foolishness.

The city attorney stood and made his way forward. "Chief

Fields," he said. "You were in attendance at all three of these disorganized free-for-alls."

The distinguished attorneys from Seattle looked at Dennis.

"Umm, objection?" Dennis said.

"Sustained," the judge said. "Ask a question, Mr. Prana."

"Chief," he said, rephrasing, "did you witness three occasions in which the defendant gathered people for building projects?"

Randy nodded, almost imperceptibly.

"Out loud, Chief," the judge said.

"Yes," Randy spat.

"Did you personally see the defendant erecting buildings without a proper permit?" the city attorney asked.

Randy sat, his face rigid.

"Randy," James said, a warning in his voice.

The judge waved a finger at James. "Pipe down, Mr. Mayor."

The crowd listened with rapt attention. Something was happening up on the stand. But what?

"Chief," the city attorney repeated. "What did you see—"

"I am not going to do this," Randy Fields said suddenly. He looked across the courtroom at the mayor. "You can fire me, James. But you and I both know why—"

"Randy!" James said, leaping to his feet.

"Permission to treat the witness as hostile," the city attorney blurted.

The judge held up a hand to quiet them all. "Chief?"

Randy took off his chief's hat, rolled it in his hands. He looked sideways at the judge.

He looked out at the courtroom full of people, a community that had formed in recent days around these building projects.

He looked at Jack.

"I don't like the defendant," he said. "Never have. But truth is, he hasn't done anything but good for this town since he come back."

"Randy!" James shouted again, although it was all but drowned out by the roar that went up from the courtroom.

Leonard Clark banged his gavel for a full thirty seconds before he got some semblance of order. "Chief," he asked quietly, when he could hear himself again, "are we having a hearing today?"

Randy looked at James, who now was sporting the white-jawed anger. It wasn't any more appealing on him.

He looked at the judge.

He looked at Jack.

He looked out across the courtroom, at one hundred people holding their breath.

And Randy shook his head.

"No, Judge," he said. "I don't believe we are." He glanced at Jack, shook his head as though he couldn't believe what he was about to say, and then he said, "The Mayfield Police Department will not present any evidence that this defendant has committed an offense."

James leapt to his feet again—but his action was lost in the rising of most of the people in the courtroom.

The judge raised a hand to Jack. Well. There you are. He struck his gavel once, and Jack could almost make out the judge saying, "Cause dismissed."

Dennis was clapping him painfully on the back, the lawyers were shaking hands with each other and with Dennis, all of them were laughing. And that was when he realized.

He looked around the courtroom, and he saw a community

of people who wanted to hope, who wanted to love, who wanted to serve.

"All these people—" he began.

And in that moment, he made his decision.

"I know what I'm going to do," he whispered.

"What's that, Twelve?" Dennis asked.

Jack shook his hand. "Great defense," was all he said. "Come on. Let's go talk to the press."

Dennis made a way for him through the congratulations, through the celebration. On his way out, Jack touched hands, bumped fists, pointed at people far off the aisle like he'd seen the president do at the State of the Union address. One of those at whom he pointed was Father Frank, who'd been sitting directly behind their table with some of his parishioners.

Again, he could not hear what Frank was saying, but he could read his lips: "Well done, boyo," he was saying, and offering two thumbs up.

Jack nodded to him. He smiled.

Frank was going to like this next part a lot.

Once they were outside, Jack took a place on the top step, and the media gathered around. Dennis took a place alongside him, not because he wanted to be on camera, but because he couldn't get back offstage without crushing someone. The Seattle lawyers tried to elbow their way on camera, but found that the media types were hungrier for a story than they themselves were hungry for publicity. They contented themselves with milling about near the doors.

"Jack," was the universal cry. "Jack." Cameras were clicking, video cameras were thrust in his direction, invading his Soviet airspace.

He held up his hands for silence, made motions that they should make a little room, and eventually—as with the judge pounding his gavel—silence fell, more or less.

"I'm going to make a statement," he said, "and then I will take a few questions."

"Finally," said a reporter who was probably itching to return to civilization and eat sushi again.

"I am grateful to Judge Clark and Chief Fields for recognizing that helping your neighbor is not a crime but a civic duty. We are only as strong as we are united. And after seeing the way people have responded to the very real needs of the elderly and the poor in this community, next week, I'm going to ask the local churches to join me in filing legal documents for a new nonprofit focused on charitable building for our neighbors. We'll call it—" He looked around the crowd, the eyes and expressions intent on his next words. "We'll call it 'Face-to-Face.'"

"Are you going back to Seattle, Jack?" came a voice from the crowd. He held up a hand, shook his head. He was not ready to take that question.

"Like many small towns in America, Mayfield, Texas, has suffered hard times. But the people here are filled with joy, courage, kindness, and more energy than I remembered. This is a good place. The people here are good people."

Some of the reporters were writing furiously on their pads. He noted that Kathy Branstetter was standing among them. She wasn't looking up at him though.

"Last year, I made a series of mistakes. I say 'series.' For the first time in my life, I was unfaithful to my wife, and then I lied about it. I refused to accept responsibility. I tried to pretend it didn't happen. In the process, I hurt her, my family, and the church I built in Seattle, Grace Cathedral, a great church with a bright future."

"Jack," someone said, and again he held up his hand.

"I am sorry for that act, for those acts that followed it, for bringing shame to those who loved me. What I did was wrong, and I apologize. To my wife, to my family, to my church, to everyone who trusted me and feels that I betrayed that trust. I know that some of you won't be able to forgive me. I know that others won't be able to forget what I did and move on. I am sorry for that, as well.

"But in the midst of that sorrow, I am grateful for everything I've learned about friendship, about family, about a God who loves us even when we fail. I'm so grateful to know that even in the midst of that sorrow, there's the possibility of moving forward, one day at a time."

He looked out at the media. "If you'll let me see hands, I'll take a couple of orderly questions now."

They were not orderly. They started shouting. He held up his own hands until some order was restored.

"Raise your hand," he said, "and I will call on you."

"You," he said, calling on the wildly waving hand of the network anchor just beneath him.

"We've been doing our show all week from Mayfield," the anchor said. "This is the real America, where people help each other and the government doesn't get in people's way—"

"Do I hear a question in there?" Jack asked.

The anchor was affronted, but he recovered and smiled smoothly. "Why did you come home to Mayfield?" he asked.

Jack smiled. "I didn't come here of my own accord," he said. "My father rescued me. When I didn't have anyplace else to go, when

I didn't deserve it, he came and brought me home. And I'm more grateful for that than I will ever be able to say. Thank you, Dad."

"Are you going back to Seattle?" a female reporter shouted. Kathy was suddenly looking up, waiting for an answer.

"You didn't raise your hand," Jack said. He looked across the crowd at Kathy.

"You," he said. "Kathy Branstetter of the *Washington Post*," he said. She looked at him uncertainly.

He nodded.

She raised her hand.

He nodded again.

"Are—" She looked down at her notes for a moment, then she stood up straight, and her voice gained confidence. "Are you staying in Mayfield, or will you be returning to your church in Seattle?"

"I'm glad you asked me that," he said. "There seems to have been a lot of misunderstanding about what I was doing here. I didn't help build a roof for a needy friend because I wanted you to pay attention to me. I didn't agree to speak at my family's church because I had a secret agenda."

He raised his hands to his chest. "I discovered that I had things I was supposed to be doing right here in Mayfield, Texas."

And he nodded at Kathy Branstetter. "So I'll be staying right here."

She nodded back, and a smile flickered across her face before she recaptured her dignity.

"The *Washington Post* is happy to hear it," she said.

Jack's phone started to ring before he could take his next question, and he pulled it from his pocket, took a look. Martin Fox. Seattle, Washington. "I'm going to make my life here in

Mayfield," he went on, shoving Martin back into his pocket. "I'm going to love my family, raise my daughter, cultivate my friendships, write, teach, try to serve God."

He shrugged, raised his palms in front of him. "It isn't going to look like ten thousand people listening to me go on about things. It's certainly not going to look like this, with the camera scrum and all of you wondering what I had for breakfast. Eggs, by the way. So I guess I have no idea what life is going to look like. But a clergy friend of mine said the other day, 'Better the battered soul who lives his life on a voyage of discovery than the timid soul who never finds out who he is.'

"So that's the story. I'm going to be a battered soul on a voyage of discovery. I'm going to be a small-town pastor, if they'll have me. I'm going to work at my family's hardware store." He laughed. "I may even do my bit to help the Mayfield Wildcats go to State again—"

"Go Wildcats!" someone in the crowd shouted, and the media actually laughed.

"So I guess what I'm saying is this: If there ever was one, there is no story here anymore. Go home to your lives. Go home to your families. Go home." He raised his hands in blessing— and he meant it. "And may God go with you."

He lowered his hands, nodded. He was done.

Dennis stepped in front of him to make a path, but it wasn't necessary. The reporters and camera operators and sound technicians began to step aside. Voluntarily, even.

Some of them held out their hands to shake Jack's.

Some of them said, "Thank you," or "Good luck," or even "God bless you."

Some of them simply nodded as he passed.

Dennis walked with Jack all the way back to the car. He held out his hand when they got there.

"You're a wonder, Twelve," he said, shaking him like a maraca. "So. I guess—thanks for staying."

"You're gonna owe me some ribs for that," Jack said, gratefully freeing his hand. "This weekend would not be too soon."

He got ready to get into the car, but he noticed that Kathy had trailed them down the street, and he stepped back out, leaned across the roof.

"Did I give you the story you wanted, Ms. Branstetter?" he asked.

She nodded.

"Are you going back to the *Post* now?"

She took a breath, considered, shrugged.

"I think I might just hang around for a while," she said. "See what happens. You know: 'Better the battered soul on a voyage of discovery' and all that." She shook her head. "Vintage Father Frank."

"Vintage," he said. "So. I'll see you around?"

She nodded. "I'm sure you will."

Jack got into his father's car, started it, turned on the radio. During the day it got nothing but static. They had no FM stations worth hearing out here, just some AM and not much of that. The music got lost in the hills and valleys, bounced away off the limestone and the water. But at night they pulled in Mexican radio, talk shows from the West Coast, and AM classic rock from Chicago.

Mayfield, Texas, was nowhere.

And it was the center of the universe.

Wherever it was, Jack decided as he drove off to see his father, Mayfield, Texas, was plenty of world for him now.

20.

Alison ran off the plane and into Jack's arms just like she had in his dreams.

On Friday evening, before dinner, Dennis took them all on a ride. Alison had never been on a horse before, and Jack knew after only minutes on the trail that she was smitten. She promised to send Lady letters from Boston, and Dennis promised to read them to the horse. Jack thought he actually would.

They visited Tom in the hospital on Saturday morning on the way to San Antonio, and he seemed weak but much recovered. He joked with Alison, and they colored Barbie coloring books together for a solid hour, comparing colors and outfits.

"You've got an eye for fashion, Dad," Mary told him.

"Second career," he said, without looking up from his work. "I think I've given everything to hardware I know how."

Tom had taken the news that Jack was staying in Mayfield without fanfare, almost as though he'd anticipated it all along. "I'm glad," was all he said.

He did not say whether he had seen Jack announce it on TV, but everyone pretty much figured that he had.

Now as Jack watched his father playing with his daughter, as he saw his sister sitting by the hospital bed, he began to imagine the future.

The elders of Saint Paul's had met on Thursday night and voted unanimously to call Jack as their minister. Salary: five hundred dollars a year.

"That seems . . . ample," he had told Bill, who had called the hospital to report the vote.

He would make it work. Jack had held a job at the Buy-n-Buy in high school to subsidize his paper route. Now he would just work in the hardware store to subsidize his preaching.

Mayfield would not let him starve.

He had started writing again, in secret for the moment, although it wouldn't be secret for long. He had already told Sheila what he was working on, and she agreed it was what people needed to hear now.

"What are you calling it?" she asked him, as excited as he had heard her in a long while.

He had given this some thought, and he thought he knew exactly what the title would be.

"*Beggars at the Door of God's Mercy,*" he told her.

It seemed only fitting, somehow.

And although this was months away and much could change, in his head, Jack was already making plans for a journey.

When Tom was fully recovered and Alison's spring break came around, he wanted them all to go to Florida—Tom, Jack, Mary and Dennis, Alison. Tracy had already given her consent. In fact, once she discovered that Jack didn't intend to fight her on the divorce, she became surprisingly generous about visitation.

They would get a place on the beach at Destin, some little mom-and-pop motel like where they used to go when Jack and Mary and Martha were children, and they would set up chairs and umbrellas on the beach and stay out all day.

Dennis would grill seven different kinds of meats. Mary would sit under an umbrella, protecting her fair skin, and read mysteries instead of tax codes for a change. Alison would build sand castles, do a fashion show of brightly colored bathing suits, play chase with the waves, flee happily from the gulls.

And Jack—

Jack would walk with Tom across the warm white sands to the water's edge, take him by the hand, ease him into the surf, hold his father upright as the waves crashed against them.

His father had always loved the beach.

And he would see it with his family, if only just one more time.

DISCUSSION QUESTIONS

1. Jack Chisholm is described early in *The Prodigal* as "the people's pastor." What does that title mean to the media in *The Prodigal*? What do you think it ought to mean?

2. *The Prodigal* is a contemporary retelling of the parable of the Prodigal Son, a powerful archetypal story that Jesus tells in Luke 15:11–32. Can you think of other contemporary stories that retell the Prodigal Son or recent events in the media that echo the story? Why do you think the Prodigal Son story resonates so powerfully?

3. Jack comes back to the small Texas town where he grew up after living for fifteen years in Seattle, Washington. What do you think would be the biggest challenges for someone making this shift? What are Jack's big challenges? Do you think the saying "You can't go home again" is true? Why or why not?

4. One of the major themes of *The Prodigal* is that we live in a celebrity culture with instant access to news and culture through both traditional and new media. What are the positive things about that reality? What are the elements

of that culture that disturb you most? How do you see celebrity culture explored in the events of *The Prodigal*?

5. Our family of origin is often the most potent influence on the people we become. In what ways does Jack's family history shape him as a pastor and as a person? How does *The Prodigal* offer hope that we need not always be stuck in the dynamics of our family of origin?

6. The news seems to offer up some scandal daily, perpetrated by someone in the public eye. In what ways do Jack's disgrace and the way he handles it seem typical of what you observe in the news? Does Jack's behavior throughout the novel offer any insight into how public figures should and should not respond when they are caught in a scandal?

7. *The Prodigal* features stories about both longtime friends and enemies with whom Jack has to interact. Are there people in your life whom, try as you might, you cannot win over? Are there friends with whom you have lost touch? What does *The Prodigal* suggest about how relationships grow and change?

8. Jack's church in Seattle, Grace Cathedral, does good work in the world, and it offers encouragement and solace to thousands of worshipers. It also seems to operate a lot like a big business with Jack as its charismatic CEO. In what ways is this bigger-is-better megachurch a good thing? Are there ways you see this model falling short of what you imagine church to be? Why does Jack feel that he has discovered a more authentic experience while preaching in the tiny church in which he grew up?

9. The character of Father Frank is based upon Brennan

Manning. Did you recognize any of Brennan's teachings in Frank's dialogue or actions? How do you imagine your life might be changed if Brennan were your pastor—or your friend? What challenges do you think you would face in that relationship? How does the relationship between Jack and Father Frank develop throughout the course of the novel?

10. Brennan Manning wanted to leave behind a novel about grace, his most enduring theme, and this book is the result of that desire. How do you define grace? In what ways do you see *The Prodigal* exploring the theme of grace? Has the novel made you think about anything differently as a result of reading it? If you discussed it with someone else, what topics would you want to talk about?

11. Brennan Manning wrote in *The Ragamuffin Gospel* that the Prodigal had mixed motives when he came home, and coauthor Greg Garrett said, "I've always wondered what happened to the Prodigal after he returned." How does Jack change as a result of the events of *The Prodigal*? What does he learn about God, community, and being a pastor? What do you imagine will happen to Jack and the characters of *The Prodigal* next? Would you like to read more stories about Jack?

ACKNOWLEDGMENTS

Brennan and Greg gratefully acknowledge Rick Christian and Andrea Heinecke at Alive Communications for bringing them together on this project, and for their support and enthusiasm across the years. Editor Natalie Hanemann worked wonders on this story, and the editorial and promotional professionals at HarperCollins, including Daisy Hutton, Amanda Bostic, and Ruthie Dean, have been a joy to work with.

Greg wishes to thank Hulitt Gloer for the use of the cabin on Turtle Creek, outside of Kerrville, Texas, where he did almost all of his writing on this book, and Baylor University, the Episcopal Seminary of the Southwest, and Gladstone's Library for supporting the planning and writing of this novel with time, space, and resources. Most of all, he wishes to thank Richard Francis Xavier Manning for bringing a message of love and forgiveness that washes over us like the waves. Rest in peace, beloved ragamuffin.

Into your hands, O Lord, we humbly entrust our brother Brennan. In this life you embraced him with your tender love; deliver him now from every evil and bid him enter eternal rest. The old order has passed away: welcome him, then, into paradise, where there will be no sorrow, no weeping or pain, but the fullness of peace and joy with your Son and the Holy Spirit forever and ever. Amen.

ABOUT THE AUTHORS

Brennan Manning was a Roman Catholic priest, a lifelong seeker of wisdom, a world traveler, a sojourner among the poor, and a sinner forgiven by a gracious God. For fifty years, Brennan offered the message that God loves us without condition or reservation, loves us as we are and not as we think we should be. It is a message of grace and forgiveness that has helped reconcile many to God, and a message that he lived out for the whole world to see, with courage and conviction, warts and all. A renowned speaker, preacher, and retreat leader, Brennan authored or coauthored twenty books, among them his memoir *All Is Grace*, *The Furious Longing of God*, *Abba's Child*, and the million-selling and life-changing book *The Ragamuffin Gospel*. He went to rest in the loving arms of his Abba on April 12, 2013, but his voice still echoes in the hearts and minds of his readers.

Greg Garrett is the author or coauthor of over fifteen books of fiction, nonfiction, and memoir, including *The Other Jesus*, *We Get to Carry Each Other: The Gospel according to U2*, and the acclaimed novels *Free Bird*, *Cycling*, and *Shame*. A frequent speaker and media guest, he is—according to BBC Scotland— one of America's leading voices on religion and culture. Greg serves as Professor of English at Baylor University, Writer in Residence at the Episcopal Seminary of the Southwest, Residential Scholar at Gladstone's Library in Wales, and as a licensed lay preacher in the Episcopal Church. He lives with his family in Austin, Texas.